Praise for *The Food Forest Handbook*

Sorting out the particulars of a Food Forest can be tricky, overwhelming and seemingly complex. But Darrell Frey's and Michelle Czolba's Book, *The Food Forest Handbook* changes all that! Through this in-depth practical book you will learn the strategies for effective planning, design, establishment and management of perennial polycultures. I found it fascinating how this design system has been utilized through the ages in many cultures to current times with a tour of successful food forests in varying climates. I recommend this book to all those who are bringing diversity to their planting schemes.

— Jude Hobbs, Permaculture land-use consultant,
designer, and educator, Cascadia Permaculture

Frey and Czolba share the valuable fruit of their decades of experience with this carbon-friendly gardening form. But they go beyond this to tour sites around the world to reap insight and inspiration. They also do a better job than any food forestry book I've seen of reminding us of the tropical origins of this form of multi-strata agroforestry.

— Eric Toensmeier, author,
The Carbon Farming Solution

Michelle Czolba's and Darrell Frey's decades of hands-on experience in permaculture and food production has allowed them to create a unique, important, and timely book. The authors have condensed two lifetimes of experience into a beautifully presented and essential volume. *The Food Forest Handbook* is an outstanding work that should be in the libraries of urban planners, designers, gardeners, property owners, naturalists, and even survivalists. "Save the Earth" isn't just a slogan; this book shows the reader how to make it a practice."

— Joseph Jenkins, author,
The Humanure Handbook,
The Slate Roof Bible, and *Balance Point*

Darrell Frey and Michelle Czolba have recovered this truth from ancient wisdom: forests are successional recyclers. What happens if we were to drop the boundary between the built environment and nature? Wouldn't we all be much better off? *The Food Forest Handbook* guides our first steps along that path.

— Albert Bates, author,
The Post-Petroleum Survival Guide,
The Biochar Solution, and *The Paris Agreement*

FOOD FOREST HANDBOOK

THE FOOD FOREST HANDBOOK

DESIGN AND MANAGE A HOME-SCALE PERENNIAL POLYCULTURE GARDEN

by Darrell Frey & Michelle Czolba

new society
PUBLISHERS

Cover design by Diane McIntosh.
Cover art © iStock. Cover illustration: Daniel Larsson.
With interior illustrations by Sarah A. Jubeck and Christine McHenry-Glenn.

Funded by the Government of Canada | Financé par le gouvernement du Canada | Canada

Printed in Canada. First printing April 2017.

Inquiries regarding requests to reprint all or part of *The Food Forest Handbook* should be addressed to New Society Publishers at the address below. To order directly from the publishers, please call toll-free (North America) 1-800-567-6772, or order online at www.newsociety.com

Any other inquiries can be directed by mail to:

New Society Publishers
P.O. Box 189, Gabriola Island, BC V0R 1X0, Canada
(250) 247-9737

LIBRARY AND ARCHIVES CANADA CATALOGUING IN PUBLICATION

Frey, Darrell, author
The food forest handbook : design and manage a
home-scale perennial polyculture garden / by Darrell Frey
& Michelle Czolba.

Includes index.
Issued in print and electronic formats.
ISBN 978-0-86571-812-8 (softcover).—ISBN 978-1-55092-622-4 (PDF).—
ISBN 978-1-77142-211-6 (HTML)

1. Permaculture—Handbooks, manuals, etc.   2. Edible
forest gardens—Handbooks, manuals, etc.   I. Czolba, Michelle, author
II. Title.

S494.5.P47F74 2017   631.5′8   C2017-901335-1
                                                                 C2017-901336-X

New Society Publishers' mission is to publish books that contribute in fundamental ways to building an ecologically sustainable and just society, and to do so with the least possible impact on the environment, in a manner that models this vision.

Contents

Acknowledgments

Any book about horticulture is a collaborative effort. This book is no exception. When my co-author Michelle asked me to help her with creating a food forest handbook for average gardeners I knew we had a big task ahead. The good folks at New Society Publishers were enthusiastic about our proposal and have been very patient with us as this book came together. We are grateful to Ingrid Witvoet and Murray Reiss for their patient edits as this work trickled in. Michelle Czolba spearheaded this book, both with her clear vision of its content and her vast experience and knowledge of designing, creating, and tending perennial polycultures. Thanks are due to the food forest designers presented in Chapter 7 for sharing their work and providing maps and photos: Glenn Herlihy and Jacqueline Cramer, Lincoln Smith, Nancy Martin, Koreen Brennan, Mary Beth Steislinger, Suzi Fields. We are grateful to the Xi'ui people of El Huizachal, Mexico, for hospitality and fruit, and to early inspiration from the late Tom Mansell, who established his Paw Paw Haven in the 1950s. We also acknowledge the many gardeners who have crossed our paths over the years.

We stand at the end of a long line of researchers and authors with the information presented in this book. Foremost among these we acknowledge researchers, designers, and authors extraordinaire David Jacke and Eric Toensmeier for their *Edible Forest Gardens* Volumes I and II. The development of permaculture design by David Holmgren and late Bill Mollison was the impetus for countless projects and we owe them our gratitude for vision and inspiration. They in turn were inspired by the work of J. Russell Smith, Robert d'Hart, Masanobu Fukuoka, and many native peoples in Australia and beyond. Thanks to Elizabeth Lynch for her work on the plant yield matrix, Nancy Martin for her contributions on water management, and to illustrators Sarah A. Jubeck and Christine McHenry-Glenn. Sarah A. Jubeck provided most of the illustrations, including the lovely apple blossoms that grace the beginning of each chapter. John Creasy, himself an urban food forester, facilitated our journey to meet native forest gardeners in central Mexico. Finally I must express my deepest appreciation to Jessy Swisher for her ongoing support and encouragement and for fruitful adventures.

— Darrell Frey

In addition to those mentioned above, I say thank you to one of my earliest teachers on the path, Chris Shaw Sanford, who helped me get over my city breeding that growing food was difficult. Also an early mentor, Joe Jenkins, whose work with composting science grew my mindset immensely. Finally, my pioneering co-founder in the food forest and permaculture business, Juliette Olshock. Also, last but certainly not least, I thank my co-author and mentor Darrell Frey. Darrell was one of my first permaculture teachers and collaborators. His wealth of knowledge and experience along with a co-operative nature helped make this process fun.

— Michelle Czolba

Introduction

The food forest is perhaps the oldest way to garden. As ancient people spread around the globe and settled the farthest reaches of the Earth, many settled into forested landscapes.

These forest dwellers soon learned that natural clearings and the edges of forests were the most fruitful places for both hunting and gathering. Across the planet people learned to utilize these clearings and edges, and later to create and manage them. Forest gardens, or food forests, were created in many diverse ecosystems.

Today, food forests are making a comeback on many scales and in many climates. This rediscovery and reimagining of an ancient practice has been led by the development of permaculture design.

Much of the early inspiration for permaculture design was drawn from the study of indigenous horticulture and from research into the value of traditional food systems based on perennial crops. Trees and perennial ecosystems stabilize soil and build fertility, reduce soil erosion, and help moderate climate change by storing carbon in biomass and in the soil.

The root of conventional modern agriculture in the Middle East, North Africa, and around the Mediterranean Sea is a way of farming that degraded soils and transformed forests and grasslands into deserts as populations grew over the millennia. Today this system relies on fossil fuels, ecologically destructive chemicals, and centralization and mechanization on a massive scale to try to maintain production in the face of changing climates and dwindling resources.

The growing movement towards local, organic, and ecological agriculture seeks to reverse course, to conserve resources, regenerate soil, restore ecosystems, help stabilize atmospheric carbon, and put people back in touch with their food systems and with nature. Organic farms, small-scale intensive market gardens, urban agriculture, community gardens, and backyard gardens are all part of this movement to reconnect with the source of our sustenance and create a permanent culture. The fruitful perennial landscape, the food forest, will play a major role in our local food systems.

Food forests are fun as well! Once you get out there and have a hand in creating an ecosystem, magic awaits. This magic is nature doing what it does—germinating seeds, growing plants you did not expect, filling in empty spaces, and becoming lush and alive. Then the insects and animals respond and become part of the system. Watching this unfold is gratifying and good living.

This book is titled *The Food Forest Handbook*. The food forest is a food-producing garden landscape built around trees and perennials. The handbook part of the title states the intent of this book: To present a practical guide to the planning, design, establishment, and management of perennial polycultures. Many possible combinations of useful perennials can be planted in a food forest. A well-managed food forest is an integrated system, and includes guilds of fruit, vegetables, herbs, medicinal plants, and plantings to promote beneficial insect habitat and balance nutrients. In this context a guild is a group of species that grow well together and interact in mutually beneficial ways. These systems can be simple, with only a few species, or contain dozens of species.

Our six chapters begin with an overview and brief history of perennial polyculture, followed by design and planning details. Other chapters will present crops to include, management and use of perennials, propagation information, and a final chapter to inspire and encourage you to actually put the book to use.

Chapter One introduces the concept of the food forest garden and perennial polycultures. We will place food forests in historical context from hunter-gatherer societies and tree crops in pre-Industrial Revolution societies to present day permaculture concepts. We will review natural polycultures and ecological communities we seek to mimic. We end the chapter with a profile of "Hazelwood Food Forest," a forest garden.

Chapter Two takes the reader through a checklist of goals, a process of site assessment, and a step-by-step design process to plan a productive, beautiful, and manageable landscape. This includes considerations of appropriate scale, place of food forests in the homestead landscape, and pros and cons of food forests.

Chapter Three continues with the design process, taking your food forest planning from concept to details.

Chapter Four profiles a range of perennial crops suited to food forest production, including fruits, berries, herbs, medicinal plants, flowers, mushrooms, perennial roots and tubers, and the integration of annual crops in the system. It discusses the role of crops in diet and nutrition, as well as harvest and storage considerations. Recipes and recommendations for how to use unusual crops are included.

Chapter Five looks at ongoing care of the food forest as it develops. Topics addressed include building and maintaining soil health with perennials, succession plantings, developing biodiversity, pollination, pest control, and pruning. Sources of mulches, choice of ground covers, and water needs are also discussed.

Chapter Six provides guidance for propagation of plants from seeds, cuttings, grafting, and division to aid the reader in creating the food forest from local resources. We also cover what to consider in obtaining and purchasing plants, and offer advice for would-be nursery enterprises.

Chapter Seven, the final chapter, presents a tour of food forests throughout North America. These examples of perennial polycultures give insight and inspiration for the design of food forests in a variety of climates. We close with some thoughts about the role of food forests, in the sustainable, regenerative society.

We want to state clearly up front that while several books have been written about food forests and forest gardens, and many such gardens are being planted around the world, food forest gardens are a living and breathing experiment. We all have much to learn about designing and managing ecological systems. In this book we present examples of existing perennial polycultures, forest gardens, food forests, and generally fruitful landscapes. Yet we also want to convey a sense of discovery. We want to encourage you, the reader, the gardener, to stretch your boundaries, to experiment, to learn as you go, to observe and interact with nature. This is the way the art and science of food foresting will evolve and grow.

Of course a food forest garden is designed around a long-term commitment. A tree planted, whether apple, pear, chestnut or oak, locust or mesquite, palm or cherry or plum, is expected to live for years and perhaps decades, even centuries. The forest garden is what we plant around the tree: berry bushes, brambles, herbs. Here there is room to play with the landscape, to plant and grow a wide range of plants, inspired by natural ecosystems. Your food forest garden is a personal journey in applied ecology, in horticultural stewardship, and in culinary adventure.

My own (Darrell) forays into perennial polycultures began with foraging wild fruits in the forests of my youth. On family hikes and camping trips I learned to use wild foods. I learned to find and gather mayapple fruits, tea berries, wild blueberries, juneberries, and other edible forest plants. Ramps and brook trout, with Indian cucumber root and birch twig tea, were a tradition at the spring fishing camp.

In my early twenties I began an intensive study of permaculture design. Permaculture as a field of ecological design has been heavily influenced by concepts of integrated design. In the horticultural landscape integrated design is expressed in perennial polycultures, companion plantings, and forest gardens. As I developed Three Sisters Farm, functional perennial plantings have been a major aspect of the farm design. Some of these plantings will be examined in these pages.

My co-author Michelle's work with food forests grew out of her earlier interest in herbalism, gardening, and urban agriculture. When she and her colleague saw a need and a niche for food forest development on the scale of vacant urban lots they got to work, creating one of the country's first urban food forests, the Hazelwood Food Forest. Her story and those of other food foresters are intertwined in the pages ahead.

Together our goal is to help you feel confident and inspired to create your own islands of paradise in your backyard, front yard, street corner, vacant lot, or city park. We foresee a not too distant time when our towns and cities are abundant with bountiful, beautiful, and fruitful landscapes.

CHAPTER ONE

Perennial Polycultures: Past, Present, and Future

The best time to plant a tree was 20 years ago.
The second best time is now.
— Chinese proverb

Perennial: a plant that lives more than two years.
Polyculture: multiple species in the same space forming interrelationships.

A food forest is an ancient concept reborn for the 21st century. As presented in these pages, a food forest garden is akin to the French potager—or English cottage—garden, a mix of perennials and annuals designed to be both beautiful and to produce an abundance of fruits and vegetables, herbs, and flowers. More specifically, the food forest is a perennial garden built around useful trees and designed to mimic a managed forest ecosystem.

In this chapter we introduce the concept of the food forest garden and perennial polycultures and their role in a sustainable food system. We begin with a review of the natural polycultures and ecological communities we seek to mimic. Next we place the food forest in historical context, from hunter-gatherer societies to tree crops in pre-Industrial Revolution cultures to present day permaculture concepts.

A close examination of Mayan—and similar Native American—horticultural practices illustrates the ancient and ongoing management of food forests by these indigenous forest dwellers. Next we walk though the development of the modern food forest movement. We conclude the first chapter by examining some examples of food forests and perennial polycultures around North America.

If you have drunk shade-grown coffee, or eaten chocolate, most likely you have tasted the products of a perennial polyculture, or food forest. Both cacao (source of chocolate) and coffee grow best in light shade under a canopy tree. The canopy tree may be a legume, such as numerous Acacia species, as well as a wide variety of fruit and nut trees including macadamia, mango, avocado, breadfruit, and useful leguminous hardwoods.

A food forest produces more than food. Many of the plants will have medicinal uses. Craft materials can be grown and gathered. Biodiversity is enhanced through inclusion of habitat for songbirds, beneficial insects, and myriad other critters, which in turn provide valuable ecological services such as pollination and pest control.

A well-designed forest garden is a place to relax and entertain in as well as work. Nature brought home with all the color, song, and buzz of life in the backyard (or perhaps the front yard), provides a connection to the living world that has become scarce in modern life.

Food forests are designed to gather and store rain, carbon, and nitrogen and activate and utilize minerals from the soil for the long term. Properly planned and managed, a food forest can build up the soil while producing yields.

A value and need that has been often overlooked in modern design and the city landscape is beauty. Aesthetics and a beautiful surrounding contribute to better health. The food forest has many opportunities for beauty—indeed it is almost impossible to avoid!

Forest Ecology

Ecology

A basic knowledge of ecology is necessary for both designing and maintaining a food forest garden. Ecology is the study of ecosystems. An ecosystem is a group of organisms living in a dynamic relationship in a shared environment. In nature, plants, insects, and animals have coevolved over millennia,

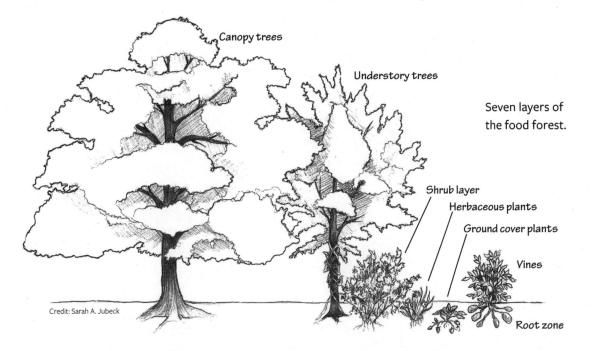

Canopy trees

Understory trees

Seven layers of
the food forest.

Shrub layer

Herbaceous plants

Ground cover plants

Vines

Root zone

Credit: Sarah A. Jubeck

adapting to each other and to the land and climate. Most ecosystems are
dominated by perennial plants, whether trees in a forest, or grasses in a
prairie. In the next section we will examine forest ecology.

Forests

A natural forest can seem to be a place of mystery. Tall trees are spaced in
seemingly random patterns. Smaller trees grow in their shade. Tangled vines
sprawl over shrubs and clamber up tree trunks. The ground may be covered
with a profusion of plants competing for space and light. Fallen branches
and leaves litter the ground, decaying into the earth and smelling of earthy
mould. Mushrooms push from the ground and other fungi cling to the trees.
Unidentified flying insects zoom past or hover near your head. Small forest
creatures scurry among the undergrowth and birds flit among the branches.
To one unschooled in ecology, a natural forest may seem wild, jumbled,
and unruly.

   Studious observation reveals a different story. Seemingly random collections of plants become complex communities woven together into networks

Credit: Darrell E. Frey

Perhaps the best use
for trees: climbing!

of interacting species. Larger trees, forming the canopy, shelter understory
companions from weather extremes and suppress grasses from dominat-
ing the ground layer. Plants share information through airborne chemicals
and nutrients through a subterranean web of roots and mycelium. Seasonal
periods of growth and dormancy are timed to maintain essential nutrients
in the community. Plants protect the soil from drying winds and heavy rain,
allowing rainfall to soak into the soil and be stored in the ground.

Examining the structure and ecology of the forest will help us understand
the patterns of natural perennial polycultures and the various roles plants,
animals, and fungi play in the forest. In Chapter 2 we will put this information to use to design and plan productive systems based on this deeper
understanding of forest ecology.

A forest is an ecological *community*. In an ecological community all members of the community interact with one another in a network of relationships. Through photosynthesis plants create new material from air, water,

and soil. Different plants have different abilities to extract essential nutrients from the soil, or in the case of legumes, the air. Plants are the base of the food chain providing food, as well as shelter, for animals. As they complete their lifecycles, dying or being consumed by animals, plants return the organic matter to the forest floor. Decomposers, including fungi, insects, arthropods, slugs, snails, and other organisms break down organic matter and return nutrients to the community. Nutrients cycle between the soil, fungi, plants, and animals. The structure of the forest itself moderates the climate, gathers and stores rainwater, and minimizes soil erosion. Pollen and seeds are moved around by air currents and by insects, birds, and other animals. Pest and predator relationships keep a balance of insect and animal populations.

The dominant player in the forest ecosystem is the tree. A natural forest tends to have a mix of tree species, usually of various ages. Different species of trees fill different *niches* in the system. Some like a dryer soil, some can handle a high water table, some like a warmer south-facing slope, some prefer the cooler northern slopes. The dominant trees form the forest *canopy*. *Understory* trees, shrubs, and plants grow best in the shade of other trees. *Ground layer* plants benefit from the reduced competition from grasses and the moderated climate provided by the upper layers.

Succession is an important concept in understanding forests. Storms, fire, and the death of older trees create clearings in the forest, allowing sun-loving annual and herbaceous perennial plants to germinate and grow. Pioneer species, such as aspen, sassafras, hawthorn, or black locust grow quickly in these clearings. As the pioneer trees mature, second-stage hardwood trees germinate and grow in their shade. When these second-stage trees mature, smaller understory trees fill in among a ground cover of shade-tolerant annuals, fungi, herbaceous perennials, shrubs, and vines.

Eventually, a native forest can develop into a climax forest of mature old-growth trees, with less diversity. An old-growth forest generally includes a mixed-age patchwork. Once again trees die or are toppled by wind storms, or consumed by wildfire. In the newly opened clearings the cycle begins anew.

As we shall see below, traditional native food forests mimic these natural forest clearings. It is likely that these food forests were inspired by indigenous people's observation of the increased diversity and productivity of the natural forest clearing. Humans have been managing forests for thousands of years. Observation and management of the landscape has been an aspect of human culture since we learned to control fire. So has utilizing plants for making crafts and tools, for medicine as well as food. Certainly our Paleolithic predecessors used fire to control forests and maintain grasslands and savanna landscapes. They first did this to promote the growth of grasses for the grazing animals they hunted. Later, when cultures worldwide developed horticulture, fire was used to reset the succession in the forest to a productive state.

More About Ecology

Community

All life on Earth exists in relationship with everything else. The basic pattern of life on Earth is the network. Also known as the web of life, this network is made up locally of interconnected communities. The forest community, the meadow community, the riverbank community, the aquatic community— each has their own species of plants, animals, and insects that live within them. Birds and animals move between these plant communities as they forage or hunt, transporting nutrients in their daily and seasonal travels.

Biodiversity

A healthy ecosystem teems with life. The diversity of plants and fungi provides food and habitat for wildlife. Predatory animals maintain a balance of animal populations over time. Insects move pollen from flower to flower to promote fruit and seed. What tree is complete without birds? When we shake ripe purple mulberries from branch to sheet on the ground, a great variety of insects falls onto the sheet as well. Leafhoppers, small cicada, fireflies, other small six-legged critters, and assorted lime-green inchworms and various spiders scramble to get out of the bowl as berries are sorted from leaf and twig. The same bird that samples our fruit also consumes hundreds of insect pests and feeds as many to their young. Field mice consume fallen fruit, seeds, and nuts, as do groundhogs, chipmunks, deer, and rabbits. All are part of the great web of life.

Edge

Edge is a term used in ecology to describe the meeting of two or more eco-logical communities. The space between a meadow and a forest is a third system. The edge may contain species of both ecosystems and many species that prefer the edge. Many plants that might not be able to compete with the dense grasses and forbs of the meadow, or grow in the shade of the forest, thrive on the edge. The edge between two systems provides unique habitats and microclimates that nurture increased diversity of life. A forest garden is often modeled on the forest edge, with a sunny side and a shady side, creating a range of niches in a small area.

Plant Guilds

The *plant guild* is an important concept in forest gardens. Bill Mollison introduced the concept to permaculture students in *Permaculture: A Designers Manual* (Tagari Publications, 1998). A guild is a beneficial assembly of plants and animals. The guild concept is derived from the study of natural ecosystems and is the basis of forest garden design. In the pages ahead we will discuss guilds in some detail. To learn more about plant guilds you only need to walk in a natural ecosystem near your home. No plant grows in isolation. Forest landscapes tend to be diverse in structure and species. Many types of plants are found together. Smaller trees and shrubs rise beneath taller trees. Vines climb trees and scramble over shrubs. Smaller perennial and annual plants grow on the ground layer and ground cover plants hug the earth. Beneath the surface roots and tubers are found among fungal mycelium. If you count the layers—subsurface, ground cover, ground layer plants, brambles and shrubs, vines, small trees, and large trees—you can see there are seven layers to the forest. The diversity of species is also plain to see.

Competition or Cooperation

Natural ecosystems include countless interactions between plants, fungi, insects, and animals. Researchers are continually discovering new ways plants communicate, store information, and interact with their environment. Nutrients are shared and exchanged between trees of the same species and, at times, with other species. Smaller shade-tolerant species live in harmony

Credit: Darrell E. Frey

with taller canopy layer trees. However, many plants also have evolved mechanisms to control their neighbors. Numerous plants have been identified that produce allelopathic compounds. These compounds, exuded by roots, bark, and/or leaves, can inhibit seed germination or plant growth. As we will discuss later in this book, various members of the walnut family produce juglone, an allelopathic chemical that can persist in the soil for decades. Many useful plants are resistant to juglone and so a walnut tree guild can be designed. Other plants, though, such as rye grass or goldenrod species, have much less tolerance for these allelopathic compounds.

This polyculture guild at Braddock Farm, in Braddock, Pennsylvania, includes an apple tree with fig, asparagus, and Jerusalem artichoke.

Perennial Polycultures

As we have seen above, in the natural world diverse perennial plant communities are the basis of the vast majority of ecosystems, whether prairie, savanna, or forest. For the purpose of this book, we define perennial polycultures as *the cultivation of perennial plants in functional groupings*. When we design perennial polycultures we are creating guilds of plants that mimic natural ecosystems, while producing a good yield. The seven layers of the forest become seven layers of food, craft materials, medicines. Some plants in the system attract and nurture pollinating insects and others help cycle vital nutrients from the soil and make them available to other plants. Mycorrhizal fungi develop connections between plants and the soil forming a network of communication and nutrient exchanges.

Everywhere I look I see perennial polycultures. In our towns and cities many are ornamental in nature, or unharvested. But most have the potential for productivity. As I am writing this book, I am seated in a bustling café in a middle-class neighborhood of Pittsburgh. Buses pass by among the busy traffic. My outdoor seating is flanked by trees. On one side a black walnut tree drops nuts on the sidewalk. These are quickly gathered by the local squirrels. On the other side a tall mulberry tree grows from a 25-square-foot plot raised planter. Around the base of the tree are roses with small rose hips, hostas, and violets. The street is lined with gingko trees, many of them with nut-bearing fruit, again to be gathered by squirrels. All these are useful plants and give a hint of the potential for productive urban landscapes. Most landscapes in this neighborhood have small trees, shrubs, and understory plantings. Replace a few plants here, add some plants there and an unproductive yard becomes a part of the home food system.

Agroforestry

There are a number of perennial polyculture systems related to food forests. We will examine some of these in more detail in Chapter 2.

Agroforestry is the use of tree crops in agricultural systems on a large scale, including pastures and croplands. These practices, which will be examined further in Chapter 2 include the following.

Alley cropping systems are annual crops planted between widely spaced rows of trees. These may be any nut or fruit, timber or legume trees. Alley cropping is more common in tropic and subtropic climates but is also used in temperate zones to obtain a second crop between tree crops, or to get a crop as the trees mature.

Silvopasture systems integrate trees and shrubs into pasture systems. Leguminous trees can add nitrogen to the pasture. Forage crops such as acorns and honey locust supplement grazing. Some specialized systems include planting acorns, apples, and hazelnuts for forage in hog pastures.

Forest farming generally involves production of crops on the forest floor. This is generally done in existing native forests and denotes a larger scale than the food forests that are the main focus of this book. In a forest farm, crops such as ramps, shiitake mushrooms, and native medicinal plants such as ginseng, blue cohosh, and goldenseal are managed beneath mature timber trees, native nuts, or sugar maples.

Windbreaks are multilevel rows of trees and shrubs which buffer downwind structures and landscapes from prevailing winds. Windbreaks and tree lines between fields offer many opportunities to plant useful crops, moderate wind speeds, and promote biodiversity.

Riparian forests protect floodplains and shorelines from erosion during floods. Riparian zones can be planted with many useful species. A riparian food forest guild might include butternuts, walnuts, paw paws, raspberries, groundnuts, vines, and medicinal herbs.

Food Forests Through Time and Around the World

Native people around the world have tended food forest gardens for millennia. This next section will briefly examine some of these societies to gain insight into traditional food forests. We begin with some concepts and strategies used in food forests, and then look a little more closely at several tropical food forest systems, as well as an historical account of a temperate food forest.

Swidden

Indigenous food forest managers around the world have employed techniques known as swidden, also disparagingly called slash and burn agriculture. While slashing and burning can indeed be an environmental disaster on

Fire is used to clear land and return mineral nutrients to the soil in a Mexican mountainside.

Credit: Darrell E. Frey

The Xi'ui people in Central Mexico practice the age old milpa system, beginning the cycle by cutting back and burning the brush to prepare for planting corn.

Credit: Darrell E. Frey

a large scale, indigenous swidden agriculture on a smaller, village scale was and is often a sophisticated horticultural technique.

In a well-managed swidden system plots of land are cleared and the trees and shrubs are selectively pruned or cut. The plots are carefully burned to release minerals in the form of ash and preserve carbon in the form of charcoal. After a period of use the plots are shifted from annual production to perennial crops or left fallow for natural rejuvenation. Below we will examine the Mayan milpa and Kichewa chacras versions of swidden agriculture in more detail.

Biochar

In the past decade the terms *biochar* and *terra preta* have come to the attention of students of regenerative agriculture. Terra preta means "black soil" in Portuguese. Terra preta is rich in carbon, in the form of charcoal or biochar. Biochar—biologically active charcoal—is extremely porous and therefore has a high capacity to store water and nutrients. This provides excellent habitat for soil microorganisms.

The formation of terra preta in the Amazon was the result of a horticultural practice that increased soil fertility by a swidden system that incorporated composted human and agricultural waste and charcoal into the soils.

Before 1492, the Amazon Basin was much more densely populated. Native people throughout North, Central, and South America practiced complex horticulture and had domesticated many crops. Recent research has shown that large areas of the Amazon region were once a cultivated ecosystem, a web of interconnected villages, garden sites, and food forests. Extensive areas of fertile soil—tens of thousands of square miles—were the product of ancient, pre-Columbian horticultural practices. Diseases introduced by European explorers and settlers decimated whole nations and greatly reduced the population of the native people. Only recently have we begun to appreciate the extent of the communities there and the well-developed agriculture they practiced.

The Mayan Milpa: Central American Food Forests

Perhaps the best documented food forest horticulture is the *milpa* system of the Maya. The Maya are indigenous inhabitants of large areas of Southern Mexico, Belize, Guatemala, Honduras, and El Salvador. The Mayan milpa system of indigenous agroecology has been practiced throughout the Americas for thousands of years. The roots of the term milpa meant "cultivated place" in the Mayan language. A traditional Mayan household maintains and intensively cultivates a home garden and a number of milpa fields located further from the home.

The Mayan Forest Garden (Annabel Ford and Ronald Nigh, Left Coast Press, 2015) documents 8,000 years of forest gardening in Central America, describing the development and role of perennial polycultures in Mayan communities and explaining the role of the food forest in sustainable agriculture for Central America today.

To create a food forest, Mayan farmers make a clearing in the forest by trimming, pruning, and cutting down forest trees. They may preserve existing useful trees, cutting them back to reinvigorate their productivity with new growth. They then carefully burn the wood to release minerals from the forest biomass and return it to the soil in the form of ash and charcoal.

Credit: Sarah A. Jubeck

The first season and for up to four years, according to Ford and Nigh, corn is the primary crop, interplanted with beans and squash and many different annuals. Over the next two to three decades the polyculture system develops in complexity as a succession of trees, shrubs, and annual crops are established. These include grains, vegetables, fruits, and medicinal and craft material plants. Crops that may be familiar to the reader include amaranth, peppers, banana, plantain, cacao, fig, papaya, and avocado. Many other crops less familiar to people outside the region are also grown.

The milpa cycle begins by clearing and burning woody vegetation. Corn, beans, and other annual crops are grown for several years as perennial crops are established and grow into a food forest. After a couple decades the cycle will begin again.

Over time the milpa goes through succession, moving from open field crops to light shade crops to full canopy (as in mature trees casting heavy shade). Perennial crops planted in the first few years provide cooling shade needed for later plantings to become established. As the soil becomes less productive for maize, other crops take precedence. A new milpa is then established for maize and a new cycle begun as the previous milpa's crop yields come from more perennial crops. Management of the milpa includes managing wildlife for hunting, late succession foraging, and beekeeping. Traditional Mayan agricultural land consists of a network of milpas in various stages of development.

The end result of thousands of years of forest gardening is that the dominant trees in Mayan forests are major crop trees for the Mayan people.

The Mayans who manage milpa systems are practicing an ancient permanent agricultural system rooted in a deep knowledge of agriculture, horticulture, soil management, water management, ecology, and the multitude of crops they tend. Traditional indigenous land management has resulted in a rich soil, high in carbon, with a high capacity to store nutrients and water.

Quechuan Chacra: South American Food Forest

Throughout the western Amazon, from Colombia south through Ecuador, Bolivia, Peru, Chile, and Argentina various indigenous people, collectively known as Quechua, traditionally practiced a horticulture similar to the milpa called *chacra*. As with the milpa, chacras are located at a distance from the home, and both are used for market production and to supplement home garden production. As described by Thomas Perreault in the article "Why *chacras* (swidden gardens) persist: Agrobiodiversity, food security, and cultural identity in the Ecuadorian Amazon," (*Human Organization*, 64(4): 327–339), the chacra does have an important distinction from the Mayan milpa.

Perreault studied the Kichewa (a sub-group of the Quechua) of the Ecuadorian Amazon at the turn of the 21st century. He found the chacras are slashed but not burned as the milpa generally are, and maize production is not as important as manioc.

Beginning with an old site, existing trees and shrubs are cut and composted for mulch. The soil is prepared by hand, with machete and hoe, and planted with manioc, bananas, and plantains. Over the next few years, other useful plants are added. Perreault reports that up to four dozen species of useful plants are cultivated in the chacras. The products of the chacras and Kichewa home gardens are grown primarily for family use, but some products may be sold at market.

Traditionally, as with the Mayan milpa, several chacra plots are maintained by a family, with a new one established every few years to produce a range of crops in rotation. The great variety of crops include maize, peppers, peanuts, coffee, banana, cacao, sugar cane, papaya, avocado, citrus, pineapple, guayausa (a relative of yerba mate), and many more useful plants.

While the Kichewa diet is becoming more dependent on imported foods, the chacra and home garden remain an important part of the local culture and food system for many communities in the region. They provide a strong element of food security and some cash crops for each household.

The milpa, the chacra, and similar food forest systems around the world have supported indigenous people while continually regenerating the soil and biodiversity of their land for thousands of years. The pattern of intensively managed home garden, supplemented with a long-term food forest holds lessons for modern food forest and food systems design. By rotating small plots, tending and replanting perennial polycultures in an ecological succession through a managed cycle of cultivation, growth, and fallow, the gardener can produce a diversity of food, as well as craft and medicinal plants, in an endless circle for generations to come.

Ancient Forest Gardens of Indonesia

The Sakuddei people in Indonesia, the subject of a 1974 documentary, *Disappearing World*, lived in communal villages and tended family food forest gardens. Their lifestyle was just one example of native food forests in Southeast Asia. Each Sakuddei village had a common house where people gathered for major events, such as weddings and funerals. Each family also had a garden camp where they planted and tended forest gardens, growing coconuts, many types of fruit, taro and vegetables, and craft materials. They also raised pigs and chickens. The roots of these highland tropical forest farmers may go back tens of thousands of years. Modern versions of forest gardens in Indonesia can include cash crops such as coffee and cacao and may have over one hundred crop species per hectare (approximately 2.5 acres).

Polynesia

Polynesians also practiced forest gardening and carried the practice, and plants, with them as they settled the Pacific. Crops such as sweet potatoes, banana, taro, and medicinal plants were grown beneath breadfruit and leguminous Acacia species. Today coffee and cacao are added to this mix, as noted earlier.

Elsewhere in the South Pacific islands, forests farms include canopy trees such as mango, breadfruit, and coconut, which shelter understories of cacao, citrus, banana, and ground layer plantings of yam, taro, cassava, and other crops.

North America

Native Americans managed forests for food and craft materials throughout the Americas. Early settlers to Pennsylvania noted the well-established agricultural systems of the Delaware and Iroquois peoples. Both of these nations of Eastern Woodland Indians practiced forms of shifting, swidden agriculture.

Land would be cleared and used to cultivate corn, beans, and squash for a period of time and then allowed to revert to forest for a while. The Delaware, who had abundant fish resources, would fertilize their fields with fish, maintaining fertility for a decade or two before shifting the garden villages. A "village" would actually utilize a number of village sites in a given year, fish camps in fish season, maple syrup camps in the late winter, hunting camps at various times. By shifting the garden village sites in regular cycles, fertility was maintained and resources conserved.

A more fully developed forest garden was documented in the late 1700s just south of Erie, Pennsylvania. When European settlers first arrived in northwestern Pennsylvania in the late 18th century, they encountered a landscape that had been managed by humans since the Laurentide Ice Sheet's retreat 10,000 to 12,000 years earlier. Savannas and meadows stretched for miles along the French Creek valley near Meadville. Native Americans maintained these meadows with fire to provide grazing areas for game animals, including deer, elk, and woodland buffalo.

At the site of present day Saegerstown, where Woodcock Creek enters French Creek, early settlers found what was most certainly a Native American food forest. This site, which apparently covered several hundred acres, was an example of tended and perhaps selected nature. A visit by early American settlers to this ancient food forest was described as follows by a Captain McGill circa 1792, as quoted in *In French Creek Valley* by John Earle Reynolds, published by the Crawford County Historical Society:

> The banks of French Creek were fringed to the water's edge with evergreen bushes and trees, while ranged along on the higher bank was a row of stately pines beautiful in their majesty as the cedars of Lebanon. In rear of the pines half a mile in extent was a very gently undulating plain on which grew great old oak trees with spreading tops, the rare old oak that tells of Centuries, a variety that now seems to be extinct. They grew with ample space between without underbrush or obstruction to the view, to the limits of this wonderful park.

Around the outer semi-circle of the park there arose a little plateau, not ten feet in elevation, and from its base flowed springs of pure cool soft water, which fed a circlet of mighty elms, unrivaled in size and beauty…there were hundreds of these great trees with wide spreading branches supplementing in grandeur the great oaks they encircled. Beneath these grew hazel bushes, blackberry and raspberry bushes, hawthorn and crabapple trees and many varieties of beautiful shrubs and plants while near the northern extremity there was a veritable orchard of wild plums bearing a great variety of large red and yellow fruit.

The ground rose from the river margin in regular successive plateaus of easy grade covered with the finest timber of the most valuable and useful kind. The view was enchanting and they moored the canoe to the bank to make further explorations. Here they were met by John Fredebaugh, who had located a claim that took in Woodcock Creek and joined on the north the land that had attracted their attention. His land…was naturally alluvial and very rich…a forest of white walnut (butternut) with here and there a great sycamore towering above and extending its weird white arms over the umbrageous growth beneath. The wild grape vine interlaced the trees and hung in festoons from the branches, forming arboreal recesses of rare and inviting beauty. Birds of bright plumage and resonant song fluttered in the trees and woodcock and grouse in great numbers clucked and crowed unawed by the presence of man.

This site was rich in resources for the native inhabitants. The oak forests would have provided acorns to feed both humans and their game animals. The elms described provided native villagers with bark to cover their longhouses and wigwams. The understory of hazelnuts, berries, and other plants described would have likely included many medicinal wild flowers. The forest understory in this part of French Creek Valley now includes ramps, ginseng, goldenseal, blue and black cohosh, trilliums, mayapples, and numerous other wildflowers that are medicinal or food plants. The wild grapes, plums, and butternuts described were all used in the native diet. Other edible plants still found in this area include the viburnum nannyberry or wild raisin, service or juneberry, and groundnut. The mixed timber trees described here would likely include black walnut, American chestnut, sugar maple, and other trees used for food, crafts, and construction.

Fungi are also abundant in this region and would certainly have been present here. Black morels, the first to appear in the spring, are followed a week or two later by white morels. At various times from summer through fall this food forest would have provided yellow, cinnabar, and black trumpet chanterelles, bolete mushrooms, sulfur shelf, and sheep's head as well as medicinal fungi such as turkey tail and reishi.

In *In French Creek Valley*, John Earle Reynolds credits Native Americans with creating and maintaining this landscape. He writes: "…for centuries this very spot has been the playground at the backdoor of the longhouse of the Six Nations (Iroquois). It was not a work of chance or enchantment. He who had planned and watched over this valley for eons of time surely had a purpose for making these acres so enchanting."

This passage is a rare documentation of the Eastern Woodland Indians' land management. It points the way towards a true stewardship of learning to farm the forest and gain sustenance from its bounty.

Food Forest Developments in the 20th Century

Next we will look at the story of the roots of the recent development of food forests through a series of book reviews. The modern temperate climate food forest has its roots in tropical systems, adapted for more trying climates, and in the study of agroforestry practices to address many problems of agriculture in the early 20th century.

In 1929, J. Russell Smith (1874–1966) published his treatise on perennial horticulture, *Tree Crops: A Permanent Agriculture*, (Island Press). Smith, a professor of geographic economics at Columbia University, made a strong case for the development of agriculture based on tree crops. Drawing on inspiration from his correspondence and his journeys to tree crop farms around the world, he proposed a radical transition to a new agricultural landscape. In particular, Smith studied the use of tree crops as human food and livestock feed. The use of chestnuts as pig forage in Corsica and the use of honey locust for livestock forage in Appalachia particularly caught his interest.

Smith researched and wrote during the North American dust bowl years, when a combination of poor tillage practices and drought led to massive windblown erosion in the US Midwest. He documents the value of tree crops not only for erosion control, but also for using marginal, sloping land for soil building and water management. *Tree Crops* makes a strong case for what Smith called a permanent agriculture featuring tree crops and pasture systems. He proposes farm pastures planted with acorn-bearing oaks, mulberry, persimmon, and honey locust to feed pigs and poultry.

Tree crops can yield a greater amount of feed than grains, while conserving and even building soil. They also can be grown on steep land and other land considered marginal for more conventional agriculture. Today this approach to integrating tree crops into pasture systems is known as silvopasture.

Smith also calls for more selection of tree crops as human food. He suggests researching chestnuts, hickory nuts, pecans, butternuts, walnuts, mulberries, and acorns to identify and develop superior cultivars and to extend their range and harvest seasons.

Much of the work of selecting useful varieties that he proposed has been begun in the United States by commercial plant breeders and individuals (see page 74, North American Fruit Explorers and Northern Nut Growers Association) but much more needs to be done.

It is well worth spending time reading *Tree Crops* and considering Smith's message. The book is in public domain and is available for free downloading as a pdf. It is also still in print for purchase as hard copy or ebook. Describing the full scope of *Tree Crops* is beyond the space available here. Full chapters are devoted to over a dozen tree crops, and other sections look at tropical plants and growing methods. *Tree Crops* was a strong influence in the development of permaculture and in food forest research in the early 20th century.

Forest Gardening, by Robert A. de J. Hart (Chelsea Green, 1996) presents Hart's pioneering work by featuring his own food forest in rural England, and served to inspire David Holmgren and Bill Mollison as they developed permaculture as a design system. Subsequent work in developing food forest design concepts were informed by both Smith's and Hart's books and research. Robert Hart's food forest work has given him icon status among permaculturists. Smith's *Tree Crops* inspired a Japanese researcher, Toyohiko Kagawa, to develop silvopasture systems in Japan beginning in the 1930s. Hart was inspired by Kagawa's work and related research to develop his own property in the English countryside into a mixed species forest garden. Hart's food forest produced fruits and vegetables.

Forest Farming: Towards a Solution to Problems of World Hunger and Conservation by J. Sholto Douglas and Robert A. de J. Hart (ITDG Publishing, 1985) presents a broad background for the use of tree crops in agricultural systems around the world. This book builds on Smith's *Tree Crops* and presents a great deal of information on the design of large, farm-scale forest farms. Douglas refers to "3D farming," using multiple perennial crops to obtain diverse yields. Included are windbreak design, use of leguminous trees for crop yields and fertility, silvopasture systems, and other examples of using tree crops for food, fodder, fuel, and oil.

Another important inspiration in the development of permaculture and food forests was the work of Japanese natural farming pioneer Masanobu Fukuoka. Fukuoka is mostly known in North America for his book *One Straw Revolution* (Rodale Press, 1978). *One Straw Revolution* documents his work in developing a method of growing summer rice and winter grains in a continuous rotation in a clover ground cover without tillage, fertilizers, or excess labor.

Less well known is his orchard management system. From the 1930s until his death at age 95 in 2008, Fukuoka managed his orchard as a food forest. His book *The Natural Way of Farming* (Bookventure, 1985) provides details of his theories and practices of farming in the image of nature. Fukuoka produced commercial yields of a variety of crops, including Mandarin oranges, grapefruits, lime, avocados, mangos, and ginko nuts.

Trained as a plant pathologist, Fukuoka left his government research post in the late 1930s to return to his family farm. There he began to put into practice his evolving theories of studying nature to develop natural farming systems. As his orchard system evolved he developed some clear practices that provided high yields with minimal input. Newly planted trees are grown with minimal pruning and allowed to find their natural form. The orchard is interplanted with a variety of leguminous trees, shrubs, and herbaceous plants, such as alfalfa and white clover, to provide nitrogen. Perennial and annual vegetables are interplanted with the fruit trees.

Fukuoka did not make compost. He practiced what we call "chop and drop," cutting back cover crops and letting leaves and other crop residue break down and return to the soil naturally. Over a couple of decades of trial and error, his orchard became highly productive while building soil and promoting a diversity of spiders, insects, frogs, and birds to provide pest control.

Permaculture Design

The creation and spread of permaculture design as a system of land use planning in the late 1970s and the development of permaculture-inspired gardens and farms since then has led to the establishment of food forests, forest gardens, agroforestry, and silvopasture systems worldwide. As stated above, Bill Mollison and Dave Holmgren were partly inspired by indigenous forest gardeners and the writings of Smith, Hart, and Fukuoka as they developed the first books describing permaculture. Even the name, permaculture, is derived from Smith's subtitle "Permanent Agriculture." Permaculture has developed as an ongoing search for solutions to the dilemma of our human impact on the land and our planet, as increasing populations continue to deplete the planet's resources and affect global climate.

Throughout this book we will refer to permaculture concepts and practices. We do not want to use too much space explaining permaculture here, as there are many good books available for that. Some explanation is in order however for the sake of clarity. In Chapter 2 we will provide a closer look at permaculture design. Here we will note the work and writings of several permaculture researchers and writers regarding food forests.

Permaculture took root in Great Britain in the 1980s much like it did in North America. In 1996 British permaculturist Patrick Whitefield published *How to Make a Forest Garden* (Permanent Publications). Written from an English permaculture gardener's viewpoint this book is a fairly basic introduction to forest gardening. Whitefield's work helped inspire food forest experimentation, building on the work of Robert Hart and other food forest tenders. Whitefield explains early in the book that he would prefer the term woodland garden, as a forest garden is more akin to open managed woodlands rather than a dense forest.

In 2005 the two-volume *Edible Forest Gardens* (Chelsea Green) was released by David Jacke and Eric Toensmeier. This two-part publication was a landmark in forest garden design theory and practice. These books are extensively researched and provide a wealth of information to the design student and professional. They are an important tool for professional designers of sustainable food systems. We highly recommend seeking them out for the wealth of charts and data on trees and their companions. The authors delve deeply into a study of ecology and the relationships between trees, other plants, and the various forest dwellers. They present many details about the design process and its application to food forests.

Food Forests in the 21st Century: The New Cottage Garden

Certainly growing plants in light shade has the benefit of protecting crops from the more direct sunlight of the tropics and subtropics. And so there has been a compelling logic to preserve polyculture systems there. But for the most part, as modern forms of agriculture developed they became more and more centralized and compartmentalized. Monoculture was the focus of agronomists and became the norm. As Western culture became more industrialized, society shifted to less interaction with their food in general and maintaining systems of gardening specifically.

In recent decades, concerns about food safety, nutrition, and the security of our food systems has spawned the growing local foods movement, with a renewed interest in small-scale regional food systems. Concurrently the development of permaculture and ecological design has helped to revive traditional practices and develop new innovative models of agriculture. Most recently, the rise of urban agriculture has accelerated the development of small-scale intensive food production. The resurgence of small farms, urban agriculture, community gardens, and home food systems has begun to include tree crops and food forests.

Today food forests are being planted around the world. In North America they are found from Nova Scotia to British Columbia, from Florida to Washington state, from Massachusetts to Texas and in cities, towns, and farms in all states. The current rise of urban and peri-urban farming and our growing understanding of ecosystem dynamics are being combined in 21st century food forests.

The earliest cottage gardens of England and the French peasant potager in centuries past were planted with a mix of small fruits, nuts, herbs, flowers, and vegetables. Each cottage garden was unique to the grower and the home, but they had common elements. More horticultural (garden cultivation) than agricultural (field cultivation), they were the base of the home food system. Walls and buildings created sheltered microclimates for more tender plants. Fruit trees were interplanted with fruiting shrubs. Herbs, flowers, and vegetables were interplanted intensively, usually in permanent beds. The forest gardens that are being planted today are similar. But we are building on the traditional knowledge of home-scale horticulture with added insights into the science behind plant dynamics. Some plants deter companions with chemicals they produce. Other plants feed and nurture one another. As we stated in the beginning of this chapter, food forest design is still evolving. We will continue to learn to get the best yields from our landscapes as we tend and grow.

A Food Forest Grows in Pittsburgh: Hazelwood Food Forest

In the summer of 2009, my partner Juliette Olshock and I (Michelle) embarked on creating the first food forest in the city of Pittsburgh, Pennsylvania, on vacant urban lots. Vacant lots here are often strewn with trash, their soil contaminated with lead from old paint. Many lots have buried dilapidated houses, in which the house had been imploded into the basement and covered with a thin layer of soil. It took almost a full year of planning, acquiring materials, and working with local government and organizations to go from idea to planting. The food forest was planted in the spring and summer of 2010.

Having recently completed my Masters of Science in sustainable systems, I had practiced many skills and points of knowledge including composting, lead remediation, creating sustainable systems, and permaculture design and

Credit: Michelle Czolba and Juliette Olshock

The site was an abandoned urban lot with little soil and tons of bricks. It was shaded to the south by a three story brick building.

really wanted to share and express that by creating a public oasis. Involved with herbalism for years, I had just begun to grow food as well. A food forest combined all of this. Creating it on vacant lots represented even more to me: a chance to make wastelands new again, evolve space, move energy, and mold this energy to form. It was also valuable in envisioning and bringing into material existence new ways of living in the world, in particular what to do with urban spaces that have become wastelands.

Our starting point was our vision: a food forest as a multi-layered, permaculture-based system of food production, specifically fruits and nuts. The permaculture-based food forest model involves three or more layers of production and is more permanent than an annual-based food system. The layers are made up of canopy trees such as pear, a bush and shrub layer with plants such as blueberries, and understory species of more traditional annual crops. Herbs figure prominently in any permaculture design, for in addition to medicinal and culinary value, they act as nectar plants, attracting bees and beneficial insects, are beautiful, and form companion relationships with other plants.

A permaculture system is intentionally created to meet the needs of humans, animals, and plants, includes food, medicine and sensual delights, and does this by mimicking nature. While working with the ecosystem, the landscape is manipulated to form microniches, for example, a south-facing, U-shaped arrangement of sun-loving plants to capture all that sunlight. Permaculture design is all about co-creation, acting in partnership with the Earth and learning from the natural systems all around us.

The Hazelwood Food Forest design included 56 species: 4 semi-dwarf trees, 7 dwarf trees, 9 bushes, 3 vines, and 33 herbs. A snap shot of plants that are at the food forest are Asian pear (*Pyrus pyrifolia*), sassafras (*Sassafras albidum*), paw paw (*Asomina trilobota*), peach (*Prunus persica*), red currant (*Ribes rubrum*), echinacea (*Echinacea purpurea*), black cohosh (*Actaea racemosa*), and comfrey (*Symphytum officinale*).

How It Started

After intense collaboration with various local groups, we found a site that suited our needs and was available. It was located on what were four vacant city lots in Hazelwood

Volunteers moved bricks, and spread compost and mulch to prepare the site.

Trees were planted and sheet mulched the first year.

Sheet mulching with cardboard and compost suppressed invasive weeds and began the soil building process.

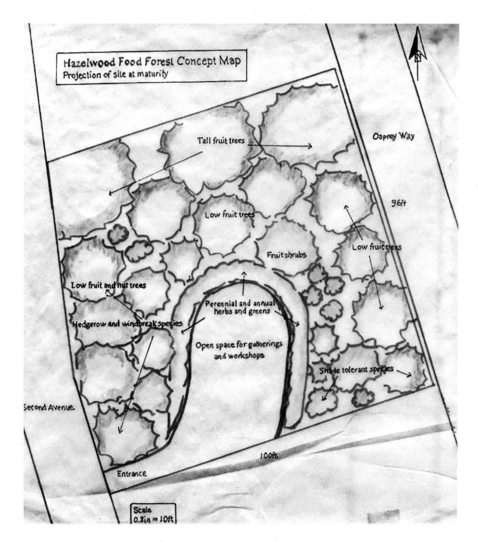

The concept map for the Hazelwood Urban Food Forest guided the site development.

(a neighborhood within Pittsburgh city limits). The site encompassed a 100-foot by 96-foot area (0.22 acre).

Much work needed to be done to go from vacant lot to edible landscape. We sheet mulched the whole site during the course of two community workshops and then weekly during many workdays. We distributed 70 cubic yards of compost throughout the site, hauled out a bunch of trash, and planted trees, bushes, and herbs. We kept many of the excavated bricks onsite and used them for various projects like creating designated beds and raising a rain barrel the requisite 18 inches.

We had harvests of elderberries (*Sambucus nigra*), strawberries (*Fragaria* x *ananassa*), peaches, plums, and pears along with tons of purslane (*Portulaca oleracea*), spearmint (*Mentha spicata*), and lamb's quarters (*Chenopodium album*) within the first few seasons.

Other cities with food forests (sometimes known as urban orchards) include Boston, Philadelphia, Los Angeles, Asheville, and Seattle's well-known Beacon Food Forest. The Philadelphia Orchard Project and Earthworks Boston were both inspirations for this concept.

Lessons Learned

It was a lot of hard physical work to keep the Japanese knotweed at bay, and paths open through the site. Knotweed is only a problem in that it does not let other plants grow. I recognize it as a useful and valuable plant with a role in the ecosystem as a protector. However, I noticed a significant decrease in its range over the course of our time at the site. I attribute that to a direct response that the plant had to our intentions, along with using a clear plastic to scorch the plants and roots.

Much of what we planted thrived. The grapevines sent out tendrils well beyond the trellis; sunflowers grew to ten feet tall; and we had milkweed throughout the central area that called in beautiful monarch butterflies. Huge swaths of medicinal and edible plants grew up from the soil bank; none of these were intentionally planted. Some of these include purslane (*Portulaca oleracea*), mugwort

Within three years the Hazelwood Food Forest was dense with foliage and flower.

Michelle's son Lorenzo enjoys the first fruit of the food forest.

(*Artemesia vulgaris*), burdock (*Arctium lappa*), coltsfoot (*Tussilago farfara*), lamb's quarters (*Chenopodium album*), cleavers (*Galium aparine*), and bull thistle (*Circium vulgare*). The tomatoes and sunflowers became volunteers, growing back from seed every year. The site became a healthy ecosystem attractive to many bird species, deer, rabbits, and groundhogs.

After five full years of working on the original site, we were both at a place of deciding what to do next and asked to leave the space. We had support in moving many of the developed plants and trees to a new site that is affiliated with a local church. The original site was then used for a commercial garden center business.

CHAPTER TWO

Food Forest
Design and Planning

Design is the process of creating a plan for a landscape, structure, or system. The design process outlined in this chapter is derived from our work as permaculture designers and teachers. Permaculture (permanent culture, permanent agriculture) is a system of design that incorporates principles of ecology, environmental science, and appropriate technologies to create ecologically sound, earth-regenerating systems. It is a design system which works with nature and natural patterns, leveraging the energy inherent in a landscape. Permaculture as a design system was developed in the mid-1970s by David Holmgren and Bill Mollison.

In many ways the food forest exemplifies permaculture at its finest. Its gardens are designed from lessons gained in the study of forest ecology. As we learned in the previous chapter, a healthy natural forest is a system in balance, with various parts supporting the whole system. A food forest follows the model of the natural forest.

This chapter begins with a review of the design process for creating a forest garden and takes the reader first through a checklist of goals, and then a process of site assessment and site analysis, providing a step-by-step design process to plan a productive, beautiful, and manageable landscape. This includes considerations of appropriate scale and place of food forests in the homestead landscape.

Permaculture Design and the Food Forest

Bill Mollison's book *Permaculture: A Designers' Manual* (Tagari Publications, 1997) lists multiple approaches to site design. Given enough land and time, one may design by random assembly, in which you randomly scatter seeds and set trees in the landscape and see what works. However, in the name of practicality and fiscal responsibility a clear and logical design process is the best choice.

Mollison's design methods include:

- Design from observing the site and expanding on the land's potential
- Design from observing nature
- Listing options and considerations and making design decisions from these options
- Data overlay, which involves making a base map and using it to inform the design process
- Flow diagrams to help you understand how you move through the site and how the site evolves over time
- Zone and sector analysis. With zone analysis you lay out the landscape in conceptual zones 1 through 5. Zone 1 contains components that need daily care and so are located around the home. Components that need less management are placed in successive zones further away. Sector analysis involves studying the energies that affect your site—sunlight, wind, weather, flood zones, wild life, fire potential, pollution, and noise—and designing to control and/or make the best use of these factors.
- Incremental design, which involves regularly adding to the design over time

While Mollison lists these as different approaches to design, in reality they are all used in a comprehensive manner. Options are researched, the site is observed and studied, lessons are drawn from nature, base maps and drawings are used to lay out flow diagrams and zones, and sector analysis informs design. Finally incremental development plans are developed based on your time and budget.

Permaculture Concepts

As we move through the design process, keep in mind some crucial permaculture principles and concepts. These will help to make your design functional and efficient, as well as ensuring it meets your goals.

Stacking

Inherent in food forest design is the idea of *stacking*. Stacking functions means using one element of the design for multiple purposes. So the plants we use can be edible, medicinal, pollinator-attracting, and soil building rather than just edible. The chicken coop houses chickens in the winter and also serves as a rainwater collection location. The garden is designed in multiple layers to make best use of space. Layers include root, ground, herbaceous, bush, understory tree, canopy tree, and vines. Each element of the design and plant should have a minimum of two separate functions.

Here are the functions we need to consider when designing:

Ecological Benefits
- Build soil
  - Fix nitrogen
  - Create mulch
  - Habitat for microorganisms
  - Organic material
- Attract pollinators and beneficial insects
- Nurse species
- Stabilize soil

Human Benefits
- Edible
- Medicinal
- Culinary
- Fibers and dyes
- Crafting and magical
- Aesthetic

Zones of Use

Part of permaculture design includes working with the concept of zones of use. Zones of use are the areas in the landscape most suitable for specific purposes. While you are identifying niches within your system, also keep zones of use in mind. If the placement of elements is inconvenient, the design is most likely not going to be successful. We want to decrease the amount of energy input required to maintain the landscape and proper placement of features helps with this.

The plants that you use on a daily basis should be closest to the door. The less tame, wilder areas fall on the outskirts or are otherwise strategically placed. Fruit trees and bushes will need adequate space to grow and not be too great a distance from home for harvesting.

Scale and Repeated Patterns

Scale will be determined based upon your goals. You may want every foot of your space part of the food forest, or you may want to leave a good portion to lawn for playing and entertaining. You may have a tiny area to work with or a large one. A beautiful point about developing food forests is repetition: you can design a specific guild and repeat it more than once. The main fruit tree can be substituted in certain instances, with the remainder of the guild staying the same. The principles remain the same in the permaculture landscape whether in a large or small area.

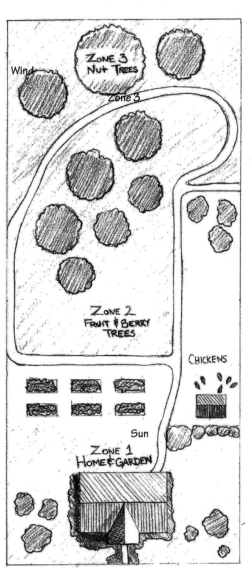

Credit: Sarah A. Jubeck

Zone systems layout of a suburban lot, based on intensity of management and use for each part of the yard. Zone One is daily use and kitchen garden, Zone Two main gardens and fruits, Zone Three larger trees and wild craft area.

Plan for Abundance

Disease, animals, pests, and other factors most likely will affect your landscape at some point. There are a few strategies for working with these natural occurrences, one of which is to plan for abundance in the first place. When you have multiple blueberry bushes, the birds eating some will not have as large an impact. As well, if wildlife is a major issue, you can strategically place crops for them. This way, your main harvest will be protected to some extent. As in nature, most plants do not occur singly, but in community. Keep your design diverse and abundant for less stress later.

Managed Increase

When your vision hits the third dimension, the larger and more complex the ecosystem you are creating, the higher the level of maintenance it will require, particularly in the early stages. On a large property it can be beneficial to implement your vision in stages, to both adjust to the work needed and experiment along the way. Perhaps all those plum trees succumb to a rot in the first year or you decide you do not want that many hazelnuts. It is great to get a reality check.

Apple tree guild in a community garden.

Make Use of Contour

A *contour* is the natural elevation curve of the slope on the site. Rather than focusing on creating curves in the design to increase edge, it is perhaps more ecologically sound to lay on the existing contour of the site. Designing with the contour in mind has a number of benefits. Planting along swales on contour allows for capture and storage of water onsite. Pathways set on contour will be level, which may be important if you are carrying your harvest. Aesthetically, planting on the contour is visually appealing.

You might be able to visually lay out a level swale on sloping land, but a few simple tools can be helpful. If you have access to a surveyor's level to mark contour lines use it. If not, the water level and the A-frame tool are low-cost tools for laying out contour lines.

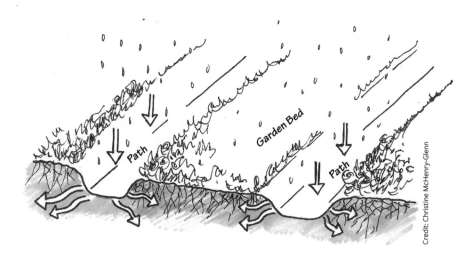

Contour beds.

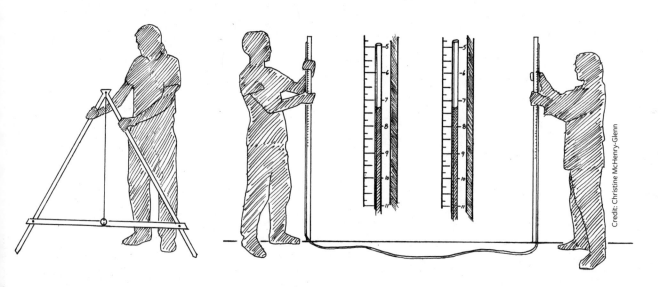

A-frame tool to lay out contour.   Water level tools to lay out contour.

Avoiding Dogma

As nature is constantly evolving, so too a permaculture design will constantly evolve, as a major focus is designing based on natural principles. Natural systems often find the path of least resistance and certainly make the most of the given situation, resources, and habitat. You can do the same with your landscape. By mixing an efficient design process with experimentation and perhaps even some capriciousness, the landscape will be diverse, abundant and, most importantly, a joyful process.

There is a plethora of wisdom to gain and utilize from permaculture design principles and perhaps the most important one is to continue to evolve. This means having lightness about the suggestions rather than looking at them as tight rules to follow. The land is the highest authority and it will speak in the language of stellar or weak growth. There is much mystery to be unfolded. On the Hazelwood site, as soon as we started to break ground, the soil seed bank sprouted and we began to have an abundance of edible and medicinal plants without any direct intention on our part.

The Design Process

The permaculture design process begins with listing goals and studying your site, and is used to create a plan for establishing and managing the food forest. In the beginning, you may dream big, state grand goals, and develop an impressive vision for a Garden of Eden. Site assessment and analysis of your available time, land, and climate considerations will likely moderate these dreams and help to narrow down the possibilities.

The process of making a base map and *assessing* the site and then *analyzing* the information gathered is the central element of the design process. The information you gather and analyze is the template that your goals and dreams for your food forest are set in. Plants are selected to fit the goal and the site. The food forest is planned to evolve over time as trees grow and mature. Management strategies are determined and polyculture interactions are considered. The final result of all this is the *site plan*. The plan may include maps and drawings of the site, written plans, plant lists, time lines for site development, and management plans.

Steps of the Design Process

Design Steps	Actions to Complete
1. Clarify overall goals	Make goals list.
2. Observe site	Note existing conditions and climatic factors and track these on the base map.
3. Create a base mapping	Create base map, visit site, take measurements, use digital mapping tools, such as SketchUp or a landscape design program.
4. Assess the site	Visit site, make observations, conduct research.
5. Analyze site	Make sense of all the information collected.
6. Research plants	Research and catalog locally available plants; research size, characteristics, and plug into concept map.
7. Sketch concept map	Create general design.
8. Create schematic design	Make a detailed overview design.
9. Detailed design with patches	Complete detailed design showing where plants will go.

Setting the Intention and Goals for Your Food Forest

Intention is the grounding element to every action in the material world. Setting an intention is letting the universe know what you want, so it can support you. The beginning of the design process involves setting this intention, this seed, for your space. Allow yourself some time to envision your ideal landscape. Use your imagination and let your mind be free. Later in the design process, we will go back to using small, slow solutions to determine what will actually work. For now, go wild.

Once you have had time to imagine your ideal landscape, start to consider in more detail what will be in it. It is helpful to create a goals list for this.

Your Goals List

Designing your food forest, or forest garden, is a way of landscaping to suit your needs for food, flowers, craft materials, medicinal plants, biodiversity, and beauty. At the same time, you will address ecological needs, working towards a self-managing system through resource cycling. One of the very first steps in this process is determining your goals. Here are some questions to get you started:

- What do you want from this space primarily? (Shade, privacy, food, ecological health, plants for medicine, dyeing, or magical use, experimentation, aesthetics, and so on.)
- How much time are you willing and able to devote to initial planting and weekly maintenance?
- What are your physical abilities or access to labor?
- How much money can you spend on resources and desired elements? Is doing it for free important to you?
- What resources do you have easy access to, or have onsite already? (Bricks, stones, manure, leaf mulch, plants, trees, and so on.)
- What is your long-term vision for the site?
- What elements on the site need to be considered as limitations or assets? (Wind, sun, shade, water; salt, pollution, buildings, poor soil, soil contamination, unwanted plants, animals.)
- How will you use your harvests?
- Do you envision earning income from your food forest?

Write down your answers to these questions. You will get a handle on your own priorities and a clearer idea of what main elements will be present in the design. These goals and ecological principles are the guiding lights for the remainder of the process.

Site Observation

During the goal setting process, take time to observe your site. It is very useful, if you can, to watch as the seasons change, see how the sun moves through the sky, where the water tends to collect, and the natural flow of energy through the space. Energy here can be defined as the movement of the elements: water, wind, solar, animals, and leaf fall. Also become aware of where the natural pathways are, for you and for any wildlife. In addition to what is happening on your site, take some time to note what is happening in the surrounding community and landscape. The potential for vandalism or theft may be a concern. All of these various aspects affect the land and the design.

Collecting data during the observation phase will be helpful later when you are designing the landscape, as you can work with rather than against what is already happening. You will also have a better idea of what to plan for, what to leverage, and what to mitigate.

There is no set or minimum time for the observation stage; it goes on throughout the design process. Actually, ongoing observation and adjustment is a major part of managing your food forest as well. The more you can observe the better. Keen observation is one of the key elements to effective design. If the space is new to you, give the observation phase some time. Let yourself be present for sunrise and sunset, different weather conditions, and times of day.

Base Mapping

A base map is the footprint of your land. The information recorded on the base map includes existing buildings, fences, property lines, trees and vegetation, utility lines (above and below ground), walkways, topography, and any other element that is currently on the property. We also determine the cardinal directions of the location and record the North arrow on the base map.

Creating the base map is essential for accurate planning. However, the intensity of the base mapping process is dependent upon your goals. If you're a home gardener, you may already have enough information through your observations and a property map to put together a simple base map. If you are just working on a small corner of your yard and want to make a sketch of your ideas to guide your efforts, that's fine. But for larger areas and to integrate your food forest into the whole landscape, the mapping process is highly recommended.

To get started on the base mapping process, you will need some maps.

1. **Property or land survey map:** The property map designates property lines and the size you have to work within. If you do not have a survey map, you might find one on file at your county courthouse or an online parcel map hosted by the county in which you live. At the least, the courthouse should have plot maps and a copy of your deed that show your property dimensions and boundaries.

2. **Aerial view map:** Getting an aerial view map is a good way to see your existing canopy cover. You will also get information on surrounding landscapes which could interfere with or assist your plans. A simple way to

obtain an aerial map is using an online tool like Bing Maps, Google Maps, or Google Earth. Type in your address and scale the map accurately. You need to know one dimension of at least one structure that appears on the map; for example, the length of one side of a house. An engineer's scale is a valuable tool for making quick measurements on the map. Some online mapping programs include a measuring tool, but be sure to check for accuracy.

3. **Topographic map:** The topographic map can be accessed via the site My Topo (mytopo.com/maps). Topography is the arrangement of features on the land. The topographic map will show the general slope of the land in contour lines. Many standard topographic maps are shown with contour lines spaced at each ten-foot change in elevation. If you have access to two-foot contour maps that is quite helpful. But a ten-foot contour map does give a sense of the landscape as well. Topographic maps are very helpful in observing water flow and in locating potential microclimates, windbreaks, and blocks. They illustrate the steepness of the landscape and can help with the layout of terraces, pathways, swales, and ponds.

4. **Cardinal points:** The base map and subsequent maps of the site should identify the cardinal points with an arrow pointing to the north. Marking the directions on the base map helps you keep in mind the directions of prevailing winds and the track of the sun through the days and the seasons.

5. **Sun sector analysis:** You should observe where the sun rises and sets at different times of the year on your property. Shade patterns are created by existing buildings and vegetation. Noting these on your base map can help plan to make the best use of your resources. Full sun, partial sun, and full shade should be noted.

Creating Your Base Map

Once you have the above three maps and relevant information, you can begin to layer them to create the final base map. If you are using a software program, import the three separate maps and match the scale. If you are not using a computer design program, use tracing paper to transfer all three maps onto the same layer.

Adobe Illustrator is one program we find useful for mapping and design; however, there are other specific landscape design programs that can be used as well.

Once you have your basic footprint map, walk the space; take measurements when in doubt. Some elements on the aerial map may have changed. What we are trying to do in this stage is simply get the picture of what is already present. This is not the time to add what you would like to be there. That comes later.

If you notice that some of the elements in your property and aerial source maps are no longer there, or that elements are there that were not represented in them, you can use either the *extension and offset lines* method or the *triangulation* method to update your maps (see sidebar on page 42).

Base Mapping To Do List

- Walk your land and make mental or written notes on observations such as water flow, solar access, existing plants, and structures (site assessment).
- Gather maps from Google Earth or find your survey map.
- Scale maps to accurate size.
- Note cardinal points.
- Double check on features in the map versus real life.
- Retrace all maps onto new paper, accurately scaled.

Site Assessment

Site assessment is the process of observing and collecting data about the site as it is now. In order to properly assess what is on the site, it is important to look at your sectors, collect some data, and take some measurements.

Relevant sectors to assess:

- soil condition
- water flow and access
- existing vegetation
- solar and shade access
- wind direction and speed

- structures on the site
- access to storage
- pathways
- views
- wildlife

The assessment phase is simply noting and recording what is there. It is a fact-gathering process. Let's go through the sectors and figure out what kind of information is important to gather.

Soil Sector

County soils maps are a great starting point for learning about your soil. The soil survey maps in the United States were developed in the mid-20th century by the Soil Conservation Service, now the Natural Resources Conservation Service. Libraries may still have copies of the original county soil survey books. These provide detailed soil maps for the county and provide a great deal of information of the type of soils found there. Today these maps have been digitized and are available free of charge through the NRCS's soil survey online tool at websoilsurvey.sc.egov.usda.gov/App/HomePage.htm. When you type in your property's location and use the tools to select your property boundaries, you can print out some basic information about your soil type and likely depth, pH, water table, and climate information for the site.

For urban soils, like Hazelwood Food Forest's, the soil survey provides limited data. Their "urban soils" category means soil made up of unknown materials whose layers cannot be designated. At HFF, we unearthed generations of rubble and debris, including bricks, sinks, trash, and more. In the case of urban soils, observation and soil testing are our main tools.

Once you know your soil type you can test it for nutrients, pH, and potential pollutants.

Testing Your Soil

Testing soil is simple: gather soil samples at different areas of your site, dry them, bag and label them, and ship them to a soil-testing laboratory. There are home testing kits as well. They can be a lower-cost method when a lot of testing is needed but require you to do the analysis as well as testing. Depending upon the model purchased, you can test for pH, organic matter, and an extensive range of minerals and nutrients.

For just a few samples, the ease and accuracy of lab testing may be preferred. We have used the University of Massachusetts' laboratory most

Updating Your Maps

Mapping terms

Plan drawing: view of site from above.

Elevation drawing: view of site plan from the side.

Scale: a drawing's proportional relationship to the actual size. A common scale is 1 inch equals 10 feet.

Tools

Simple drafting tool sets can be purchased at college book stores, art supply stores, and online.

The most basic tool sets include an engineer's scale, rulers, drawing compass, triangles, and drawing curves. A large drawing board and T-square are helpful. Pencils and drawing pens come in various line thicknesses to aid in drawing and illustrating the maps clearly.

Locating elements of the landscape for mapping can be done in two ways: extension with offset lines method or triangulation.

Extension with offset lines method

At Three Sisters Farm we made all our garden and landscape maps with the extensions with offsets. Starting at a known point, such as a corner of your house, lay out a long measuring tape at a right angle to the building. This is the extension line. A 100- or 200-foot tape is best. Then measure the distance off that line to the feature at a 90 degree angle. So a tree may be plotted as being 15 feet south and 20 feet west of the corner of your house. Continue this process for all elements on the property and transfer them to the map. Care must be taken to

be sure you are measuring at 90 degree angles for accuracy.

Triangulation

Triangulation sounds complicated but it is based on simple geometry. And it is easier to be accurate with triangulation than with the extension with offset method. Tools required include a 100- or 250-foot measuring tape and small drafting kit. The drafting tools should include an engineer's ruler, dividers or drafting compass, and drawing board.

1. Start from the location of two elements on the map, like two corners on the side of a building.
2. Next, simply measure all existing features, trees, shrubs, and garden corners from the two known points.
3. Record all data accurately.

It usually takes two people to measure by triangulation. One holds the measuring tape at the starting point and notes the distances. The other person measures to the elements being mapped and reports the distance to the note taker. Be sure to record the measurements accurately from each starting point. It is a good idea for one person to shout out the distance to each point and the other to record the numbers.

Then, using the ruler or drafting compass, drawing tools and tracing paper, transfer the measurements to the paper, again starting from the known locations on the map. Using a drawing compass, measure from the first known location to the first element, say a tree, and make an arc on the paper. Then, using the measured distance from the second known location to the tree, make another arc. Where the two arcs overlap is the location of the tree. Repeat this process for all elements you wish to add to the map.

It is necessary to have a sheet for recording the data which includes the names of the elements and the number of measurements. Make sure to properly name elements so that you will remember them at a later date. It is quite easy to get confused if there are any unclear notes.

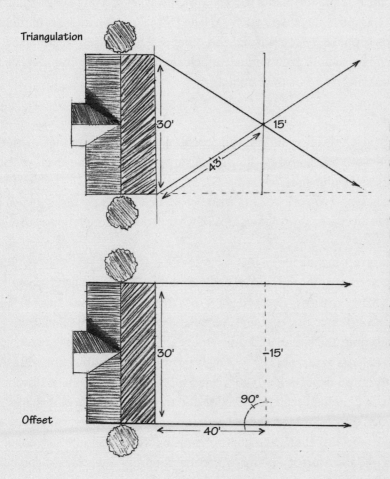

Mapping by triangulation involves location of site elements by measuring from two known points on the landscape to locate other points. Mapping by extension and offset involves laying out a line (extension) from a known location and measuring with right angles from the extension (offset) to locate other points.

frequently because of the range of things they test for. Thorough instructions on collecting soil samples are included in either the home testing kits or from the laboratory of your choosing.

Comprehensive soil testing tells you:

1. If there are any heavy metals or other contaminants in the soil. If you do have contaminants, you can decide upon remediation strategies and if you want to take that on yourself.
2. The amount of organic material present in the soil. This will tell you how much soil building will be required to obtain a good yield. Remember, feed the soil and the plants will grow themselves (to a large degree).
3. The type and amount of nutrients needed for plant growth. Most of these can be supplied by composting and other soil building strategies. However, if you want to grow annuals which are more nutrient intensive, you will know what needs to be added.

Soil Profile

Digging a post hole into your soil will provide a lot of important information about your soil. The side of the hole reveals the soil profile. The layers of the soil profile are called horizons.

Once again, if you are dealing with urban soils, you may not get clean, designated layers. You will get an idea of what is there though (glass, rocks, and so on).

These layers include:

- **The O horizon or the top layer of organic matter:** This is the layer of sod, fallen leaves, partially decayed plant materials, and mulches. In a natural ecosystem it also contains animal and insect droppings and, from time to time, the bodies of dead creatures.
- **The A horizon or topsoil:** The topsoil is the most lively part of the soil. It is usually a richer color. It contains a mix of particles from the lower levels, and perhaps materials eroded and transported from elsewhere or added by the gardener, mixed with organic matter, roots, worms, insects, fungal mycelium, and microorganisms. Topsoil should also contain a good portion of air—up to 25 percent pore space is ideal—and be capable of holding moisture, while draining away excess water.

- **The B horizon or subsoil:** This will also contain plant roots but will have far less organic matter. The transition from A to B horizons is usually clearly marked by a lighter soil color. Some soils contain more graded changes.
- **The C horizon:** This is the part of the subsoil less influenced by the surface layers. It is mostly made up of weathered bedrock or whatever parent material underlies the site.

Below the C horizon is the parent material such as bedrock. In glaciated areas the base material can be deep layers of sand, clay, and gravel mixed with larger stones and rocks.

Often the transition from horizon to horizon is gradual and there may be graduations within a layer. Generally, when moving from the O horizon to parent material, the soil becomes denser and contains less life. Clay particles tend to settle into the lower layers.

Sand, Silt, and Clay

Soil particles are classified by size. Sand is the largest, silt intermediate, and clays are the smallest. Soils high in silt are considered ideal. Sandy soil may drain too fast, drying out too quickly and losing minerals and fertility to lower layers. Clay soils can easily be too compact, slow to drain, and low in air that roots and soil organisms need to thrive.

A good soil has all three particle sizes in the right balance. Clay has a high potential to catch and hold minerals until plants and fungi need them. Sand is needed to help with drainage but does not contribute much to holding available nutrients. Silt can catch and hold nutrients and drains better than clay.

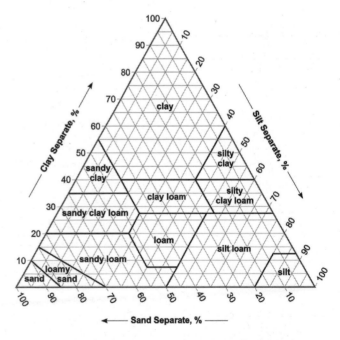

The soil triangle illustrates soil type based on relative amounts of sand, silt, and clay found in the soil.

Water Sector

Assessing water flow and access can be done in a few ways. The topographic lines on the maps you made will show the direction of water flow. The steepness of the topography will give you an idea of its speed.

On the site, observe the natural paths formed by water flow. Water flows from high areas and collects in low lands. If there is slope onsite, remember that water will take the path of least resistance. Under canopy cover, water will evaporate more slowly and so there will be more moisture in general. Take note if excessive dripping from structures pools in any areas. If you are in a dry climate, keep these principles in mind as you move through the design process as possibilities for how to keep water in your system.

Other areas of water assessment include quality, noting access to plumbing, available roofs from which to collect rainwater, and features that would either block or collect water, such as stones, vegetation, buildings, or anything else, natural or built.

Vegetation Sector

Here you identify the existing plants, trees, shrubs, and vines on your site. Once you know what is on your site, you can adapt the design to make best use of what is there as well as what will complement it. You may learn there are already many edibles or useful plants present. Also note nearby vegetation. Neighboring vegetation could be helpful, providing windbreaks and habitat for beneficial creatures. It can also be detrimental, a source of invasive plants, pest animals, and excess shade.

Here are some plant identification resources to get you started:
- *Newcomb's Wildflower Guide*
- Peterson Field Guides
- The USDA's Interactive ID Keys
- Plant identification applications
- Local plant identification classes (often offered by state parks)
- Plant identification social media groups
- Herbal medicine walks and edible plant group gatherings

Solar Sector

Understanding the daily and seasonal cycles of sunlight on your food forest is crucial to the design process. At the Hazelwood Food Forest, a three-story building adjacent to the site on the south side of the lot was a major influence on the design.

Take the time to really study the site. Will any structure be built next door? Will nearby trees grow larger and shade the site? Will your planting goals maximize the site's potential? Will your food forest shade the neighbor's garden? How will the food forest affect buildings and other gardens on the site? You will not want to shade the solar panels you just installed, (or your neighbor's). But you might want to shade your south-facing windows in the summer time.

In assessing solar access, you can supplement your visual observations with a solar pathfinder tool, or plug your Google Earth map into SketchUp (which has a feature for solar access). Solar assessment successfully shows where the shadows are cast and at what time of year.

Wind Sector

The prevailing direction and average speed of wind can influence your landscape and therefore modify the design plan. If you are not sure about prevailing winds, ask your neighbors, and pay attention to the weather.

Knowing how wind direction and intensity vary through the year will inform the design process. In northwestern Pennsylvania our prevailing winds and most storms blow in from the west and northwest. Occasionally a storm system pushing up the east coast will give us winds from the east. In southwestern Pennsylvania, the prevailing winds are west and southwest.

The food forests at Three Sisters Farm are designed so the outer semicircle of shrubs on the west and north side of the Spiral Garden food forest provides a windbreak from prevailing winds for the rest of the garden and the bioshelter adjacent to the garden. At Three Sisters Farm we also get wind speeds of up to 60 miles per hour at least once a year. These can topple a tree and have pushed a couple of our apple trees on their side in a wet year. A windbreak food forest should be designed with maximum wind gusts in mind, so they will break the wind rather than be broken by it.

Beyond general observation, the wind sector can be explored through a wind rose for your area.

As defined by the Natural Resources Conservation Service (wcc.nrcs.usda.gov/climate/windrose): "a wind rose gives a very succinct but information-laden view of how wind speed and direction are typically distributed at a particular location. Presented in a circular format, the wind rose shows the frequency of winds blowing from particular directions. The length of each 'spoke' around the circle is related to the frequency of time that the wind blows from a particular direction. Each concentric circle represents a different frequency, emanating from zero at the center to increasing frequencies at the outer circles."

Wind roses are available on the Earth System Research Laboratory's website under the meteorology section: esrl.noaa.gov/gmd. This shows the general direction and speed of wind for your area. Within your site, there could be other factors that will affect the wind flow, such as topographic features, wind breaks formed by trees or houses, or wind tunnels created by natural and built environment. Carefully note these for design consideration.

Built Sector

You should represent existing structures on your base maps. Walk around the buildings and structures and make notes about their relationship to the food forest. Be sure to preserve access for building maintenance and access. Proper placement of trees and shrubs can provide summer shade and winter wind protection for your house

Many states have a call number for locating buried infrastructure, power cables, and water and gas lines. Locate these and note them on the map. Overhead power lines are also

Credit: Sarah A. Jubeck

> 11.05
8.49–11.05
5.40–8.49
3.34–5.40
1.80–3.34
0.51–1.80

A windrose is a graphic representation of the annual average wind direction and speed in your area.

a concern. Avoid planting trees that will need to be pruned away from the overhead lines. In locations with onsite sewage processing, septic tanks and septic drainage fields should be kept clear of trees so that the pipes do not clog. Occasionally the septic tank will need to be pumped clean of accumulated sewage, and so access should be preserved for that process.

Site assessment is also a good time to plan for future site development. Many a tree has been removed to make way for a patio, garage, or other construction projects.

Nearby roads and parking lots can be sources of runoff water in storms. This can be a problem if oils, brake fluids, and other chemicals are spilled on the pavement. Non-edible vegetative swales may be needed to catch and hold such water before it enters your property.

Legal Concerns

It is a good idea to assess potential legal issues. Many municipalities have restrictions such as right of way and setback rules for structures on a property. Right of way clauses and restrictions also exist in many deeds. The highway department may have legal rights to widen roads as needed. Be sure you know the rules.

You may wish to have chickens or ducks in your food forest plan. Restrictions are likely to exist on the number of birds allowed. Beekeeping may also be regulated. It is best to be on good terms with local officials. Treat them with respect, ask honest questions, and seek options if a rule stands in your way. Often a group of like-minded citizens will help get new ordinances passed if regulations restrict your plans. Urban farming is a growing movement, and part of the answer to local food security everywhere. Community food forests are taking root in many towns and cities, often with the blessing and assistance of local governments.

Site Analysis

Creating the Sector Map

Site analysis is where you analyze what role each sector plays in the system and how they interact with and influence other sectors as well as the whole. It is where you start to get a better understanding of what you may need to do to bolster or quell an influence. It is where you go through all the data you've collected for all the sectors and turn it into useful information.

According to Bill Mollison's *Permaculture: A Designers' Manual*, (1988, 49), zone and sector analysis is "a primary energy-conserving placement pattern for the whole site." It looks at both the energy available onsite including people, resources, and machinery, and the energy flowing through the site. The *sector map* is where we record all of this information and use it to overlay our base map. It then gives a full picture of what needs to be put into the design to make the ecosystem healthy and abundant.

Once you know what is onsite, you can then refine your goals and timeline based upon what is realistic or achievable. For example, if you want to grow a decent-sized annual garden in the first year, surrounded by fruit tree guilds that will mature over time, and you find that your soil is very low in organic material, you will need to spend some energy and time amending the soil with compost, cover crops, sheet mulching, or other soil-building strategies.

The site analysis process leaves you with a set of refined goals you will then use in the next phase, the concept design, or concept sketch. The concept design is the first phase in which you put together existing

Sector analysis of a suburban lot, showing some of the factors that affect the property.

Credit: Sarah A. Jubeck

and desired elements on the same drawing. Up until now, we have been creating all of the pieces needed for this stage. Now we are ready to begin the actual design.

The Soil Sector

Once you get your results back either from the lab or your home testing kit, take time to read through the results and background information about each. Different nutrients will be present in differing amounts and the results will give you an idea of what will grow best on the site at the moment. For example, apples appreciate a fair amount of calcium in the soil and so if there are high levels in the soil it is a tree that could fit well.

Soil testing tells you:

1. If there are any heavy metals or other contaminants in the soil. If you do have contaminants, you can decide upon remediation strategies and if you want to take that on yourself.
2. The amount of nutrients needed for plant growth. Most of these can be supplied by composting and other soil-building strategies. However, if you want to grow annuals which are more nutrient intensive, you will know what else needs to be added.

```
                           ANALYSIS REPORT

SAMPLE ID: 314-17 2ND AVE
SOIL TYPE:

SOIL PH    8.0        ALUMINUM (AL):   19 PPM (Soil Range: 10-300)
BUFFER PH  7.5

NUTRIENT LEVELS:_PPM_|     LOW      MEDIUM       HIGH_____VERY_HIGH
PHOSPHORUS (P)    21 |XXXXXXXXXXXXXXXXXXXXXXXXXXXXXXXX
POTASSIUM  (K)   260 |XXXXXXXXXXXXXXXXXXXXXXXXXXXXXXXXXXXXXXXXXXXXXXXXX
CALCIUM    (CA)12940 |XXXXXXXXXXXXXXXXXXXXXXXXXXXXXXXXXXXXXXXXXXXXXXXXXXX
MAGNESIUM  (MG)  200 |XXXXXXXXXXXXXXXXXXXXXXXXXXXXXXXXXXXXXXXXXXXXXXXX
NITRATE  (NO3-N)  14 |XXXXXXXXXX

CATION EXCH CAP       PERCENT BASE SATURATION
   67.6 MEQ/100G         K= 1.0 MG= 2.5 CA=96.6


MICRONUTRIENT___PPM__SOIL_RANGE     MICRONUTRIENT___PPM___SOIL_RANGE
Boron      (B)  1.1    0.1-2.0      Copper    (Cu) 32.0    0.3-8.0
Manganese  (Mn) 19.4   3 - 20       Iron      (Fe) 1.6     1.0- 40
Zinc       (Zn) 63.0   0.1- 70

EXTRACTED LEAD   (PB)   98 PPM.     ESTIMATED TOTAL LEAD IS    830 PPM.
EXTRACTED CADMIUM (CD)  0.5 PPM.
EXTRACTED NICKEL (NI)   0.5 PPM.    EXTRACTED CHROMIUM (CR)   0.2 PPM.
                           COMMENTS
```

Soil test results give help to plan the improvement of your soils with the proper amounts of composts and rock minerals. A good soil test will tell you micro-nutrient levels and the presence of lead in the soil.

The Composting Process

Composting is defined as an aerobic process of decomposition of organic matter into humus-like substances and minerals by the action of microorganisms combined with chemical and physical reactions.

There are four main phases in the composting process, depending on which microorganisms are active: mesophilic, thermophilic, cooling, and curing. While the first three phases will happen naturally, the fourth, curing, is an additional step that could be left out. In the mesophilic phase the oxidative action of bacteria, actinomycetes, fungi, and protozoa (which grow between 10–45 degrees Celsius) increases the temperature. This leads into the thermophilic phase, which occurs when temperature reaches 45–60 degrees Celsius. It is the peak of degradation of fresh organic matter. After the peak, the cooling phase is characterized once again by mesophilic microorganisms which continue to degrade complex organic compounds and produce humus-like substances. During the cooling phase, the work of earthworms, fungi, and insects further helps the process of turning organic matter into humus. The fourth stage, a curing phase, is where the pile is left alone for up to a year after the cooling stage to assure pathogen destruction. This specifically applies to composts which incorporate human, pig, and dog manures.

A general equation for the overall composting process is:

$$C + O \rightarrow CO_2 + energy \text{ (heat)}$$

Four necessities for good compost are moisture, oxygen, high temperature, and a "balanced diet." The diet consists of organic materials with a total carbon to nitrogen ratio (C:N) of between 20:1 and 35:1. Organic materials include manure, plants, leaves, sawdust, grass clippings, food scraps, urine, etc. Basically, anything that will rot will compost.

Nitrogen can easily be lost if there is an imbalance with carboniferous "brown" materials. Humus is the result of the composting process and is a brown or black substance that holds moisture and is chemically stable. It holds nine times its weight in water (900 percent), compared to sand (2 percent) and clay (20 percent). Problems with slow or no heating in the compost pile most commonly stem from a lack of nitrogen, moisture, or air. The solution is to add more nitrogenous material or water.

There are numerous benefits to both composting and compost. As an amendment, compost enriches soil by adding organic material, increasing water retention, introducing beneficial soil organisms, and adding nutrients. It both prevents future pollution and fights current pollution by binding heavy metals and other toxins and reducing material going to the landfill, which can produce methane gas and a host of other problems. The composting process can destroy human and animal pathogens and finished compost has been shown to decrease plant pathogens that cause disease. Finally, it is economically viable, both in saving money for waste disposal and the potential to sell the finished product for profit.

General results for soil testing include:
- Soil pH
- Macronutrients including phosphorus, potassium, calcium, magnesium, and sulfur
- Micronutrients including boron, manganese, zinc, copper, and iron
- Aluminum
- Lead
- Base saturation percentages of calcium, magnesium, and potassium
- Scoop density

You will learn if any minerals need to be added to the soil. Test results tell you the levels of phosphorus, potassium, calcium, and magnesium, expressed as levels of very low, low, optimum, and above optimum. Generally you can choose which crops to provide basic analysis for and the results will have comments about what to add in what amount based upon that crop's needs.

The Water Sector

Water collection is an important consideration. Water is precious and essential for life. We need to use it wisely. The soil's ability to absorb, store, and conserve water while also draining properly is essential to plant health. In drylands the ability to capture and store rainwater for later use, and the selection of appropriate plants, is critical to the design of the food forest. Regulations on the collection and storage of rainwater vary from state to state, and can vary between municipalities in a state, so be sure to check with your local and state laws.

Drainage and runoff patterns are additional ways of analyzing the water sector onsite. If you have hills and valleys, remember the water will collect in the valleys. These can be good areas for rain gardens, designed with plants specific to marshy landscapes. Rather than attempting to grow dry-loving plants and trees, work with the natural flow.

There are a number of strategies for making the best use of rainwater in a food forest garden. The common standard for irrigation is that a garden requires the equivalent of an inch of rain each week in the growing season.

With larger perennials a heavy dose of water is needed to soak down to the root zone and recharge the soil's water store.

Storage and Release

The general concept is that a portion of the rain that falls and snow that melts on a given site should stay onsite to be used for irrigation, or be allowed to slowly sink into the soil for groundwater recharge.

Directing rainwater runoff from our buildings to storage structures or to our gardens is an essential part of good permaculture design. A few basic concepts of hydrology can help create successful gardens and help us avoid problems. These include understanding how much rain falls in a given area and how it moves across the surface and into the ground.

Rainfall

Rainfall patterns vary from place to place and year to year. A general understanding of your rainfall patterns can greatly aid the design and help reduce the need to irrigate.

In our part of the country, southwestern Pennsylvania, we expect to receive 40 to 45 inches of rain each year. It is evenly distributed throughout the year. During the summer, rainfall generally comes in the form of storms and downpours. Spring and fall we are more likely to get long, steady, lighter rain. Winter snows can be light or heavy but the snow tends to accumulate for weeks at a time and can melt gradually over weeks or in a few days.

Summer storms average less than an inch of rain. Rain that delivers 4 inches in 24 hours happens once every 25 years in our area. Even heavier rain occurs on average every 100 years. These 25- and 100-year rains tend to cause flooding.

A light rain might not infiltrate the soil and can evaporate quickly without contributing to the water supply. When rain falls heavily or snow melts quickly, much of it will run off to ditches and streams. Lighter rains and slowly melting snow tend to soak into the ground, until the ground is too saturated to hold more water, and then it will begin to run off.

The capacity for water to infiltrate the ground also depends on the soil type and surface features. Steeper land drains faster. Impervious surfaces like roads and parking lots have little or no infiltration. And they can contain a mix of potential pollutants ranging from sediment to varying quantities of nutrients, organic chemicals, petroleum hydrocarbons, and other constituents that cause water quality degradation.

Storage Strategies

There are a number of strategies to reduce runoff and collect water from impermeable surfaces and store it either in the soil or in containers for later use. *Rain barrels* and *cisterns* allow us to gather stormwater for irrigation. A *rain garden* is a garden designed to absorb water runoff. A *swale* is a long shallow trench for collecting water and allowing it to soak into the ground or flow into a storage structure such as a pond or rain garden. A *bioswale* is a swale planted with water-tolerant plants. A *vegetative strip* is a sort of swale, often on roadsides or parking lots, designed to slow runoff and allow it to soak into the ground. Often a vegetative strip is intended to filter out debris and pollutants before they can enter streams and groundwater.

Rain Barrels

Rain barrels are inexpensive and easy to build and install. Many sizes and styles of rain barrels are available. Generally they hold around 50 gallons of water. Several rain barrels can be connected to each other to hold more water. A good rain barrel should be designed with a screen to filter out debris such as leaves and twigs. It should have an overflow hole near the top and a faucet connection near the bottom.

Take advantage of gravity! You will want the barrel to be higher than where you want the water to end up in the landscape. Water does not run uphill, so keep it at least 18 inches from the ground level or watering surface. This will increase water pressure for your hose or irrigation system. The barrel should be also elevated high enough off the ground to allow for filling buckets and connecting hoses. It is preferable to have the rain barrel faucet set so that the water flows out by gravity from the rain barrel to the garden. Because a 50-gallon rain barrel will weigh around 400 pounds when full, it needs to be set level, stable, and secure.

Water is healthiest when cool; shading helps to prevent the growth of algae in your vessel. Consider shading your barrel(s) with a perennial such as a creeping vine like the Trumpet vine, or with a canvas tarp or other cover.

Larger aboveground tanks can also be set to collect rainwater off a building. These have the same design considerations as a rain barrel.

Bear in mind that this water is not potable for humans and animals. Be sure to check your filter regularly to prevent blockages and overflow. And remember to detach the downspout in the winter

Not all rooftops are created equal. Rain barrels and harvested rainwater are not recommended for use on edible plants with the following roof types:

- Wood shingles or shakes that have been treated with chemicals to resist rotting and moss growth
- Zinc (galvanized metal) anti-moss strips at your roof peaks
- Copper roof or gutters
- Asphalt shingles with zinc embedded in the surface

Rain barrels are simple to build and easy to use.

Credit: Nancy Martin

Cisterns

A cistern is a larger structure, usually buried in the ground, with a holding capacity of 500 to several thousand gallons. Many older homes were built with cisterns before municipal water supplies became common. Modern cisterns are made of either potable-water-grade plastic or concrete. Water is usually pumped from a cistern for use. A cistern may make sense for some locations. They are expensive to purchase and require excavation to install.

Rain Gardens

A simple rain garden is a depression approximately 18 inches deep that is filled with absorbent materials such as compost, sand, topsoil, and mulch and planted with suitable native plants. Native plants are best because they establish deeper roots (which help the soil hold water), are adapted to the local climate, should not need excessive care, and attract local pollinators, birds, and butterflies.

Rain gardens absorb water and allow it to slowly soak into the earth. As with rain barrels and cisterns, rain gardens help to prevent watershed pollution in the form of polluted runoff. They also aid in preventing flood and stream bank destabilization, and of course they contribute to groundwater recharge and healthy soil.

Some people opt to have the overflow from a rain barrel or cistern drain into a rain garden—the best of both worlds!

The square footage of your rain garden should generally be about 20 percent of the area draining into it. To capture runoff most efficiently, a rain garden should be longer than it is wide and aligned perpendicular to the slope.

Swales

A swale or bioswale is simple to construct with a rototiller and rake. The top soil is tilled, along a marked contour, to the width desired for the swale. Then the soil is raked down the slope to create a wide and shallow depression. On relatively level land soil is raked to the sides to create the shallow depression. This can be tamped and then planted as desired. Rain runoff from the catchment area is directed into the swale.

The swale is sized to catch and absorb the desired amount of rain. A swale can be sloped gradually downhill to lead rain runoff to a desired storage area, such as a rain garden or pond.

Variations on swales include adding below-ground gravel beds or pipes to increase storage or drainage as desired.

Vegetative Strips

Vegetative strips are often used along roads or in parking lots to slow runoff, filter out pollutants, and allow water to infiltrate the ground. Vegetative strips are small green spaces at a slightly lower elevation than the drainage area. They are sized to absorb water running off from rain storms.

Because stormwater management features are designed to catch, store, and slowly release rainwater and snow melt the water level for your food forest will fluctuate. Plant selection should take this into account. At Three Sisters Farm, a vegetative infiltration strip along our driveway is home to a natural, self-sustaining polyculture of Joe Pye weed, milkweed, and jewelweed. These three plants have medicinal values and provide habitat for butterflies, honeybees, and other beneficial insects. Other plants that may do well in swales, rain gardens, and vegetative strips include ground nuts, elderberry, willows, viburnum species, butternuts, and alder.

Benefits of Storage and Release

Rainwater harvesting using rain barrels, cisterns, and rain gardens serves many purposes in the landscape.

1. Storing water for later use in the landscape: Depending on the number and/or size of the collection vessel, a significant amount of water can be harvested from rooftops during the rainy season and used later when rains diminish.
2. Reducing flooding: Redirecting water from municipal storm drain systems can greatly reduce the amount of water directed to water treatment plants and/or rivers, streams, or lakes. Alternatively, water absorbed onsite can work its way slowly and gently underground to recharge the groundwater. On its way it is filtered as it passes through soil, sand, rock, and the roots of trees and other vegetation. This process acts as a natural and effective filtration system.

3. Reducing nonpoint source (nps) pollution: Water is the universal solvent; it dissolves more substances than any other liquid. It washes everything that it passes over. Therefore, as it passes over impervious surfaces and rooftops it picks up numerous contaminants that are then dumped into waterways.

4. Recharging groundwater supplies: Water is a crucial factor in maintaining healthy soil. Soil is alive and needs air and water to support the life it carries within.

5. Filtering/purifying water via onsite absorption/infiltration: Roots are very effective at filtering pollutants from water. The earth itself acts as a giant water filter.

Calculating Quantity

For stormwater management, the general rule is to design the storage, whether rain barrel, cistern, rain garden, or swale, to hold up to two inches of rain running off a section of roof. In western Pennsylvania this will happen every few years. It is also important to allow for safe overflow of excess water.

The area of collection is the section of the roof feeding the storage. A building may have multiple roof sections and multiple downspouts. From a house with just a 1,000 square-foot-base one can harvest 24,000 gallons of water annually in southwestern Pennsylvania. Based on the calculation below it is easy to see that rain barrels fill quickly! You may want to consider either a larger vessel or numerous connected 55-gallon rain barrels.

Water harvest calculation:

- The square footage of the house (not the roof) × 0.6 × annual rainfall in your area = Annual Harvest
- In Pennsylvania we get 40 inches of rain per year. Thus, a 1,000 square-foot-house × 0.6 × 40″ = 24,000 gallons per year.
- A 2-inch rain generates 1,200 gallons on a roof covering a 1,000 square-foot base.

If you have a roof that is not ideal for harvesting usable rainwater you may want to build a small structure over your rain barrels from which to collect roof water. This structure will serve a dual purpose: it will provide shade for the vessel; and it will provide a suitable roofing surface for harvesting rainwater. Ideal roofing materials include slate, clay tiles, and stainless steel.

Make sure that the rain barrel/cistern is placed securely on level ground. At 8.34 pounds per gallon, water is quite heavy. A 55-gallon drum, when full, weighs well over 400 pounds. Be sure to check your filter regularly to prevent blockages and overflow, and if you live in a cold climate remember to detach from the downspout in the winter to prevent damage to your roof and your rain barrel. Finally keep in mind that this water is not generally considered potable.

These photos show the setup of a watering system for a rain garden.
Rainwater is collected in a 500-gallon tank and slowly released into the rain garden.

The cistern set up on stone foundation.

Cistern for rain garden connected to house.

Rainwater flows from house to cistern.

Cistern outflow connection for rain garden.

Now that you have assessed the water flow and access onsite, you can apply this data to your needs. In this phase, you also want to consider the water needs of the plants that you would like to include. For example, most fruit trees prefer well-drained soils and have medium water requirements. However, each species is different and it is important to do your research upfront. It is much simpler to find the best place for each plant than to try to modify the site to suit the plant.

If the site is on a high water table or in a valley, there are specific rootstocks that many fruit trees can be grafted on which work with wet conditions.

A banana circle is watered by grey water piped underground from outdoor showers at Surylila Yoga Retreat Center in Andalucia Spain.

A "mulch sponge" in the center of the circle absorbs grey water slowly releases water and nutrients to the circular bed of bananas, bird of paradise flowers, fava beans, nasturtium, edible mallow and other crops

The Riparian Food Forest Garden

A riparian zone is land along a stream or body of water that is flooded occasionally and is vegetated with water-loving plants. Riparian zones along stream banks are best kept in permanent vegetative cover and so offer a perfect opportunity for food forest development. If land is classified as a wetland, there may be management restrictions.

Please consult with your regional USDA Natural Resources Conservation Service Office if working with a wetland. Generally, you can plant and manage a wetland area as long as the soil is not drained.

As always, the first step is to assess the existing plantings. Many wetland plants are quite useful. Native plants play key roles in local ecology as well, while many native trees and shrubs provide valuable services.

The black walnut guild is a good example of a riparian food forest. The black walnut guild is commonly referenced in food forest books. There is good reason for this. Because black walnuts are allelopathic to many other plants they need special considerations. The trees exude a chemical compound, juglone, from their roots and leaves. Juglone can persist in the soil for decades. As a nutritious and widespread tree, the black walnut deserves a place in the landscape and in our diet. Similarly, the butternut is a valuable addition to the diet. The guild of plants that will grow under a black walnut or butternut include understory trees such as red bud, persimmon, paw paw, and crab apple. Shrubs include viburnums, rose of Sharon, and wild roses. Other plants that do well in this guild include black raspberries, red raspberries, Virginia creeper, grapes on wild grape rootstock, ground nut, ostrich fern, and morel mushrooms. Many native wildflowers are also juglone tolerant. Some annual vegetables also fit into the black walnut guild. These included corn, beans and squash, potatoes, beets, melons, and onions.

The Vegetation Sector

Once you've identified the plants and trees on your site, you can decide what stays and what you would like to remove. Each plant currently in an ecosystem has a role and you can decide if you would like to replace it with another that has more uses or keep it.

You may discover that there are a few or many invasive plants. These are typically quick growing, tough competitor plants that quickly fill in open land. They are difficult to remove and make it difficult for other plants to establish themselves.

Additionally, there may be some trees that can act as nurse species. A nurse tree is a tree that provides services such as shading, symbiotic fungi, or leaf mulch to saplings as they grow. Once the saplings are strong enough, the nurse trees are generally pruned back or removed.

The Solar Sector

If you used a solar pathfinder to measure your solar access, you will have the results in a format that includes the percentages of available solar radiation in a given area per month. As the pathfinder does not necessarily include factors such as shadows created by buildings and large trees, make sure to consider that in your analysis. Also run the solar pathfinder at different times of day to obtain a clearer picture of the way the sun moves across the sky through the day as well as through the year.

For most fruit trees and many perennials, you will need access to full sun, which we define as at least eight hours per day. There are many edible plants that can grow in the shade as well, including paw paw, varieties of currants and berries, mesclun, leafy greens such as kale, root vegetables, and many perennials.

Directional access is another important part of solar analysis. How much space do you have facing south? Facing north? Most fruit trees will do well in south-facing situations. Also consider the height of trees and place the tallest ones on the north side so that they do not create shade for shorter plants. Shade will be created with the placement of trees so plan for shade-tolerant plants in the understory.

Shade Ecosystems

Many plants will get scorched in full or even part sun. Edibles such as mesclun, leafy greens, and tender understory herbs need shady areas. You can grow salad greens and valuable herbs such as ginseng or goldenseal in your shady spots. For more tropical climates, the shade is a place to grow many native rainforest plants and to create comfortable relaxation places.

Shade ecosystems can be used in a number of ways. In the Northeast, there are many native plants that need shade, so a native plant guild is one way to utilize the space. Several of these plants are medicinal, including American ginseng, goldenseal, blue cohosh, black cohosh, sassafras, witch hazel, and hawthorn.

For food production, lettuces and greens (such as kale, chard, kohlrabi) prefer cooler, less sunny areas. Mix those with some mushroom logs and you have a fairly diverse edible landscape in your shady spot.

There are also shade-loving or tolerant fruit trees and bushes, for example, paw paw, black currant, mulberry, and black raspberry. Here is an example of a shade-tolerant guild that you can use if you have the space:

Hazelnut Guild	
Hazelnut	*Corylus* spp.
Elderberry	*Sambucus nigra*
Paw paw	*Asimina trilobata*
Eleagnus	*Eleagnus multiflora*
Black currant	*Ribes nigrum x*, Crandall, Greens Black, Hill's Kiev Select
Black raspberry	*Rubus occidentalis*
Wild onions	*Allium* spp.
Columbine	*Aquilegia vulgaris*
Violets	*Viola odorata*

The Wind Sector

Depending on your location, wind could be a minor or major consideration in design. In heavily urban areas, wind tends to be dispersed by buildings and so does not generally create a challenge for growing plants. In open areas, wind could wreak havoc on trees and plants you are trying to establish and so needs to be addressed.

If you know your site well, you probably have a general idea of the wind flow. Analyzing the wind rose gives you further information to use. It tells you what direction the predominant winds come from and the average speed. Of course, wind gusts are always possible as well.

Once you know the direction the winds come from and the average speed, you can plan for windbreaks or wind-tolerant species, if necessary. Likewise, the general direction could be insignificant if you have a unique geography that blocks or creates a wind tunnel. You can gauge this by time spent on the site.

The Built Sector

When analyzing the built sector, keep in mind issues around storage, access, pathways, flow of traffic on the site, views you would like to preserve or block, shadows or other microniches created by the buildings, and zones of use.

The built sector can also include the surrounding community and how that will affect your site and future landscape. For example, is there a noise issue, unsightly views, or air pollution coming from a nearby mill? Are you making your space private or welcoming to people outside the site?

When looking at the built sector, consider the big picture, including how the layout of structures relates to plants. Also, consider where good sitting areas or other built areas can be placed, based on factors like available shade, quiet, good scents from plants, and proximity to house.

Bringing It All Together

The main point of site assessment and analysis is to understand your site as it relates to your design goals. Take the goals that you made early on in this process and refine them now based on what you found on your site. The goals may have changed somewhat through finding out what is more manageable and what may require more energy input. Your planning process will also move from general to specific. For example, generally you may want more food independence; specifically this may mean you want several fruit tree guilds, space for an annual garden, and chickens. Generally you may want a space for healing and peace; specifically this translates to blocking the noise and view of a busy street, along with planting passionflower vines on a trellis.

Once you have assessed and analyzed your site, it is time to put together a sector map to organize the information gathered.

Ginseng and Goldenseal

Many plants used medicinally are common weeds found throughout the United States, while others are more fragile. Two of the latter are American ginseng and goldenseal. They both have roots that are used medicinally and limited habitat ranges. They are native to the eastern broad-leaved deciduous woodlands and require shade. With loss of habitat and a long history of wild collection, both are considered threatened species. These two plants are also considered to be companion plants, in the sense that they help each other to thrive.

In order to continue to use these plants for their valuable medicine, conservation efforts must be made. A major way to do this is to grow them. In Pennsylvania, their habitat is present throughout the forested areas. Growing ginseng can be economically profitable; however, there are many other benefits to medicinal plant husbandry: ecological, social, and spiritual.

be cross-pollinated. The seed germination requires 18 to 22 months average. During the process of seed dormancy, the seeds must remain moist (not wet) and exposed to the alternating cycles of cold and warm. Ginseng requires a tree and/or shrub cover of 60 to 90 percent shade. The appropriate soil varies but, in general, is loamy, moist, and high in organic matter. The pH is slightly acidic, from 4.5 to 6.0 and high calcium levels are associated with higher survival and production rates.

Ginseng does best on a northern or eastern aspect, however niches within a system will work if they are facing these directions. Finally, there are certain plant, tree, and shrub indicator species that tend to grow in association with ginseng (Table 1). American ginseng is listed in Appendix II of CITES (the Convention on International Trade in Endangered Species of Wild Fauna and Flora). Husbandry

American Ginseng
(*Panax quinquefolius*)

American ginseng is in the family Araliaceae (ginseng family) and is native to the eastern United States. Every county in Pennsylvania has reported a wild ginseng population at some point in time.

The plant has a four-stage life cycle. It flowers in Pennsylvania from early to mid-June through mid-July. It is both self- and cross-compatible and so does not need to

Table 1: Selected plants commonly found in association with American ginseng.

Trees	Shrubs	Herbs
American basswood	Spicebush	Trillium
Sugar maple	Witch hazel	Jack-in-the-Pulpit
American beech	Blackhaw	Goldenseal
Black cherry	Red elderberry	Blue cohosh
White ash	Hazelnut	Wild yam

Adapted from "Penn State Forest Finance 5: Opportunities from Ginseng Husbandry in Pennsylvania" (2007) and Eric Burkhart, personal communication. This table of plants can be used to create a guild in your design.

of ginseng, and other endangered species, can help conserve native plant resources and serve to increase our connection with the Earth and nature.

The ginseng root is the part highest in ginsenosides, the bioactive components of the plant. It is used as an adaptogen (helping the body and mind adapt to stress), a longevity tonic, to restore energy and augment mental clarity, and to increase resistance to disease and ill health. Up to 90–95 percent of the wild root from the US goes to Asia, where American ginseng is highly valued for its medicinal qualities.

Goldenseal (*Hydrastis canadensis*)

Goldenseal is in the family Ranunculaceae (buttercup family). It produces a solitary flower with greenish-white sepals in April or May. Also a native to the eastern United States and Canada, goldenseal prefers the rich soil and abundant organic matter found in hardwood forests, especially in the Ohio River Valley region. A pH between 5.5 and 7.0 produces vigorous and reproductive populations.

In Pennsylvania, wild distribution seems to be limited to the southern and western portions, in habitat where seasonal flooding or moistness occurs. It is also found in association with certain deciduous trees, shrubs, and herbs. Some consider it easiest to grow through rhizome propagation, rather than from seed. It prefers well-drained, humus soils and 60–80 percent shade.

The golden rhizome is the part most used medicinally and holds a host of therapeutic properties. It is used internally and locally for its antiseptic and anti-microbial actions. Traditionally, it has been used as a dye as well. It is one of the most widely used herbs, second only to ginseng in commercial importance.

Concern over sustaining the wild goldenseal trade can be found as early as the mid-19th century. Market and price instability discourage the commercial husbandry of the plant and roots only go for about 20 to 30 dollars per dry pound. Therefore, it is best to grow for reasons other than strictly profit, such as personal use or ecological reasons. There is also no market niche for forest-grown goldenseal, unlike ginseng.

Table 2: Selected plants commonly found in association with goldenseal. Use this as a guide to creating a guild.

Trees	Shrubs	Herbs
Sugar maple	Paw paw	Jack-in-the-Pulpit
Tulip poplar	Spicebush	Black cohosh
Red oak		Trillium
Slippery elm		Wild yam
Black walnut		Mayapple

Creating a Sector Map

Identifying the sectors onsite is the first step in creating a concept sketch. This will be a layer that you can place over your base map which shows how the sectors work as a whole on your site. You will take the information gleaned through the site analysis process and label the sections on your site where the sectors play out.

For example, you may have found areas that are sunny or shady; wet or dry; subject to high wind or loud noise, or open onto unsightly views. The sector map labels these areas.

The Design Concept Map

A design concept map is also called a site concept map. In this phase, we are working in broad strokes based upon the information we have collected and our goals for the site. At this stage we can also integrate the various sectors and begin to imagine what plants and structures we may use to offset the site's undesired effects.

Prior to drawing a site concept map, revisit your top goals for the space. This informs your concept and final design, and eventual implementation.

An example list of site concept goals is as follows:

1. Block wind from east
2. Block view of street
3. Decrease noise from neighbors and traffic
4. Capture water from roof and slope
5. Diversify useful vegetation
6. Add composting system
7. Plan for odor control (chickens)
8. Decrease lawn
9. Create container (establish property microclimate)
10. Grow a good portion of seasonal produce

Possibilities Abound: Microniches on Your Land

Once you have done the steps of site assessment and analysis, followed by plant research and coming up with a sector map, you may find that many of the plants you intended to grow are not fit for your site due to constraints of the ecosystem. This is a great time to view what you do have as an opportunity. Each combination of sunlight, moisture, and placement is a niche. Each plant and tree has a niche that it prefers. So now is the time to look at what you have to work with and find the plants that love exactly that. You can also modify existing conditions to an extent if there is a non-negotiable that you want to grow.

Micro and Macroclimates

Based on the results of your site analysis, you can begin to see what the micro and macroclimates and niches are on your site. Microclimates form based on a unique combination of biotic and abiotic factors, creating a system within a system which can provide the groundwork for a niche. Microclimates can be of varying sizes and may form in very small areas of a few square feet. Elements that contribute to a microclimate include slope aspect, heat radiation in urban areas, being near a body of water, or under a tree. A south-facing brick building creates a microclimate that would be warmer than land not adjacent to the structure.

While the microclimate is about what defines the climate, the climate creates the conditions for a niche to develop. Mollison defines niche simply as "an opportunity in space." A niche includes all of the biotic and abiotic factors that a species needs to survive and thrive. So the area by the south-facing brick building will create a niche for warmth- and dry-loving plants to thrive, such as fig, sage, and peach.

Consider your site now based upon microclimates and potential niches. Here are more examples of microclimates that may be present:

- *Cool and shady*: It tends to be cooler and shadier under trees.
- *Damp*: The bottom of slopes and hills tend to be wetter drainage areas.
- *Dry and windy*: Conversely, the top of slopes and hills are usually more dry and can be windier.
- *Hot and polluted; reflecting bright light*: Land adjacent to streets would be hotter and more prone to environmental pollutants and car exhaust.

Based upon the microclimate present, begin to consider the type of niche that *could* form (combining climate with the biotic factors of soil organisms, plants, and insects). So a cool and shady microclimate could become the niche for plants that need just that, including mosses, mushrooms, and understory plants. A hot and polluted microclimate can become the niche for plants that are hardy and can withstand stressors. You can also offset the way the pollution impacts your site. For example, at Hazelwood Food Forest, we used a combination of elder and hazel as a buffer.

We will go into some niche case studies to show what abundance abounds when you look at what you have as an asset rather than a liability.

Hazelwood Food Forest Species List

In the five years that the food forest was on the original site, many plants survived, some did not, and many were added as the site evolved. It is also interesting to note that the different people involved in a project will naturally expand the plant palette, as people are attracted to different plants. As management changed hands, new volunteers came and went, and friends offered plant cuttings, our final species list reflected this.

Plant Research

Once you have your concept design sketched out, with the general guilds and niches you want to include, it is time for research to hone it down to specific plants. In this phase, you can start with general research and go increasingly deeper. The plant research phase will overlap with the remainder of the design process, as you find the varieties and plant types that you like and will work the best for your landscape. In Chapter 3 we provide more details to aid you in selecting plants for your food forest.

When selecting fruit trees, take time to research and choose the most disease-resistant cultivars for your area. Choosing varieties that will be hardy and less susceptible to disease is the first and most important step in food foresting.

Plant Selection

During the research phase, keep in mind some important points. Oftentimes, the design will begin with the main, or largest and longest-living species in the guild. This is because the longer a plant will be there and the more

Case Study: Hazelwood Food Forest

Niche: urban / polluted / salt

In urban environments, special considerations need to be made. At the Hazelwood Food Forest, we needed to consider air and soil pollution, street salting in the winter for de-icing, preventing easy access for littering, and rodents, especially rats.

We determined that salt from street de-icing could be an issue for any plants we wanted to grow against the busy main street that the food forest abutted. To deal with that, we decided on an elderberry guild, made up of elderberry, hazelnuts, quince, blueberry, serviceberry, and strawberries.

Elderberry trees are quite hardy and salt tolerant. They also provided a decent block to the wind and therefore air pollution. In the second year, the elderberry bushes bore a good amount of fruit and the plants were strong.

Credit: Michelle Czolba and Juliette Olshock

Hazelwood Food Forest elderberry guild.

Comprehensive Final Species List at the Hazelwood Food Forest

Edible

Asian Pear — *Pyrus pyrifolia*

Asparagus — *Asparagus officinalis*

Blackberry — *Rubus* spp.

Blueberry — *Vaccinium angustifolium*

Borage — *Borago officinalis*

Bronze fennel — *Foeniculum vulgare*

Chinese chestnut — *Castanea mollissima*

Chives — *Allium schoenoprasum*

Chokecherry — *Aronia prunifolia*

Currant — *Ribes* spp.

Dandelion — *Taraxacum* spp.

Dock — *Rumex* spp.

Elderberry — *Sambucus canadensis*

Fig — *Ficus carica*

Garlic — *Allium sativum*

Gooseberry — *Ribes uva-crispa*

Grapevines — *Vitis* spp.

Hazel — *Corylus americana*

Jerusalem artichoke — *Helianthis tuberosus*

Lemon balm — *Melissa officinalis*

Milkweed — *Asclepias syriaca*

Mint — *Mentha* spp.

Mulberry — *Morus rubra*

Nasturtium — *Tropaeolum* spp.

Nectarine — *Prunus persica* var. *nectarina*

Nodding onion — *Allium cernuum*

Oregano — *Origanum vulgare*

Ostrich fern — *Matteuccia struthiopteris*

Paw paw — *Asimina triloba*

Peach — *Prunus persica*

Persimmon — *Diospyros virginiana*

Plum — *Prunus* spp.

Purple flowering raspberry — *Rubus odoratus*

Quince — *Cydonia oblonga*

Red raspberry — *Rubus* spp.

Sage — *Salvia officinalis*

Serviceberry — *Amelanchier arborea*

Shiitake mushrooms — *Lentinula edodes*

Sorrel — *Rumex acetosa*

Spicebush — *Lindera benzoin*

Staghorn sumac — *Rhus typhina*

Stevia — *Stevia* spp.

Strawberry — *Fragaria* spp.

Sunflower — *Helianthis annuus*

Sweet cherry — *Prunus* spp.

Thyme — *Thymus vulgaris*

Yarrow — *Achillea millefolium*

Yucca — *Yucca* spp.

Medicinal

Bee balm — *Monarda* spp.

Black cohosh — *Actaea racemosa*

Borage — *Borago officinalis*

Bronze fennel — *Foeniculum vulgare*

Chamomile — *Chamaemelum nobile*

Cleavers — *Galium aparine*

Comfrey — *Symphytum x uplandicum*

Currant — *Ribes* spp.

Dock — *Rumex* spp.

Echinacea — *Echinacea purpurea*

Elderberry — *Sambucus canadensis*

Feverfew — *Tanacetum parthenium*

Garlic — *Allium sativum*

Joe Pye weed — *Eutrochium* spp.

Lamb's ear — *Stachys byzantina*

Lemon balm — *Melissa officinalis*

Mint — *Mentha* spp.

Motherwort — *Leonurus cardiaca*

Mugwort — *Artemisia vulgaris*

Mullein — *Verbascum* spp.

Oregano — *Origanum vulgare*

Plantain — *Plantago* spp.

Raspberry — *Rubus* spp.

Sage — *Salvia officinalis*

Shiitake mushrooms — *Lentinula edodes*

Snakeroot — *Ageratina* spp.

St. John's wort — *Hypericum perforatum*

Thyme — *Thymus vulgaris*

Wild geranium — *Geranium maculatum*

Wild ginger — *Asarum canadense*

Wormwood — *Artemisia absinthium*

Yarrow — *Achillea millefolium*

Beneficial Insect Attractors

Bee balm — *Monarda* spp.

Buttonbush — *Cephalanthus occidentalis*

Comfrey — *Symphytum x uplandicum*

Daffodil — *Narcissus* spp.

Dead nettle — *Lamium amplexicaule*

Joe Pye weed — *Eutrochium* spp.

Milkweed — *Asclepias syriaca*

Mint — *Mentha* spp.

New York ironweed — *Vernonia noveboracensis*

Oregano — *Origanum vulgare*

Queen Anne's lace — *Daucus carota*

Rose of Sharon — *Hibiscus syriacus*

Sage — *Salvia officinalis*

Tansy — *Tanacetum vulgare*

Thyme — *Thymus vulgaris*

Tobacco — *Nicotiana* spp.

Wild columbine — *Aquilegia canadensis*

Yarrow — *Achillea millefolium*

Nutrient Accumulators

Comfrey — *Symphytum x uplandicum*

Dandelion — *Taraxacum* spp.

Jerusalem artichoke — *Helianthis tuberosus*

Sorrel — *Rumex acetosa*

Sunflower — *Helianthis annuus*
    (draws lead from soil)

Yarrow — *Achillea millefolium*

Nitrogen Fixers

Alfalfa — *Medicago sativa*

Blue false indigo — *Baptisia australis*

Crown vetch — *Securigera varia*

Good Resources to Get Started with Plant Research

Seed Savers Exchange (seedsavers.org) was founded in 1975 to promote the preservation of rare vegetables through a member-based seed exchange. Early on the exchange expanded to include fruits and nuts and other plant materials. Their website provides access to their online catalogue of rare and heirloom vegetables and flowers and their members' seed and plant exchange: exchange.seedsavers.org.

The North American Fruit Explorers (NAFEX, nafex.org) is "a network of individuals throughout the United States and Canada devoted to the discovery, cultivation, and appreciation of superior varieties of fruits and nuts." Members include professional pomologists, nurserymen, and commercial orchardists and many amateur growers. NAFEX members share ideas, information, experiences, and propagating material.

United Plant Savers' (unitedplantsavers.org) mission is "to protect the native medicinal plants of the United States and Canada and their native habitat while ensuring an abundant supply of medicinal plants for generations to come." They are a member-based organization. The website contains resources and links for native plant preservation, growing and harvesting. They maintain a 350-acre botanical sanctuary in southeastern Ohio (goldensealsanctuary.org), host workshops, and offer a certification program for sustainable plant and herb harvesting.

Northern Nut Growers Association (northernnutgrowers.org) offers information and resources and hosts plant material exchanges among members. According to the website the Northern Nut Growers Association "brings together people interested in growing nut trees. Our members include experts in nut tree cultivation, farmers, amateur and commercial nut growers, experiment station workers, horticultural teachers and scientists, nut tree breeders, nursery people, foresters, and beginning nut growers."

The Apios Institute (apiosinstitute.org) "exists to share experience and knowledge about perennial crop polyculture systems (variously known as home gardens, food forests, and forest gardens) for all climates, through a collaborative network of farmers, gardeners, and researchers, in order to fill critical knowledge gaps regarding the design and management of these systems."

Plants for a Future (pfaf.org) maintains a donation-supported database of over 7,000 plants. Their main aims are "researching and providing information on ecologically sustainable horticulture, as an integral part of designs involving high species diversity and permaculture principles."

The **Lady Bird Johnson Wildflower Center** (wildflower.org) at the University of Texas at Austin hosts the Native Plant Information Network (NPIN), whose goal "is to assemble and disseminate information that will encourage the sustainable use and conservation of native wildflowers, plants and landscapes throughout North America." This site's database includes over 8,500 species native to North America. Listings provide photos, plant range, growing conditions, and uses by people and wildlife. While this service is free, they are a membership organization and do accept donations.

The **Germplasm Resources Information Network** (GRIN, ars-grin.gov) "provides germplasm information about plants, animals, microbes and invertebrates."

The **PLANTS Database** (plants.usda.gov) is a service of the Natural Resources Conservation Service that provides general information about plants, including classification, images, distribution maps, and links for further information.

i-Tree (itreetools.org) is "a state-of-the-art, peer-reviewed software suite from the USDA Forest Service that provides urban forestry analysis and benefits assessment tools. The i-Tree Tools help communities of all sizes strengthen their urban forest management and advocacy efforts by quantifying the structure of community trees and the environmental services that trees provide. i-Tree Tools are in the public domain and are freely accessible."

Gardenology.org is a wiki site, written and edited by registered users, with a database of over 20,000 plants. Listings include images, variety descriptions, history, uses, information on cultivation and propagation, and links to related resources. Some listings are quite extensive and others need further contributions.

Eat the Weeds (eattheweeds.com) is forager and author Green Deane's website, with a database of over 1,000 wild edible plants. It provides a wealth of information on wild plants as food, medicine, craft materials, and more.

The **Web Soil Survey** (websoilsurvey.sc.egov .usda.gov) a free service courtesy of the USDA's Natural Resource Conservation Service is a valuable tool for site analysis. The web soil survey is used to generate a property's soil maps and reports on land use characteristic of the site's soils and hydrology.

difficult it is to move around, the more foresight you want to put into its placement. Understory plants can be moved around if necessary, replaced, and are less of a commitment.

Not every food forest will have all the layers listed below. But it is good to keep the model of nature in mind and to allow for additions and changes over time.

In this section we look more closely at the anatomy of the food forest. In the next chapter we will study the various plant layers more thoroughly.

The Canopy Layer: Trees

The larger trees in the food forest dominate the system and have a strong influence on the rest of the design. The mature size of the trees, both height and spread of branches, and the extent and depth of the root systems influence the layout of everything else. If you are beginning with a mature yard tree, say a large maple or oak, you will be designing around a large space and a lot of potential shade. If your polyculture is built around an apple tree your food forest will have a smaller footprint. If, like the Hazelwood Food Forest, your system has a number of fruit trees, you will design under, around, and between the trees. If you plan to follow the pattern of the milpa food forest, the central trees may be pruned heavily every few years to harvest useful wood products and allow more light to reach lower levels.

When planning for fruit trees, there is a variety of sizes to choose from, including standard, semi-dwarf, and dwarf. Depending on the size of your landscape and your harvesting goals, you can choose which size will be best.

Standard: Large fruit trees typically grow 25 to 30 feet tall and require a 15- to 30-foot- diameter space, depending on fruit type. Large size makes pruning, spraying, and harvesting trickier. Trees begin bearing after three to five years and live long enough that your great-grandchildren can harvest fruit.

Semi-dwarf: Medium-size trees (10 to 16 feet tall), needing a 15-foot-diameter space. Annual pruning is vital to maintain height and shape. This tree size yields hundreds of fruits per season. Trees start bearing in three to five years. Semi-dwarf trees grow to 15–20 feet generally and have a longer lifespan than dwarf trees.

Dwarf: Small trees (7 to 10 feet tall) suited to an 8-foot-diameter space. Fruit is normal size; trees start bearing in three to five years. Dwarf trees have the shortest life spans. They are the easiest to prune, spray, and harvest without special equipment. Their downside is a shorter lifespan.

Surrounding the fruit trees is a 5–10-foot buffer zone filled with a mix of annual vegetables, perennial bulb flowers, nitrogen fixers, insectaries (plants that attract beneficial insects and bees), and nutrient accumulators to create fully functional guilds. The guilds will require maintenance to keep out weeds and fill in any bare spaces.

At this stage, you can also consider succession planting. The dwarf trees bear fruit in less time than the standard and also die sooner. So to begin, some dwarf trees can be planted while you wait for the standard trees to catch up.

Understory Trees

Understory trees are smaller trees planted beneath taller trees. A classic example is planting paw paws under walnut trees. In the eastern woodlands of the United States common native understory trees include dogwood and redbud trees. There are several things to consider at the design stage. If your understory and canopy trees are planted at the same time, be sure to allow room for both to fill. Some understory trees may grow faster than the canopy tree and could slow the growth of the canopy. Succession is also a consideration. Your understory trees may be thinned out when the canopy fills in. At this point long-range planning is important. Visualizing the food forest a decade or two ahead and understanding the size and lifespan of the various trees will help you mix and match the right combination.

Shrub Layer

The shrub layer consists of woody perennials, usually with multiple stems, that grow from 2 feet to 12 feet high. Shrubs may provide fruits and berries, habitat, medicinal herbs, craft materials, or nitrogen. Many, of course, have multiple uses and provide multiple functions.

Shrubs generally may not live as long as the trees in your food forest. So, again, planning for succession and transition as the system matures is important. Shrubs may be started closer into the canopy trees in a young food forest. As the system matures they can be replanted further out to be replaced with more shade-tolerant plants.

Herb Layer

The herb layer consists of non-woody perennials, biennials, and annuals that grow one foot to several feet tall. Non-woody perennials grow anew from a perennial root each year. Herb layer plants with harvestable roots are discussed in the root layer section of Chapter 4, but in the design process we should consider their role above ground as well. It is important to know the size, growth habit, and spreading habit of all plants, and especially the herb layers. This layer adds the most potential for diversity in the food forest. Some plants will be on the sun side of the garden, some on the shady side, and some in full shade. Keep in mind that this layer will need the most tending, weeding, mulching, and replanting.

Ground Cover Layer

The ground cover layer is a variation of the herb layer, with plants hugging the ground and keeping under a few inches high. A number of plants can grow densely and close to the ground. We generally avoid grasses in a food forest because they spread fast and can overwhelm the rest of the food forest. Examples of ground layer plants include strawberries, wild ginger, chickweed, various clovers, ajuga, thyme, and numerous native wildflowers. Annual ground covers could include sweet potatoes, squash, nasturtiums, and other low-growing annuals.

Vines

When adding climbing plants to the food forest, you should again consider the growth habit and size of the plants. In a Three Sisters Guild of corn, beans, and squash, the pole beans should be a variety that will not overwhelm the corn stalks and pull them down. The Three Sisters are also planted in a proper ratio to keep a balance. Too many bean vines can also pull down the corn stalks. Balance is important. Vines should be accessible for pruning and not too vigorous for the trees and shrubs. Most varieties of hardy kiwi grow too densely for most polycultures. Adding trellises and other plant supports is a good option to consider. Hops are another vigorous grower. The inclusion of hops should keep in mind their potential to overwhelm other plantings if not pruned and managed properly.

Root Zone

When we speak of the root zone, we are talking not just about roots we harvest, but also about all the life and plants that live underground. The soil biota is of particular concern. We want a living, healthy soil. Earthworms, while not native, are here now and play a big role in recycling decaying plant material. Many small creatures are part of the soil ecosystem. Ground-dwelling bees nest in the soil as well.

In the food forest we try to minimize disturbing the soil. Holes are dug to plant new plants and to harvest roots, and weeds and unwanted plants are uprooted, but generally we try to avoid disturbing the soil ecology. Mulches are usually applied annually to suppress unwanted plants and to feed the system. In and below, the fungal mycelium thrive and interact with virtually all the plants in the system. Mycelium are the tiny threadlike "roots" of fungal organisms. Mushrooms are the "fruit" of the mycelium. A diversity of fungi in a food forest helps maintain the health of the whole system, by recycling nutrients and by exchanging minerals for sugars from plants. Many fungi will naturally find your garden when the soil is not disturbed too much. In Chapter 4 we will discuss adding useful fungi to the food forest.

In the food forest root crops grow best in the margins between the trees and shrubs and in deep soil beds. Jerusalem artichokes prefer the sunnier edges of the system, while ginseng, goldenseal, and wild ginger prefer the shaded areas. Designing for proper placement and harvest of root crops will help prevent damage to trees and shrubs.

Invasive Plants

Non-native plants, insects, and animals, also known as invasives, can be a major problem in a natural ecosystem. For the purposes of this discussion, a non-native plant is a plant that was not native to an area prior to 1492. Countless plants have been introduced to North America from Europe, Asia, Australia, and South America since the Europeans first arrived. The vast majority have become naturalized or integrated into the cultivated landscape and natural world with minimal problems. Many are useful and edible. But a number do cause problems. They can invade natural landscapes and supplant native plants, running rampant and disrupting ecosystems. Some plants are invasive in some areas but not other areas. Examples of invasive plants include garlic mustard, Japanese knotweed, multiflora rose, privet, and Japanese honeysuckle.

The list of introduced insects and other creatures is long as well. Japanese beetles, gypsy moths, emerald ash borers, and other insects cause millions of dollars in crop damage each year. Earthworms are also an introduced species and are still extending their range in North America. While earthworms perform important functions, they can impact and alter native forests when they first arrive. Climate change is an additional factor affecting this issue. As natural ecosystems are stressed and the plant mix changes in our fields and forests, invasive species have even more opportunities to spread.

From a design point of view, we must be careful when choosing plants to avoid unleashing a menace on our natural landscape.

Multifunction Plants

Before deciding on which plants to put into your design, research how many functions they can be used for. Always strive to choose a plant that fulfills at least two functions and preferably more. Remember to stack functions. For example, a multifunctional plant often used in food forest design is staghorn sumac (*Rhus typhina*). Staghorn sumac is a small tree which can grow to about 16 feet. It is very hardy and stabilizes poor soils while blocking strong wind. This makes it valuable for the edges as a windbreak and to prevent soil erosion. It is also a very useful plant for humans, being edible, medicinal, and valuable as a plant dye. The berries are used in pies or drinks and the twigs and branches can be used as a natural toothbrush, being astringent and antiseptic. The stems can be used as a tap for sugar maple trees or as a flute. With all these characteristics, Staghorn sumac is a great choice for urban areas on the edge where you want to build soil fertility and water retention.

Pollination

Considering the pollination needs of each species is critical when making your variety selections. Each fruiting tree is pollinated in a different way and checking this upfront will ensure that you harvest nice yields. Fruit trees can be self-fertile, partially self-fertile, or need cross-pollination with other varieties of the same species.

Self-fertile trees can be fertilized by pollen from blossoms on the same tree or another tree of the same cultivar, as well as another cultivar of the same species.

Partially self-fertile trees will bear a small amount of fruit without cross-pollination.

Cross-pollination is the transfer of pollen from one cultivar to the flower of a different cultivar. Trees that require cross-pollination must have a compatible variety nearby to produce fruit.

Most nurseries will have pollination charts or knowledgeable staff. The best way to be sure to have fruitful trees is to plan for their pollination needs and have a honeybee hive if possible. For most plants and trees, bees and other pollinators do the work of spreading the pollen to the stigmas. Some plants—especially most nut trees—are pollinated by windborne pollen. But for the most part, fruit-bearing plants rely on insect and animal pollinators. The agent transferring the pollen is called the pollinator; the source of pollen is called the pollinizer.

While most plants have both male and female parts on the same flower, some species, including persimmon, ginko, and kiwifruit, do not. They therefore require both a male and female plant in close proximity. The female plant bears fruit but must be pollinated by the male plant.

There are many very useful and precise charts available, including those that show pollinizer ability by varieties. Definitely check in with those before making your purchases. Here is a general guide to fruit tree and shrub pollination that may be used in your design.

Most apples, European and Asian pears, Japanese plums, and sweet cherries depend on cross-pollination so more than one compatible cultivar is necessary for proper fertilization. These cultivars must have overlapping bloom times. There are exceptions where certain cultivars may be self-fertile. Be sure to check with the source of plant stock.

Peaches, nectarines, apricots, European plums, and sour cherry are self-fertile and assisted by honeybees in the transfer of pollen from one flower to another. While cross-pollination is not essential for fruit set with these types, having multiple cultivars of each species can increase the number of fruits that form.

Most nut trees including black walnut, Chinese chestnut, pecan, hickory, and hazelnut require cross-pollination. Again, there are exceptions so check with the plant source.

Mulberry can be monoecious (female and male flowers on the same plant) or dioecious (female and male flowers on separate plants). Mulberries are wind-pollinated and generally do not need cross-pollination.

Paw paw has an interesting pollination story. It is self-incompatible, requiring cross-pollination. The stigma ripens before the pollen does, guaranteeing that the flower will not pollinate itself. It is largely recommended to hand pollinate, as the natural pollinators (flies and beetles) are inefficient.

Elderberry is a good example of a partially self-fertile plant. Cross-pollination is not required to produce fruit, but flowers that are cross-pollinated will produce larger and more fruit.

Blueberry needs to be cross-pollinated and sometimes with more than one cultivar with similar bloom times.

Strawberry, blackberry, and raspberry are self-fertile.

Currants and gooseberries are considered self-fertile and produce well on their own. A few varieties are partially self-fertile and will have higher fruit yield when planted with more than one cultivar nearby.

When considering where to plant new trees or shrubs, it is important to properly space the cultivars which will cross-pollinate. It is recommended to place trees no more than three rows apart, so they can be efficiently fertilized by bees. In permaculture design, we may not be working with neat rows, so space based on the room needed and research into the pollination requirements of that plant.

Pollinators

When we think of pollination, most people think about honeybees. Honeybees are an important pollinator and provide us with many valuable products. But they are only part of the picture. An observant gardener will notice a great diversity of pollinator insects visiting flowers in the garden. Pollinators forage flowers for nectar, pollen, and insects, and in the process spread pollen from flower to flower. They come in many shapes and sizes. We have observed bumblebees that are all black with a few touches of yellow, or perhaps white, and some that are all yellow with a touch of black. There are over 40 species of bumblebees in North America, in a range of color patterns and sizes. Dozens of species of mason bees, metallic bees, wasps, syrphid flies, and butterflies and moths are important native pollinators. Hummingbirds also are important pollinators. In a food forest, with a wide range of flowering times among the different plants, we need to provide for a wide range of pollinators throughout the growing season.

Fruit Tree Polyculture

Moving from the selection of "must-haves" in the design (the plants that you love and want to invite and welcome into your life) to supporting and functional plants, we begin to create a community of plants, known as a polyculture or guild.

A polyculture is a group of plants that work well together, providing for the needs of the ecosystem and the designer. When we move to this level of the design, systems thinking helps pull the elements together into a working whole. This means having a holistic view of each element and how it will affect and contribute to the whole. It

Locally adapted figs were donated by a neighbor for the food forest.

Asian pears were quick to produce bumper crops in just a few years.

First crop of apples from Hazelwood Food Forest.

also means creating a regenerative system that will continue to thrive without major external energy inputs.

Plant Palette

Once you have worked on a design or two, all of the guilds and polycultures that you come up with become part of your working plant palette. This is like an artist's choice of colors in that you have worked with certain plants over time and found them to be successful. Each designer and each region will have a different palette. The possible combinations are endless. Having a plant palette also simplifies future design projects and limits the amount of time needed to do plant research. This will be explored more in Chapter 4.

Example of Fruit Tree Polyculture

The overall design of the fruit tree polyculture would be in a spiral shape to provide insulation for more delicate and frost-susceptible nectarine and peach trees. A mix of standard, semi-dwarf, and dwarf fruit trees would provide a diversity of life span and years to harvest.

A small shed in the center would provide a roof for water catchment, space for a bat house, and a place to store tools and buckets. Bats are skilled and valuable insect hunters which will lessen the need for pest management.

Species List

Canopy Fruit Trees (30 feet tall)
Apple (*Malus domestica* or *Malus pumila*) x
  Empire and Granny Smith, Fuji and Golden
  Delicious
Pear (*Pyrus* sp) x Bartlett and Anjou

Sub-Canopy Fruit Trees (10 to 30 feet tall)
Mulberry (*Morus* species)
Elderberry (*Sambucus* species)
Asian pear (*Pyrus* species) x Shinko and Olympic

Shrub Layer (maximum 10 feet)
Nanking cherry (*Prunus tomentosa*)
Goumi (*Eleagnus multiflora*)
Roses (*Rosa rugosa*)
Red currant (*Ribes rubrum*) x Johnkeer von Tets
Gooseberry (*Ribes grossularia*) x Invicta

Herbaceous Layer
Comfrey (*Symphytum officinalis*)
Asparagus (*Asparagus officinalis*)
Chicory (*Cichorium intybus*)

Pear Tree Guild
Option A
Daylily (*Hemerocallis*)
Columbine (*Aquilegia*)
Virginia mountain mint (*Pycnanthemum
  virginianum*)
Borage (*Borago officinalis*)
Crimson clover (*Trifolium incarnatum*)

Scallions/Welsh onion (*Allium wakegi*)
Calendula (*Calendula officinalis*)

Option B
Chives (*Allium schoenoprasum*)
Oregano (*Origanum vulgare*)
Bee Balm (*Monarda*)
Dill (*Anethum graveolens*)
Yarrow (*Achillea millefolium*)
Chicory (*Cichorium intybus*)
Daikon radish (*Raphanus sativas*)
Dutch white clover (*Trifolium repens*)
Garlic (*Allium sativum*)

Types of Pears (will cross-pollinate each other)
Barlett: mid/late August harvest; best canning
  variety
Anjou: winter desert pear

Apple Tree Guild
Comfrey (*Symphytum officinalis*)
Mint (*Mentha*)
Red clover (*Trifolium pratense*)
Yarrow (*Achillea millefolium*)
Strawberry (*Fragaria* sp.)
Carrot (*Daucus carota*)
Parsnip (*Pastinaca sativa*)
Lupine (*Lupinus*)
Goumi (*Elaeagnus multiflora*)
Lemon balm (*Melissa officinalis*)

Species List (cont'd.)

Types of Apples (will cross-pollinate each other)

Empire: McIntosh-style; long shelf life; September harvest

Granny Smith: mid- to late-October harvest

Fuji Apple: mid- to late-October harvest

Golden Delicious: mid- to late-September harvest

Fruit Guild #1: Peach and Plum

Dwarf peach trees (flower early):

Southern Sweet (*Prunus persica*)—early summer harvest

Garden Golden (*Prunus persica*)—late summer harvest

Guild

Anise (*Pimpinella anisum*)

Garlic (*Allium sativum*)

Borage (*Borago officinalis*)

Peas (*Pisum sativum*)

Lupine (*Lupinus*)

Daylily (*Hemerocallis*)

Chives (*Allium schoenoprasum*)

Fennel (*Foeniculum vulgare*)

Feverfew (*Tanacetum parthenium*)

Plum Trees

European cross plum (*Prunus domestica*)

Guild

Artichoke (*Cynara cardunculus* var. *scolymus*)

Daffodils (*Narcissus*)

Nasturtium (*Trapeolum*)

Dill (*Anethum graveolens*)

Dandelion (*Taraxacum*)

Chicory (*Cichorium intybus*)

White Clover (*Trifolium repens*)

Fruit Guild #2: Nectarine and Cherry

Dwarf nectarine (flower early):

Nectar abe (*Prunus persica* var. *nectarina*)—good bee pollinator plant

Southern Belle (*Prunus persica* var. *nectarina*)—early fruiting

Guild A

Stinging nettle (*Urtica dioica*)

Garlic (*Allium sativum*)

Dill (*Anethum graveolens*)

Coriander (*Coriandrum sativum*)

Parsley (*Petroselinum crispum*)

Caraway (*Carum carvi*)

Marigold (*Tagetes*)

Sunchoke (*Helianthus tuberosus*)

Cherry Trees

Blackgold (*Prunus avium*)

Guild B

Chives (*Allium schoenoprasum*)

Horseradish (*Armoracia rusticana*)

Parsley (*Petroselinum crispum*)

Oregano (*Origanum vulgare*)

Parsnips (*Pastinaca sativa*)

Garlic (*Allium sativum*)

CHAPTER THREE

Food Forest Design: From Concept Sketch to Detailed Designs

Concept Sketch

This stage of the design process is when you take the information and observations gathered so far and start putting them down on paper in illustrative form. The concept sketch, also called concept design or concept map, is the first drawing phase of the design process. This is where zones of use, niche ideas, climatic areas, and basic ideas go.

Lay the sector map over the base map and make a copy of the two of these combined. This will give a full picture of the niches and zones that are present. Next you can start to add in areas of use.

For example, if you get full sun on half of your property and have a large shade tree covering the other half, your concept sketch would have circles with short descriptions in these areas. In the sun zone, you can plan your peach tree guild and sunflower hut, while the shade zone will be labeled for a native medicinal understory with a sitting area.

This stage is called "arrows and bubbles" because it is very sketchy and not precise. It is for getting patterns down so that you can work with the existing energy flow, rather than against it.

Design Schematic

The schematic is the first more detailed phase of the design process. In it the guilds identified in the concept sketch are drawn with more depth and specificity. Generally this level is created at a scale of 1 inch to 15 or 20 feet.

Within each of the zones that you created in the concept design, consider which specific plants will fulfill those functions and do well given the ecological factors. For fruit tree guilds, place your trees first and then the supporting shrubs, herbs, and vining plants around it. Consider issues of shading and directional access, especially for the large trees.

Be sure to research the mature size of plants you chose. Find the heigth and width of your desired trees and shrubs and measure these out for your designs. A good rule of thumb is to give a slight buffer for each plant to grow but not too much for unwanted plants to move into. In the schematic design stage, you may place marks where a swath of herbaceous and understory plants will go.

If you are doing your design by hand, first sketch out your concept design ideas in more depth. Make the measurements accurate using an engineer's scale and allow room to experiment and move elements around. This is obviously simpler when using a design program; however, drawing it on paper helps to make the decisions more concrete. Do you really want to make five iterations or is this the best placement for the tree? Consider it in your mind's eye before committing to paper.

Plants will most likely need to be coded with abbreviations that are recorded in a key.

Once you feel like you have a well-functioning schematic design, transfer it onto another layer as your final copy. You can color code if you like. Here are the features required to make your design understandable:
- North arrow
- Scale used
- Key of the plants included with abbreviations
- Name of the project and date of the design
- Designer name

This is where you will develop your species list. Species lists can vary in extent. A shortened species list with only the basics assumes that you have done your background research and are presenting and keeping track of the final results. This means you've done all the necessary research on pollination needs and recorded the compatible cultivars. All of the sectors can be included for each plant, if you want to get very technical. You can also use the species list for recording where you will purchase the plants.

The basic requirements for a species list are:

- Common name
- Scientific name
- Cultivar
- Height at maturity
- Width at maturity
- Solar needs
- Additional notes about plants that do not fit into these categories

Additional factors can include:

- Bloom time
- Fruit time
- Preferred soil
- Pollination
- Rootstock
- Source of plant

Detailed Patch Designs

A patch design is the most detailed of all the drawings and includes plants and other elements represented at the scale of 1 inch equals 5 feet or less. In this stage, you include as much detail as possible so that you can also use these designs as the planting plan. This is where you decide on every plant that will be put in the ground, including the understory and herbaceous layer. In addition to providing an accurate visual plan, they are done to mathematically determine the exact number of plants that will fill up a space and therefore the number of plants to procure, propagate, or purchase.

For the detailed patch designs, you may need to use an architect's scale to measure accurately. When the patches are complete, they can be taken into the garden on planting day and used as a fine-tuned guide to the location of each plant. This minimizes waste and can help the installation phase flow smoothly. It can also be interesting to find that when the design meets the ground, changes need to happen. Flexibility is a designer's friend.

Customizing the Design Process to Fit Your Goals

Perhaps you do not need an exact planting map or one of your goals is to experiment. In this case, you can end the formal design process at the concept sketch stage. Working with a sketch, you can make a species list that is more general and find plants that suit your broad goals. The sketch will get you some limited specificity. Be sure that you do not waste time or money when purchasing plants due to errors in projecting how many plants could fit in a space. Some quick calculations based on the size of the area and the plant sizes will be needed.

For example, a five-foot-square area may seem like it could hold many plants, but at full maturity you may find that your space is overcrowded and needs to be thinned. These are the exact questions that are answered in the deeper phases of design. If you have easy access to plants and that is not as much of an issue, then a concept sketch may suit your needs well.

Food Forest Pros and Cons

Before embarking on planning and designing your food forest, we want to mention some issues to consider. Keeping these in mind will offer perspective and a dash of realism. In general, food forests require more upfront work and take longer to bear harvest than a traditional agricultural system. Tending the soil is a critical factor and can take years to build to the black gold state. Fruit trees typically take three to five years for first harvest.

Over time, however, input lessens and the system becomes much more self-sustaining and, ideally, regenerative. Rather than needing to repeat the initial garden establishment in consecutive years, the work shifts to pruning, adding mulch, light weeding, continuing to plant new species, and propagating.

Learning how to properly grow and manage a food forest takes more sophisticated knowledge and skills. Depending upon your perspective, this can either be a pro or a con!

A really fantastic benefit of the food forest model is that annual crops can be incorporated into the system, giving you the option to diversify what is grown. So as the trees are maturing, you can still have a harvest of annual crops.

Of course, the pros and cons of your food forest design are relative to your goals. If a main goal is low maintenance and a self-sustaining system, then the maintenance aspects will be lessened. Something like intensive fruit growing will require much more maintenance.

Annual gardens require the same work year after year. In general, there are few perennial plants and compost and mulch need to be reapplied annually. Also many annual gardens do not function like a system, where the plants, soil, microbes, and humans interact in beneficial ways.

A major ecological benefit of any perennial polyculture system includes maturation of perennials, closing the loop through existing resources like leaf drop, and increase in soil health and diversity. For the food forester, this means less effort in the long run maintaining a highly fertile soil.

Patterns of Design

Food forests can be arranged in patterns to provide multiple functions in the landscape. These functions include acting as windbreaks, creating microclimates, defining borders, giving privacy, and promoting biodiversity. Below we examine some of the common patterns for food forest design.

Tree Lines, Hedgerows, and Windbreaks

A *tree line* is a row of trees that springs up, is planted, or is allowed to grow between fields or along property lines. A *hedgerow* traditionally is a specific type of tended tree line. Common in Britain and Europe, hedgerow design and management is a centuries-old art form. A *windbreak*, or shelterbelt, is a hedgerow or tree line strategically placed to moderate the climate downwind.

Tree lines can naturally spring up along fence rows and between fields where the soil is undisturbed and the land is not mowed. Over time, as trees mature the diversity increases. Native plants take root, trees mature, and shrubs fill the understory. As the shade increases the shrub layer expands towards the open edges and understory plants and vines take root.

Hedgerows tend to be planted densely and pruned to provide a definite barrier. The term implies moderate tree heights, often under 25 feet tall. In England, hedgerows have traditionally been created by planting hawthorn (*Crateagus* spp) and/or blackthorn (*Prunus spinosa*) saplings in a close spacing and weaving the thorn trees together with hazel rods to form a dense barrier. This weaving process is known as pleating.

These hedgerows and similar but unwoven hedgerows are also planted with other useful fruits, herbs, forage plants, medicinal plants, and wild

Case Study Designs for a Fruit Tree Planting Foundation: Polyculture Guild Plantings

One of the projects of Three Sisters Permaculture Design was to work with the Fruit Tree Planting Foundation to design and plant a food forest garden at a community garden. The Fruit Tree Planting Foundation (ftpf.org) is a nonprofit organization dedicated to "planting fruit trees and plants to alleviate world hunger, combat climate change, strengthen communities, and improve the surrounding air, soil, and water." It works with community groups worldwide to purchase and plant orchards in school yards, public spaces, and other locations "where the harvest will best serve communities for generations." We donated our time to design and implement a food forest plan as part of a Pittsburgh-based FTPF project.

The orchard includes apple, pear, peach, cherry, juneberry, and redbud trees. We chose to focus the work on two trees in the system—a pear tree and a peach tree—as polyculture systems, based on the budget allowed for plantings.

For both guilds we chose a keyhole bed design to allow access to harvest fruit and to the understory plants. We left out the vine layer for simplicity. The plants selected were chosen to provide herbs for sale, beneficial insect habitat, nutrient cycling, and ground cover.

Species included:

- spearmint
- lemon balm
- thyme
- chives
- purple sage
- tansy

- lime mint
- catnip
- ajuga
- oregano
- lavender
- valerian

- comfrey
- yarrow
- chamomile
- bronze fennel
- lamium

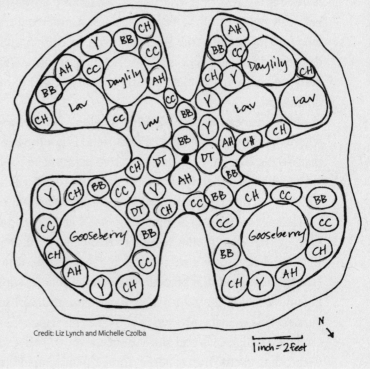

This design sketch shows planting plan for a Peach tree guild. This guild includes fruit, insect habitat, and nutrient cycling plants: peach, gooseberry, anise hyssop, chives, crimson clover, daylily, dwarf tansy, lavender, and yarrow.

Credit: Liz Lynch and Michelle Czolba

1 inch = 2 feet

N

edibles. Over time a hedgerow naturally tends to become more diverse as seeds are carried in by the wind, birds, or animals.

The traditional English woven hedgerow may be a bit sophisticated for the average food forest planting. Part of the hedgerow concept is that it serves as a living fence to keep livestock enclosed. A hedgerow may also have an earthen mound, or stone-wall base to help contain livestock. So if livestock control is your aim, it might pay to more closely study the ancient art of weaving trees together into a living fence. But a dense planting of useful trees, shrubs, and other perennials can serve well as a hedgerow. The spacing density of a hedgerow does not allow each tree or shrub to attain full growth and will reduce the yield of each individual plant. Still a diverse hedgerow

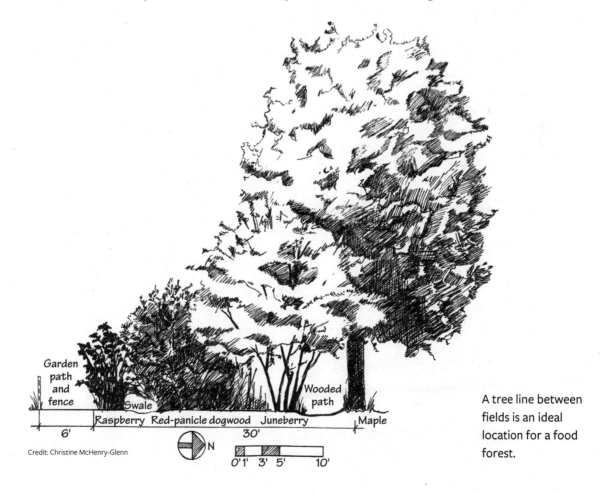

Credit: Christine McHenry-Glenn

A tree line between fields is an ideal location for a food forest.

can provide a high yield of mixed harvests, while functioning to moderate climate and provide fencing.

In comparison, the term "hedge" in the United States usually refers to a single species planted and pruned heavily and maintained as a border or landscape feature. For the sake of clarity we will refer to hedgerows as a more diverse planting that is not pruned intensively.

Windbreaks are designed to slow the wind but let some pass through. Allowing some wind to pass through prevents wind resistance, which could damage the trees, and prevents turbulent air flows on either side of the windbreak. The windbreak should have multiple layers, widespread canopies, and full understory to avoid gaps. When space allows, a windbreak can have a central row of taller and shorter trees and shrubs on one or both sides. A windbreak will modify the air speed anywhere from five to ten times its height. That is, a 30-foot-tall windbreak will slow the wind for somewhere between 150 feet to 300 feet downwind. The effect would be strongest within

Hedgerows can be planted with sturdy trees, such as nut pines, on the windward side and a mix of useful trees and shrubs on the leeward side.

Credit: Sarah A. Jubeck

the first 50 feet downwind. Windbreaks help moderate the climate. Slowing the wind will help keep soil and plants from excess drying and will lessen airborne erosion and wind chill. Lowering wind chill can help protect plants from extreme weather and will reduce heat loss from buildings.

Hedgerows and tree lines are perfect for food forest design. If you have an existing tree line with minimal understory, you can easily begin to add useful plantings between and around the trees. The existing trees will give clues to possible guild combinations. The size and natural form of existing trees will help plan the layout to maximize productive potential. If your goals are to create a closed canopy to grow shade-loving forest plants and mushroom inside plant you will want to create a denser canopy.

The ideal tree line runs east to west. With this orientation you will get a side in full sun most of the day. Sun-loving plants would be on the south side. Shade-tolerant plants go between the larger trees and to the north of the existing trees. If the tree line tends to run north to south, you can add sun-loving plants on either side and use the understory for shade-tolerant species, with each side getting at least half a day of full sun.

When establishing a new tree line where none exists, you will need to plan more for succession over time. The larger trees should be placed at a reasonable distance apart for full growth and a succession of plants can be planted between or underneath. Trees can be placed to allow for the spacing desired. A well-designed tree line has width as well as height, if space allows. The higher trees form the central line and smaller trees are planted on either side. As trees develop, a succession of crops can be grown between the young trees. Small fruits such as raspberries make a good transitional crop. Soil building understory should also be included in the early years of tree line development. As the trees mature and the canopy spreads, the understory can be planted with a more diverse mix of food forest crops.

Both tree lines and hedgerows can greatly enhance biodiversity. They offer birds nesting sites and food. They provide shelter and food for a wide range of insects, spiders, reptiles, and small mammals. They also can harbor pests, such as groundhogs and squirrels, and their predators—fox, hawks, and snakes. Essentially, the more diverse the plantings are the more diversity the landscape will have.

Sample Hedgerow Species

Selected useful trees:

- Eastern red cedar
- Red maple
- Sugar maple
- Serviceberry
- Black birch
- Shagbark hickory
- Redbud
- Hawthorn
- Flowering dogwood
- Persimmon
- Black walnut
- Plum
- Wild black cherry
- White oak
- Sassafras
- Basswood

Selected useful shrubs:

- Chokeberry
- New Jersey tea
- Hazelnut
- Filbert
- Witch hazel
- Northern bayberry
- Currant
- Gooseberry
- Staghorn sumac
- Blackberry
- Black raspberry
- Nannyberry

Vines:

- Wild grape
- Grape
- Virginia creeper

Some Other Multifunctional Arrangements

Suntraps

A suntrap is a design pattern presented in *Permaculture One* by David Holmgren and Bill Mollison (Tagari Publications, 1979) and further developed by Bill Mollison in *Permaculture Two* (Tagari Publications, 1979) and *Permaculture: A Designers' Manual*, (Tagari Publications, 2nd ed., 1997). A suntrap is a U-shaped row of trees, open to the south or sunward side, framing a field, garden, and perhaps a home site. They can be relatively small, a few hundred to a couple thousand square feet, surrounded by a narrow band of small trees and shrubs, or up to several acres, with larger trees and more width to the food forest.

Edible Trails

A tree-line food forest is a good pattern for public spaces. Edible walking paths can be planted with a full range of edible and otherwise useful plants. Trees will provide shady spots to place sitting benches. As discussed elsewhere in this chapter, food forests do require maintenance, including weeding and mulching. So scale comes into play. On a farm a long tree line can be allowed to be a bit more wild. But in a park or other public space, be sure to plan on having enough labor to keep things as tidy as required. Keep your designs small enough to manage. Once trees and shrubs are established they may need less tending. A mix of medium-sized fruiting trees and shrubs can be quite fruitful and self maintaining when mature. Management of these systems is more fully discussed in Chapter 5.

Credit: Sarah A. Jubeck

The Forest Edge

The edge of a woodland can be an excellent place to locate a food forest. The potential design depends on the woodland edge's orientation to the sun. A sunward-facing edge protected from prevailing winds by the forest is ideal. A major concern will be the potential for wildlife from the woodland to harvest your crop. Deer, rabbits, and squirrels are likely to frequent the woodland edge, and so extra care to protect plants and harvests is needed.

The suntrap builds on the windbreak concept to create a sheltered zone for home and/or gardens.

If you find your site has lots of shaded areas, growing lettuces and other salad greens can be a great use of the space. Salad greens grow well in the partial shade areas and can be incorporated into the food forest. In hot climates full shade may be required to grow many salad crops in the summer. In milder climates a number of salad ingredients can be grown in the shade of the food forest.

For example, violets love the deepest shade. Both leaves and flowers are used in salads. In moist soils watercress and other cresses also enjoy the shade. Chervil, bronze fennel, mallows, and various mints also do well. Wild edibles such as dandelion, ox-eye daisy, yellow dock, wood sorrel, and chickweed have a place in the shade in hot months. The young leaves of both basswood and mulberry trees can be eaten raw or cooked.

Credit: Michelle Czolba

Mixed salad greens grow well in the partial shade of a food forest.

How to Grow Mesclun

The French term for a salad mix of fresh, young greens is *mesclun*. It is a combination of lettuces and other greens (commonly from the Brassicaceae or mustard family) that are cut when young, and seasonal wild edibles. The mix is ideally tender, with a balance of sweet, bitter, and spicy flavors. Mixes can be as creative as desired in terms of texture, color, and flavor and changed throughout the season. Growing your own ensures exceptional quality and freshness of the final product.

The Process

Growing salad mix is fairly simple. The soil is prepared as for any other seed, with the exception of adding additional organic matter. Maintenance includes weeding, watering, rotational sowing, and, of course, weekly harvesting. Weeding is a meticulous process since the plants are very fragile and shallow rooted.

The first step in mesclun production is purchasing seeds. You can make a custom mix based on your favorite lettuces and greens. Peruse several seed catalogs to find the exact mix you want to create. Considerations when purchasing seeds include cost, organic or heirloom status, color and flavor of greens, local adaptability, and best growing season for different varieties.

Prepared mixes are also available, but these have a few drawbacks. This is because brassicas and lettuces are easiest to manage when they are separated. Brassicas have specific pest problems that lettuces do not and the germination and growing times of each are different.

There are many layouts you can use to grow the mix. The easiest to manage are swaths of separate varieties in six-inch rows separated by enough room for a stirrup hoe (available in three- and six-inch widths). Weeds are much easier to both see and remove with this layout and harvesting is simpler due to a more consistent size. Another benefit of keeping the two separate comes during harvest when a desired balance between the two tastes can be measured. When planning for a season of salad mix, a rotational planning system or calendar is helpful. An sample sowing schedule is every 10 days, give or take 3 days, May through August. Every 10 days a swath about 3 feet by 4 feet can be planted of both brassicas and lettuces.

Here is a list of some of our favorite lettuces and greens to grow for the salad blend.

Lettuces

- Red Salad Bowl
- Strela Green
- Green Deer Tongue
- Royal Oak leaf
- Black Seeded Simpson
- Antares
- New Red Fire
- Merlot
- Tango
- Hyper Red Rumple Waved
- Revolution
- Lollo di Vino
- Rossimo

Greens

- Hopi Red Dye Amaranth
- Tres Fine Maraichere
- Mispoona salad selects
- Wrinkled crinkled crumpled cress
- Chervil
- Olesh
- Aurora Orach
- Beet greens
- Swiss Chard

Other specialty items added to the mix as available can include: chives, sorrel, fennel, pea shoots, nasturtium and calendula flowers, and salad burnet.

Defying the Season: Growing Mesclun in the Summer

Salad is in demand in the heat of the summer. It is a cooling food for many people. As the common name "spring mix" implies, though, lettuces and greens prefer cool weather. They are traditionally late-winter, spring, and fall crops. In the heat of the summer, lettuces tend to bolt quickly and are generally less vibrant. Brassicas tend to become very spicy, especially the mustards, which is unappealing for a general salad mix. Weeds and pests become more of a problem as well in the summer.

Again, the shady understory of the food forest beats the heat and provides a great place to grow your greens through the hot months.

Pest Management

Common pests in the salad mix include flea beetles, slugs, and leafminers; slugs can also be an issue and somewhat of a nuisance when the weather is wet. Flea beetles prefer warm and dry weather conditions. They are only an issue with the brassica greens, as they do not tend towards lettuces.

While preventing the problem with floating row covers can help, the greens tend to become leggy trying to reach for the sunshine. It also creates a hotter environment under the cover, an undesirable side effect for cool-loving crops.

Urban Considerations

Growing food in the city brings special challenges. Access to land is often an issue and a detailed discussion of that topic is beyond the scope of this book. Mainly we want to say that vacant land, churchyards, and community garden land is available more often than you might think. Rooftops too can provide opportunity for edible green space. A little searching, networking, community action, and creative planning can yield space to those wishing to create food forests in the city.

he issues of concern we will address here include air quality, water quality, light pollution, sources of organic materials and soil. Soil issues were discussed in more detail in chapter two.

Air Quality

Urban air quality is a concern for the food forest designer. While mature trees can help mitigate air pollution, especially when there are a lot of them, they are still affected by bad air. Air pollution results from fossil fuels and industry. Often called smog, it includes dust particles, evaporated hydrocarbons, ground-level ozone, sulfur dioxide, and nitrogen dioxide. All these man-made pollutants also occur as a part of natural processes, but, when concentrated and out of balance, they cause health-related issues for people, animals, and plants.

Ozone is good in the right concentrations in the upper atmosphere. But at ground level it can cause us trouble. Oxygen is most stable when its two atoms are joined—O_2. Ozone is O_3, a molecule made up of three oxygen atoms. Ozone forms in the lower atmosphere when sunlight reacts with hydrocarbons and other volatile organic compounds in smog. High concentrations of ground-level ozone, above 100 parts per billion (ppb), can cause tissue damage in humans and other animals. It can also damage leaves and negatively impact tree health. Specifically, excessive ozone absorption by leaves can interfere with photosynthesis and reduce plant growth.

Two other pollutants that can harm plants are sulfur dioxide (SO_2) and nitrogen dioxide (NO_2). These are both also found in smog, and mainly originate in the burning of fossil fuels. Both contribute to acid rain.

From a design point of view, it is best to locate an urban food forest in an area with a lot of mature trees and away from main traffic arteries. Until we, as a society, have moved away from internal combustion engines, pollution from ground-level ozone, sulfur dioxide, and nitrogen dioxide will be an issue. We all must heed warnings issued on ozone alert days. When the air is still and the sun shines brightly, reducing the use of gasoline- and diesel-powered engines is our main tool for fighting ozone.

Because leaves can absorb these pollutants, they do help to reduce air pollution. But there is a limit to what they can absorb before their own productivity decreases. The solutions are simple: reduce fossil fuel use and plant more trees.

Water Quality

Plants, like people, need contaminant-free water to grow best. Finding it in the city could be a challenge. Issues of concern include chlorine, acid-rain water, and local pollutants.

The EPA has established four parts per million chlorine as safe for drinking water. However, chlorine will kill soil organisms. Soil biology will rebound and chlorine becomes bound in the soil particles and is rendered relatively harmless. But we suggest that regular doses of chlorine are not a good idea for the soil ecosystem, and there is reason to avoid the buildup of chlorine in your soil. It is also important to know what process is used to purify your drinking water. Chlorine gas will evaporate from standing water in 24 to 36 hours. So some gardeners fill a vented tank with tap water and leave it sit a few days before watering. However, many water treatment facilities use chloramine. This is more stable in the water and requires a chemical process to remove from the water. The processes used for removing chloramine are a little beyond our scope here, but with a little research you can find small-scale methods. On the scale of a garden or food forest, chloramine removal may be costly and hard to manage.

Whenever possible it is far better to irrigate with rainwater or other non-chlorinated water.

Rainwater, though, can have its own problems. Acid rain still occurs downwind of industrial areas and coal-fired power plants, though perhaps not as severely as in prior decades. Roof materials and local air pollution can also reduce rainwater quality as discussed elsewhere in this chapter. Pay attention to the pH of your rainwater and adjust it by adding pulverized limestone to the rain barrel if needed.

Use of greywater, from sinks, baths, and other non-sewage household uses is becoming more common. Care must be taken to not use excess soaps, chlorine, or synthetic chemicals that harm the soil and plants in a home that directs greywater to irrigation uses. Unless the greywater is sterilized, it should be not be applied directly to edible parts of plants. Subsurface irrigation of your forest garden is a great use. The sooner the greywater reaches your soil after use, the safer it is. Storing greywater can lead to stagnation and bacterial growth. (We recommend further research on this topic. Greywateraction.org is a great source of information.)

Light Pollution

Trees are sensitive to day length. Generally they time their seasonal cycles based on the seasonal variation between daylight and darkness. Excess light, such as streetlights or security lighting, can throw off these natural cycles for leaf growth, flowering period, and fall/winter dormancy. Continuous lighting is definitely not good for plants. With excess light at night trees can grow larger leaves, which might make them more susceptible to air pollution. Pollination may also be affected.

When lighting is unavoidable a few lighting design options can be considered. Outdoor lighting should, when possible, be set by timers for peak hour operation only. Security lights should use a motion detector so they are not shining (and using power) all the time. Lighting should be directed to paths and open areas, and shielded from vegetation. High-pressure sodium and incandescent lights can cause the most trouble with plants. Mercury vapor, metal halide, or fluorescent lights are better choices.

Mulches in the City

Plenty of mulch material can be found in most cities. Examples include wood chips, municipal composts, and annual leaf collection. The problem with these is that the materials may treated with herbicides and insecticides, and could contain other pollutants and litter. Care must be taken when gathering and using leaves and mulch materials to avoid unwanted contaminants. Whenever possible you should compost organic matter before using it in the forest garden. Wood chips and bark mulches should also be from a known source, and please, do not use dyed mulch! Sawdust may include treated wood residue and glues, formaldehyde, and synthetic materials. So again, know your source!

Site Preparation

Before moving on to the planting stage, the site needs to be prepared so that planting is smooth and easy, and the plants get what they need. Depending on the conditions of your space, the site may need soil amendments, plant and tree removal, bed creation, sheet mulching, or more.

Site preparation is a good time to lay out beds and create a compost area. You can put any sod or topsoil removed into the compost bed and begin planning right away for onsite regeneration. Early fall is a good time to design and begin site preparation with the addition of compost or mulch to the beds. This will give time over winter for the new richness to be worked into the existing soil, increasing biodiversity and moisture retention. By spring, the beds will need tending and may not be recognizable but the soil will be richer. You can shape your beds at this time and plant in the spring when the time is right.

The site preparation needed will depend on all the information you have gathered thus far and where you are heading next. For the Hazelwood Food Forest, site preparation was a major consideration and included removal of large amounts of trash and debris, incorporating 70 yards of compost into the existing ground, and sheet mulching a quarter-acre site using cardboard, 25 yards of leaf mulch, and 8 yards of bark mulch!

We needed to do some grassroots lead remediation using compost and a strategy of primarily growing fruit trees. Five years later, the soil on that site could be classified as black gold and its fertility was apparent through an abundance of over 70 species, so all the work paid off.

Humus is a stable component of organic material which results from the breakdown of plants and other natural decaying substances. It happens both in the soil and in compost production. Humus is extremely fertile soil and so calling it black gold signifies its high value in growing plants.

Seed Resources

Fedco Seeds: Cooperative seed and garden supply company.
fedcoseeds.com   207-873-7333

Seeds of Change: Organic seeds, plants, and foods.
seedsofchange.com   888-762-7333

High Mowing Organic Seeds: Organic seeds.
highmowingseeds.com   802-472-6174

Farmtek: All manner of farm equipment, including shade cloths.
farmtek.com   800-327-6835

The Brenmar Company: Biodegradable produce bags and compostable products.
brenmarco.com   800-783-7759

Capital Roots: Garlic and pepper spray.
cdcg.org/pests.html#garlic

CHAPTER FOUR

A Food Forest Feast:
Selecting Plants for Your Food Forest

In the previous chapter we discussed the process of designing a productive fruitful landscape. In this chapter we take a closer look at selecting the plants and fungi you might include in your food forest. We begin with a review of the role of fruit and other food forest products in your diet.

We then present a cornucopia of food forest crops to consider. Chief among these are fruits, nuts, and herbs. Leafy greens, edible flowers, root crops, and wild edible plants also have a place in the food forest. Fungi and medicinal herbs complete the menu. We will examine each of these below.

We conclude with some recipes and ideas for using your harvest.

Why We Eat Fruit

Fruit has been a part of the human diet throughout the vast majority of our ancient lineage. Our hominid predecessors in Africa had a diet heavy in fruit and nuts. As our ancestors emerged from the forests to scavenge and hunt in the savannas they kept their connection to the forest. Through our intertwined senses of taste and smell, sweet and sour flavors indicate the ancient evolutionary roots of our fruit-full diet. The English language gives testimony to the prevalence of fruit in our diet with its wealth of words to describe fruits' tastes, such as sweet, pungent, fragrant, sour, tangy, tart, juicy, aromatic, acidic, bland, and insipid.

When modern humans emerged over the last several hundred thousand years, our use of fire was a key element in diversifying our diet. Cooking

Credit: Lincoln Smith

American black currant.

Credit: Michelle Czolba

Asian pear.

Credit: Darrell E. Frey

Hardy kiwi.

allowed us to include more varied plant proteins and harder-to-digest complex carbohydrates, and to better digest meat. Today a healthful diet consists of a mix of fruits, vegetables, fats, and proteins. Though fruits remain an important part of a healthful diet, most people do not eat enough each day.

We are drawn to eat sweet things for the calories they contain, to obtain quick energy. This taste for sweets, combined with the availability of inexpensive processed sugar, has led to a modern epidemic of obesity, and has been shown to contribute to diet-related illnesses. What is a natural tendency to consume fruit sugars becomes an unhealthy craving.

Eating fruit daily can satisfy this craving for sugar, while providing fiber, minerals, vitamins, and many phytonutrients. Fresh fruit is actually mostly water. Its sugars are easily and quickly absorbed by our bodies. Vitamins found in fruits include vitamins C, E, and A. Many fruits contain essential minerals, including potassium, calcium, magnesium, phosphorus, iron, zinc, and other trace minerals. Phytonutrients are healthful compounds found in fruits and vegetables. Thousands of types have been identified so far, and most have not been researched. Those that have include carotenoids, flavinoids and bioflavinoids, phytosterols, resveratrol, and chlorophyll. These compounds promote wellness in various ways. Because many are anti-inflammatories and antioxidants, they both reduce the risk of and help our body to fend off diet-related illnesses: coronary and vascular diseases, cancer, and diabetes. They can help

Fruit All Year: Fresh Fruit on the Table Spring Through Fall; Preserved Fruit in Winter and Spring

Given enough land, good design, and proper planning it is possible to have fresh fruit on the table from late spring through early winter. The Crop Yield Chart on page 129 gives potential yields of various fruits and the space they require. The data given are for optimum yields in a good year, but they do give a general idea of what to expect from a mature plant.

On a small plot it is especially important to plan well to get the most production from your space and time. Careful integration of plantings in a food forest garden can provide a succession of harvests. It bears repeating that we do not want to space our plants too densely. Allowing each plant to reach nearly its potential growth will give the best yields. A good strategy is to plant enough of your favorite fruits to preserve excess for the off season. Late varieties of apples, pear, and quince can be stored in a cool cellar or refrigerator.

May
- Edible honeysuckle
- Everbearing strawberries, such as Tristar and Alpine varieties will give a continuous yield from late spring until fall.

June
- Edible honeysuckle
- Juneberry
- Cherry
- Strawberry
- Mulberry

July
- Red raspberry
- Blueberry
- Black raspberry
- Currants
- Bush cherry
- Rose hip

August
- Blackberry
- Gooseberry
- Peach
- Plum
- Blueberry
- Apple
- Pear
- Elderberry
- Rose hip

September
- Apple
- Pear
- Grape
- Kiwi
- Chokeberry

October
- Apple
- Grape
- Quince

November
- Apple
- Quince
- High bush cranberry
- Harvest and storage
- Preserves
- Sauces
- Frozen
- Juiced
- Dried

Credit: Darrell E. Frey

Yellow Transparent apples for sauce.

repair cell damage and boost immunity. While some of these beneficial compounds may be stored in our body, nutritional guidelines recommend daily consumption of a range of fruits and vegetables to keep levels high.

The best way to eat most fruits is fresh. Some fruits, like elderberry, aronia or chokeberry, and quince might taste better cooked and sweetened. But in order to have fruit available throughout the year, preservation of your harvest is essential. Fruit can be dried, frozen, canned, preserved in jams and jellies, juiced, and made into wine.

My favorite fruit is the fruit that is in season. The first juneberries and strawberries are amazingly welcome after a long winter with no fresh local fruit. Mulberries soon follow, with a slightly different flavor and sweetness level on every tree. Red raspberries, black raspberries, currants, and gooseberries follow in quick succession. When the first apples, Yellow Transparent, begin to ripen in July and we make sauce, it brings back my earliest memories of my father cooking these deliciously tart apples. Blueberries, blackberries, peaches, plums, pears, and a succession of apple varieties all are savored and enjoyed as each in turn comes to ripeness. Late fall brings paw paws and quince and more apples and pears.

Stored Fresh

Some fruits will keep for weeks or months with refrigeration or cool storage in a root cellar. Choose fruit that is not overripe or bruised. When storing bins or baskets of fresh fruit you should check the supply for spoilage regularly as you use them.

Dried Fruit

Most fruit can be dried in a food dryer. Dried fruit will keep through the winter at least if fully dried and stored in airtight containers. Drying concentrates the flavors of fruit but loses some of their vitamin C and A content.

Fruit Leather

Fruit leather is made by drying a puree of fruit on a sheet of plastic. Fruit leather can be rolled up and stored in a cool dark container for a few months. It will keep longer in the freezer.

Preserves

There are a number of ways to make fruit preserves. Common types of preserves include jam, jelly, preserves, and conserves; they're also known by many other regional terms. Basically jams, preserves, and conserves are whole fruit and sugar. Pectin, derived from fruit, is often added to thicken jams. Jelly is made from fruit juice or strained juice, sugar, and pectin. Fruit spreads are made from whole fruit with no added sugar.

Rose hips, the fruit of the rugosa rose, is rich in vitamins and stores well dried. They prefer the sunny edge of the food forest and fit well into a windbreak.

Chutneys are made from a mixture of fruits and spices with vinegar and sugar added to help preserve the fruit. Fermented chutneys are made by adding a lactobacillus culture to a chutney and allowing it to ferment at room temperature for two days before refrigerating. Added sugar is not used, but some recipes call for adding a salt brine.

Vinegars

Vinegar is the stable product of a process whereby fruit juice is converted by yeast to wine and then the alcohol is converted by bacteria into acetic acid. Vinegar is shelf stable for long periods of time. It is used to preserve other foods for long periods of time as well. Many of the phytonutrients found in fruit will still be found in their vinegar.

Shrub

Shrub is a word for fruit vinegar-based beverages. Shrubs were a common drink in colonial America, a way to preserve the flavor and nutrition of fruit without refrigeration. Shrub recipes mix fruit, sugar, and vinegar. Some recipes cook the mixture, some do not. Cooked shrub is strained after it cools. The uncooked recipes steep in the refrigerator for a few days and then are strained. It is best to store shrub in the refrigerator. It should keep a few weeks or even up to a few months. Shrub can be drunk as is, mixed with carbonated water, or used in mixed drinks.

Fruit Brandy and Other Alcohol Concoctions

Fresh fruit will keep very well in alcohol. Simply place cleaned fruit in a clean jar and cover it with brandy, rum, whiskey, gin, vodka, or your favorite spirits. Be sure the alcohol completely covers the fruit. Many traditional recipes can be easily found. Some mix spices with the fruit. We prefer to use brandy distilled from wine, but any alcohol that is at least 80 proof will do. Some people add a sweetener—sugar, honey, or maple syrup—depending on the fruit and their taste. The fruit can be strained and used as needed and the remaining liquid is a fine flavored cordial. If you are leaving the fruit in the jar for more than a few weeks it might be best to store it in the refrigerator. The strained liquor can be kept indefinitely stored in a cool cupboard.

Freezing

Most fruits can be frozen with good results. Vitamins are mostly retained in frozen fruit. The downside of freezing fruit is the need for adequate storage space for a large supply and the energy required to keep the freezer going. Berries and sliced fruits are best frozen on trays and then packed into tightly sealed containers and returned to the freezer. This keeps the fruit from freezing into a solid mass, making it easier to use small amounts. Frozen fruit should be used within the year. A few fruits, like paw paws and melons, are best preserved by freezing.

Canning

Canning fruit is a common way to preserve the harvest. Fruit is often canned in a sugar syrup to maintain sweetness. Fruit juice can be used to replace the syrup.

Lacto-fermentation

The process of lacto-fermenting is quite old. Lactic bacteria are responsible for the fermentation and are naturally present on the surface of all plants. By combining finely chopped vegetables with sea salt and adequate water, the resulting fermented vegetable is highly nutritious, delicious, and great for digestive health. The lactic acid is a natural preservative as well. Examples of traditional fermented foods include sauerkraut, kimchi, beet kvass, fermented dairy (yogurt and kefir), pickles, relishes, and grape leaves.

Fruits can also be fermented using the same basic method; however, they are likely to produce an alcoholic ferment due to the high sugar content and yeasts present on fruit.

Basic Sauerkraut Recipe

Ingredients

1 medium head of cabbage

1 to 3 tablespoons sea salt (varies according to personal taste preference)

Optional: caraway seeds, other vegetables such as carrots, turnips, garlic

Directions

1. Chop or shred the cabbage. Sprinkle with salt.
2. Knead or pound the cabbage for about 10 minutes or until there is a fair amount of liquid.
3. Stuff into a quart jar, making sure to press the cabbage underneath the level of the water. Use a weight to keep the cabbage submerged. Add more water if necessary.
4. Cover with a tight-fitting lid.
5. Allow the cabbage to culture at room temperature for two to four weeks. Remove the lid every few days to release the pressure that can build.
6. Move the finished sauerkraut into cold storage. It will continue to ferment over time, but more slowly. Finished sauerkraut in cold storage has a shelf life of at least one year (and sometimes much longer).

Taxonomy 101

Taxonomy is the classification of organisms for accurate identification. Each organism is given a unique Latin name.

Domain, Kingdom, Phylum, Class, Order, Family, Genus, Species

For the purpose of this book we mostly present plant genus and species and also specific varieties. Occasionally we will provide the plant family in our discussions.

Plant Nomenclature Example
Yellow Transparent Apple: *M. domestica*
Family: Rosaceae
Genus: Malus
Species: Domestica
Variety: Yellow transparent

Other terms to know:

Variety: A plant with specific characteristics or traits that should carry on through seeds to the next generation (true to seed).

Hybrid: Plant varieties that result from a cross of two or more varieties to make a unique variety; generally hybrids do not grow true to seed.

Cultivar: A plant variety developed through selective breeding and generally reproduced by cuttings, division, or grafting, but not by seeds.

Heirloom: A plant variety that has been maintained by gardeners and small-scale growers and seed companies for decades or longer. Generally heirlooms are not grown by commercial large-scale growers, though in recent years they have come into demand by chefs and consumers.

Nuts

Nuts should be an important part of a good diet. We should obtain around 20 percent of our calories from oils. Most nuts are great sources of healthful oils. Nuts also have high levels of protein, minerals, and B vitamins.

Nuts may be full-size canopy trees, such as chestnut, oak, hickory, walnuts, pecans, butternuts; understory trees such as almonds and filberts; or shrubs such as hazel and chinquapin chestnut. Trees in the walnut family, as discussed elsewhere, can be allelopathic, and so are a special design consideration.

Acorns were a staple food and livestock feed in many regions in past centuries. Many Native American nations used acorns extensively. Acorns usually contain high levels of tannin, which must be leached out by soaking in numerous changes of water before the nuts are eaten. White oak species were preferred because they have less tannin. Some selected varieties of burr oak have been known to produce a "sweet" acorn, requiring little or no leaching before being consumed.

Preservation

Most nuts will keep fine in the shell or out of the shell when stored on a cool dry and dark cupboard. Chestnuts are an exception. They will dry out or can get moldy easily. To store a large harvest of chestnuts it is best to peel the shell and freeze the chestnut meat for later use. Chestnuts can also be frozen in the shell. Chestnuts are low in oil and are mostly starch when the husks first open. Over a period of a few weeks they continue to ripen and become sweeter as the starch converts to sugar. So, before freezing them you should sample the chestnuts every week until their flavor and sweetness develops. When they first fall off the tree the nut is full and tight against the shell. The nut meat loses moisture and shrinks a bit as it ripens. You will know they are ready to be eaten or frozen when the shell is looser.

Acorn meal and acorn cakes.

Credit: Lincoln Smith

Herbs

Culinary herbs provide multiple functions in our diets and in the food forest ecosystem. In addition to providing added flavor to our food, many herbs contain health-promoting compounds. These include phytonutrients and aromatic compounds.

Herbs provide important habitat for beneficial insects and act as attractors for many. Pollinator insects and predatory insects benefit from having a wide range of herbs and flowers blooming at various times of the year. These insects need pollen and nectar in their diet to fuel their flights and feed their young. As companion plants, aromatic herbs and flowers are said to repel or

Go Wild

The intrepid plant explorer can often find native and naturalized plants in their own area. Our own foraging places include swamps and marshes, stream banks and river banks, forest and fields. We gather nuts, berries, wild fruits, mushrooms, and medicinal plants. Abandoned farmyards are a great place to look for apples gone wild and other interesting plants.

The first two rules of foraging are to properly identify a plant or fungi before you use it and to never overharvest. You can easily be poisoned by consuming the wrong plant. So please be sure you know what you are doing. Foraging requires an ethical attitude on the part of the forager. Rare and endangered plants should not be harvested. You should never overharvest wild plants. A third rule is to seek permission on other people's land before you harvest. Trespassing rules vary in each state and locality, so be sure you have permissions.

We should all be on the lookout for more productive and flavorful specimens of our regional wild plants. For several millennia native people harvested and managed nature in North America and elsewhere. Surely they had preferred selections of many wild foods. Several centuries of cultural disruption and the subsequent poor land use practices of European settlers meant the loss of those centuries of selection. Today we have found or bred named varieties of native walnuts, pecans, hickory, and other nuts, and fruits such as blueberry, blackberry, raspberry, juneberry, and paw paws. Improved varieties of others, such as elderberry, aronia, wild rose hips, nannyberries, fox grape, and many other wild plants await discovery and further refinement.

When you do find a promising new cultivar of a wild plant, you can collect seeds, make cuttings, or try grafting branches onto seedlings. Just remember to follow the rules above.

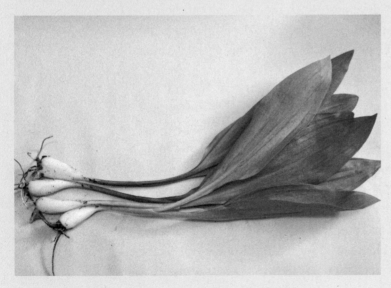

Ramps, a wild allium native to eastern North America are a grow early in the spring as an understory crop.

confuse insect pests. A food forest is an ideal place to grow herbs, because it offers a wide range of potential niches to fill.

Greens

Many types of leafy greens will do well in the food forest. Some prefer full sun in cooler weather, but many will appreciate partial shade in hot summer months. Greens are very important in the diet, being rich in vitamins, minerals, and phytonutrients. Many are eaten raw.

Edible greens such as chervil, chickweed, violets, and some wild edibles prefer shade.

A few trees have edible leaves when they are young. These include mulberries, basswood, and hawthorn and the tropical moringa tree. Sassafras leaves are dried and powdered and used to thicken soups. Mallow leaves, and hibiscus leaves are also eaten cooked.

Edible Flowers

A number of plants with edible flowers can be grown in the food forest. Edible flowers, while containing vitamins and minerals, are more of a flavor and aesthetic component of the menu. As with culinary herbs, and ornamental and medicinal flowers, edible flowers provide food for our insect allies. Most culinary herb flowers are edible, and prefer partial to full sun. Nasturtiums, roses, calendula, marigolds, pansies, chives, garlic chives, and beans like the sunnier or partial shade sections. Violets, violas, and pansies prefer the shade. Wild bergamot and bee balm like the partly sunny edges. Various mallows grow in full or partial sun.

Roots

Root crops need special consideration when being placed into the food forest system. It is important to not disturb or damage the roots of trees and shrubs when harvesting root crops. The key is to plant root crops on edges or in deep soil beds reserved for them. Jerusalem artichokes like to grow in patches in the sunnier part of the food forest. Annual beds for crops of potatoes, sweet potatoes, and other root crops can be included in the layout and rotated with beds of greens. These can be planted shallowly or grown

Credit: Darrell E. Frey

Woodland sunflowers, a relative of Jerusalem artichoke and ground nut, a wild bean with edible tubers, both grow well in the root zone of the food forest.

just below mulch to ease harvest and minimize damage to perennial crops nearby. Horseradish will do well in full or partial sun. Wilder edible roots, such as leguminous vine groundnut and woodland sunflowers can do well in partially shaded edges. Comfrey and horseradish also fit in, but their deep roots require deep digging to harvest, so locate them where they can be harvested as needed. Masanobu Fukuoka discussed planting daikon radishes in his orchards, both for harvest and for the soil-conditioning action of their deep roots.

Wild Edible Plants

A wide range of wild edible plants will fit into the food forest. As often stated, please be sure you properly identify the plants you eat. Naturalized wild edibles are plants that came from other continents and are now widespread in our landscape. Plantain, ox-eye daisy, purslane, and dandelion all have nutritious edible leaves and are all naturalized plants in North America. Daylilies, originally from Eurasia, are also widespread naturalized plants with edible tubers, shoots, and flowers. Each of these is a great candidate for the food forest.

Numerous native wild edibles may be included as well. Many common fruits are native to North America. These include strawberries, blueberries, raspberries, and blackberries. Wild berries may not be as productive as selected varieties but they may have unique and intense flavors. Many new varieties are out there waiting to be discovered. If you are short on space, you may prefer selected varieties for their known qualities. But if you are adventurous and have lots of space, wild fruits may have a place in your landscape.

Woodland edibles, such as ramps, sweet cicely, wood sorrel, violets, wild ginger, and even trilliums, if you can bear to harvest the leaves for food, do well in deep shade. Ramps are spring ephemerals, growing and producing a crop before the trees are in full leaf. Ostrich ferns are another wild edible plant worth considering. They need a little room to spread but will produce edible fiddleheads each year for decades once established.

Fungi

Mushrooms and other fungi have a special place in the food forest. As previously discussed, mushrooms are the fruiting bodies of fungi. For much of their life cycle fungi exist as a hair-thin masses known as mycelium. The individual strands of the mycelium are known as hyphae. Hyphae can literally grow into plant roots and exchange nutrients with the plants. In a natural forest the network of mycelium serves as both the nervous and circulatory systems of the ecosystem. Chemical cues are passed between trees and even between different species of trees via mycelium. At the same time, soil fungi act as decomposers, working with other soil organisms to break down organic matter and return nutrients to the ecosystem. Certainly not all fungi are beneficial. Many fungi plague our gardens as parasites and disease organisms. But those in the soil are generally helpful.

Credit: Darrell E. Frey

Shiitake mushrooms.

To better understand the roles of fungi, you should read the work of Paul Stamets. His book *Mycelium Running: How Mushrooms Can Help Save the World* (Ten Speed Press, 2005) contains a wealth of information on the many uses of fungi. And *The Mushroom Cultivator: A Practical Guide to Growing Mushrooms at Home* (Agarikon Press, 1984) is the bible of the topic.

As you manage your food forest, you may find mushrooms appear on their own. Honey mushrooms, morels, and wine caps may naturally find their way into the system. Shaggy manes might make an appearance after doses of compost. Puffballs, meadow mushrooms, and giant puffballs could also enter on their own. Always use extreme caution when identifying mushrooms. Even after you are sure of the identity of a mushroom, you should consume a small sample first. Some mushrooms can cause allergic reactions in some people.

You can also purchase spawn to establish beds of shaggy mane, wine caps, and morels in mulch in the food forest. Morels may require special soil and plant relationships to establish them long term. You can always try to establish fungi by dropping spore-producing mushrooms in your food forest. I have established giant puffballs and even chanterelles this way, but there is no guarantee of success.

The shadier sections of the food forest are good habitat for cultivating fungi on wood as well. Logs inoculated with spawn from shiitake, reishi, maitake, lion's mane, and oyster mushrooms can produce for many years if tended properly. Each of these fungi has a preferred type of wood on which they grow best.

Medicinal Plants

The list of medicinal plants for planting in the food forest is vast, and beyond the scope of this book. Most plants seem to have some medicinal properties. Plants may be tonics, rich in minerals and plant chemicals which can have a rejuvenating effect. Many of these are used in herbal teas. Many plants are curatives, useful to fight infections and aid in minor health issues, such as the calming chamomile, the refreshing mints, and the pain-easing willow bark. Other plants are the source of more powerful medicines that require professional advice to prepare and use.

Tea plants are most abundant in the herbaceous plant layer of the food forest. These include bee balm, lemon balm, various mints, anise hyssop, catnip, and many more. Annuals such as calendula and borage prefer the sunny side but can handle some shade. Vines such as wild yam and hops are also used for their medicinal properties. Perennials include valerian, ginseng, goldenseal, and many other shade-tolerant medicinal plants. Trees with medicinal uses include beech, birch, oak, slippery elm, and basswood.

Uncommon Fruits

It is difficult to avoid using part of the title of writer and researcher Lee Reich's *Uncommon Fruits for Every Garden* (Timber Press, 2008) in this section. A number of the plants listed here are described in detail in his book. We recommend you check it out. Many fruits not commonly grown can be planted in the food forest.

Paw paws have been emerging as the new cool fruit for years. But because they do not ship or store well they have not been an economically successful crop. They are late to ripen and are best eaten when they are soft, with

Cornelian cherries and edible dogwood.

Cornelian cherry sauce.

Credit: Darrell E. Frey

Credit: Darrell E. Frey

a texture similar to pudding. The flavor varies, and is hard to describe, but is sort of a mix of melon, banana, and vanilla. Many selected varieties are available. Two are needed for pollination.

The Cornelian cherry dogwood, *Cornus mas*, is popular in eastern Europe. Their fruit is slightly tart but tasty. The cherries ripen more fully after they fall off the tree, and are used for a variety of preserves. You will need to plant two for good pollination. The trees can grow over 30 feet tall, but we have seen coppiced specimens that are more accessible. The other edible dogwood, *Cornus kousa*, is commonly planted in parks and yards as a small ornamental tree. The fruit is sweet and flavorful, but the skin tends to be tough.

A number of varieties of currants and gooseberries are available. Because they flower later in the spring, they are reliable producers each year. The musky flavored black currant is an acquired taste, but in high demand for those in the know. The leaves of black currant also make a flavorful tea. Jostaberry is a cross between currants and gooseberries. The plants are similar to the bush form of currants, but a little larger.

Jujube, also known as Chinese date, is a small tree or shrub that produces a date-like fruit. We grow them in the bioshelter, but they are known to do well outside in temperate climates.

Maypop, also known as passionflower is a fast growing perennial vine native to eastern North America. The vines die back each fall and grow again each year from the roots. The egg-size fruits ripen in mid summer.

Mulberries, *Morus alba*, are so common in many cities that they seem to be weeds. Indeed they may be considered invasive. The fruit ripens in June. A dozen trees planted as unselected seedlings at Three Sisters Farm have a wide range of fruit types. Some are white, some purple, some in between. Some are very sweet with little flavor. Some not as sweet with lots of flavor. One tree ripens a few weeks later than the others, extending the season. Nearby a native red mulberry ripens fruit in July and August. Selected varieties of mulberry are available.

Alpine strawberries and other day-neutral strawberries yield through the warm months until frost and make excellent ground cover plants.

Soil-conditioning Plants

A number of plants may be grown in the food forest for their capacity to condition the soil. A good example is the biennial taproot plants. These plants, such as burdock, yellow dock, chicory, curled dock, and evening primrose have tap roots that grow into the subsoil. The first year they grow from seed and form a rosette of leaves and a deep root system. The second year they send up their flower stalk, set seed, and die. The taproot becomes a channel of organic matter that feeds the soil, and helps to increase soil depth, soil aeration, and drainage.

In the classic book *Weeds: Guardians of the Soil* (Devon-Adair, 1980), Joseph Cocannouer describes the soil-conditioning abilities of a number of plants considered weeds. Plants such as purslane, lambsquarters, wild amaranth, and even ragweed are described as having the ability to mine the deeper layers of soil for nutrients and create channels for other roots to follow. Of course, many of these plants have edible or other useful parts as well.

Nutrient-cycling Plants

A number of plants are known for their ability to concentrate various minerals. Often called *dynamic accumulators*, they gather various essential minerals in the soil; when they shed leaves or die back, the nutrients are returned to the soil in a bio-available form, enriching it. Some of these, such as stinging nettles, can be added to the compost pile if you do not want them in the food forest. In addition to nettles, other accumulator plants include comfrey, dandelion, yarrow, yellow dock, curled dock, burdock, sorrel, and various legumes. The leaves of most deciduous trees are good sources of minerals as well. Comfrey is one of the most common plants added to food forests. Comfrey flowers over a long season and therefore provides habitat for pollinating and other beneficial insects. Its roots go deep into the ground and access nutrients beyond the reach of many more shallowly rooted plants. Comfrey leaves provide a source of nutrient-rich mulch when cut and dropped several times each season. Comfrey can spread, though, and should be placed judiciously to avoid crowding other plants.

Habitat Plants and Ecological Niches: The Birds and the Bees

We want a healthy ecosystem in the food forest. Songbirds help keep insect pests under control. Beneficial insects pollinate the flowers. Predatory insects also help control pests. As managers, we keep an eye on things and assist nature in maintaining a balance.

Most flowering plants provide pollen and nectar for insects. In trade for nectar, pollinators move pollen from flower to flower. But some types of flowers provide better habitat to keep pollinators supplied with food. These include composite flowers, such as daisy, sunflowers and purple coneflower, umbrellifer flowers, such as dill, cilantro, and Queen Ann's lace, and many herb flowers. When designing for pollinator habitat the goal is to support a diverse range of pollinators through the growing season.

Creating Your Food Forest Guild

As we discussed in the previous chapters, a plant guild is a group of plants that can grow together in an ecologically sound community. The canopy layer tree or trees can have a strong influence on the selection of the other members of the guild. If you are beginning with an existing mature tree as the canopy tree you will do best to research its natural characteristics and build a guild to complement that tree and provide for your needs. When starting with an open space, you can build your guild from scratch. To review, key components of the ecological food forest include nitrogen-fixing plants, pollinator and beneficial insect habitat, nutrient-cycling plants, and fungi. Your guild may only have one layer of trees, but the key elements—canopy, understory, herb layer, ground cover, roots, and vines—all have many options. In the next section we offer the concept of the plant or species palette to aid you in creating a unique and evolving system to suit your needs.

Species Palettes

A species palette is a list of plants with a common theme. Using one helps simplify the design process by indicating which plants to choose in a given situation. A drawback to this tool is that you may overlook plants not listed, so it is best to develop and add to your own lists over time. In this book we provide some examples of species palettes. Any species may include dozens of cultivars, or varieties, to choose from, which adds more options for selecting the right plant for your food forest. Specific varieties of a species offer options of fruit size, flavor, ripening time, pollination requirements, hardiness, and variations on size and shape of the plant. At Three Sisters Farm our apple varieties include fruit ripening every few weeks from the Yellow Transparent in July to Northern Spy in October. While we do suggest specific cultivars from time to time, we are primarily focused here on species selection.

The following lists suggests possible plant palettes you can create to guide your planning.

Location Palettes

Full sun

The canopy layer trees receive full sun. Other plants for the sunny side of the food forest include most culinary herbs and sun-loving vegetables.

Partial shade

Currants	Gooseberry	Elderberry

Deep shade

Violet	Ginseng	Ramps
Valerian	Goldenseal	Shiitake mushroom
Woodland wild flowers		

Wet soil

Poorly drained soils can be bad for many species. A high seasonal water table in the spring will kill roots that grew in the drier season the summer before, often due to lack of oxygen. Plants that do well in wet soils are specialized to gather oxygen and other nutrients from wet soil. Trees include swamp white oak, alder, which fixes nitrogen, and willows. Other plants that can be tolerant of wet soils include elderberry, bee balm, mints, jewell weed, swamp milk weed, swamp rose, and ground nut, to name a few.

Riparian zone/rain garden

A riparian zone is the land along a stream or lake shore that experiences occasional high water in storms and in the spring when snow melts. Plants that naturally grow in the riparian zone can also do well in the rain garden and bioswale.

Butternut	Groundnut	Jewel weed
Black walnut	Wild bergamot	Willows
Paw paw	Bee balm	Bamboos
Nannyberry	Mints	
Serviceberry	Joe Pye weed	

Acid soils

Blueberry	Cranberry	Potatoes
Huckleberry	Lingonberry	Rhubarb

Slightly acid soils

Elderberry	Gooseberry
Currants	Wildflowers

Functional Palettes

Nitrogen fixing

Legume:

Redbud	Mesquite	Acacia
Black locust	Carob	Chinese silk tree
Honey locust	Tamarind	Kentucky coffee tree

Other nitrogen fixing trees:

Alder	Russian olive
Autumn olive	Gumi

Shrubs:

Caragana	Eleagnus

Vines:

Wisteria

Bamboo

Bamboo is an extremely useful plant. Mature bamboo can be made into trellises, poles, and when strong enough, many other useful implements. Some species are edible. Bamboo can also be invasive. Clumping bamboo is less likely to spread, but running bamboo can spread quickly from underground roots. Besides escaping from your garden, bamboo can overrun your food forest. If you choose to grow bamboo put it a place where you can control it. For example, you can grow it between a building and a mowed yard or driveway, or between a pond and cultivated area. Some people keep it contained in large planters. When you plant bamboo as part of your food forest garden, you can also contain it by intensive harvest of shoots for food and by cutting back excess growth. You will likely find the maintenance is worth the effort to have the materials available close at hand.

Herbaceous perennials:

Lupines	Groundnut, vining	Birdfoot trefoil
Kudzu, vining	Hog peanut, vining	Licorice
Clover	Alfalfa	
Sweet clovers	Trefoils	

Annuals:

Peas	Soybeans
Beans	Peanuts

Choosing Your Plant Varieties

Once you know the type of fruit and other plants you want to grow, you will need to choose varieties to plant. The selection of varieties for good fruit is an important decision and one you will live with for years to come. Half the fun of planning a food forest is browsing catalogues to find your selections. If you are lucky enough to have friends and neighbors who grow fruit, you can ask for advice. Many modern varieties have been developed with the idea that you will use an arsenal of fungicides and pesticides to wage chemical warfare on pests and diseases in your orchard. It is best to search out varieties that are known to produce well with organic culture in your area. Old-time, heirloom varieties are mostly tried and true.

Of course you will want to select the best varieties of fruit for your needs. You may want fresh eating apples, pie apples, cider apples, or some of each. If you only have space for one or a few apples, you will want a multipurpose apple. Whatever the fruit, adaptation to your area is important, as is harvest time, yields, and flavor.

Many fruit varieties require pollination from a different variety to have good fruit production. Be sure to check the requirements of the varieties you chose. Disease resistance is another important consideration. Study the diseases that may affect the fruit in your region and choose plants that will be resistant.

Crop Yield Chart

This chart is intended as a tool to help you know what yield you might expect from your perennial crops. The yields listed give a general idea or range of possible yields for healthy well-tended trees.

Keep in mind that some fruit trees do not yield every year. Frosts during flowering time can limit fruit set and some varieties naturally produce better crops on alternate years.

Plant	Yield per Plant (lbs)	By When? (years)	Preservation
Grapes	15	3	drying, juice, canning
Hardy kiwi	25–200	5–9	drying, freezing, canning
Passionfruit vine	20	3	
Asparagus	3–4 per 10 ft row	3–5	freezing, canning
Strawberry	2 lb	1	drying, freezing, canning
Blackberry	2–10+	2–3	drying, freezing, canning
Blueberry	8–15	3–5	drying, freezing, canning
Bush cherry	12–15	2–4	drying, freezing, canning
Currant	11	3	drying, freezing
Cranberry	4.5	2	drying, freezing
Elderberry	12–15	2–4	drying, freezing
Gooseberry	11	3	drying, freezing
Raspberry	3	2–3	drying, freezing
Aronia	20	3–4	cooked or juiced
Goji berry	2	3–4	drying, freezing
Dwarf apple	55–120	3	drying, freezing
Semi-dwarf apple	77–155	4	drying, freezing, juice
Standard apple	100–400	5–8	drying, freezing, juice
Dwarf Asian pear	56 (1 bushel)	3–7	drying, freezing, juice
Semi-dwarf Asian pear	56–112 (1–2 bushels)	3–7	drying, freezing, juice
Standard Asian pear	170–450 (3–8 bushels)	3–7	drying, freezing, juice
Cornelian cherry	30–50	3–13	drying, freezing, canning
Sour cherry	50–100 (1–2 bushels)	4–5	drying, freezing, canning
Sweet cherry	50–100 (1–2 bushels)	4–5	drying, freezing, canning
Paw paw	25–50	5	freezing
Peach	200	5–6	drying, freezing, canning
Pear	100–300	5–6	drying, freezing, canning, juice
Plum	150	5–6	drying, canning
Chestnut	20–40	15–20	
Hazelnut/Filbert	2–4	5–8	
Pecan	20–100	15–20	
Walnut	20–100	15–20	

Staghorn Sumac (*Rhus typhina*)

Any one of the sumac's uses make it worth establishing and together they make it a valuable addition to an agricultural landscape. We manage a small stand of sumac along the north tree line. It is a key part of our native plant gardens, providing the dappled shade typical of a forest edge.

A native to North America, sumac can be found from the Northeast to the Midwest and south to Alabama in the mountains. Staghorn sumac grows quickly to a height of 30 feet in well-drained soil.

Sumac flowers are a major midsummer nectar source for honeybees if the weather is hot and dry. The golden honey is often strongly scented and bitter when new, but matures to an excellent flavor by fall. The scarlet fruit spikes make a delicious, thirst-quenching iced tea and can be used medicinally. The flowers can be dried for later use.

The seeds, which remain on the branches through winter, are an important wildlife food. Many beneficial birds, such as catbirds and thrushes, as well as game birds such as grouse, turkey, pheasant, and quail rely on sumac seeds in winter when other food is scarce. Rabbits, deer, and other hoofed browsers eat the bark, twigs, and fruit. *American Wildlife Plants* reports that "captive quail" fed "a 50% diet of sumac seed…with other high caloric feed stuff thrived and gained weight," and that the seeds are a good source of provitamin A. Sumac seeds are eaten by chickens and could be incorporated into their forage yards.

Sumac grows well as a mid-story edge species between forest and field or as part of an "ecological island" between fields. Dense plantings on steep sites will control erosion. As a pioneer in reforestation, sumac will provide shade for young hardwood trees. At one of our previous homes, a dense stand of sumac acted as an effective dust barrier between the dirt road and the garden. Its fernlike foliage, with its tropical appearance and fall colors, gives sumac high ornamental value.

A major problem with sumac is control. It will spread rapidly by root and seed, and is difficult to eradicate. Cutting off unwanted growth is the best control. New growth cuttings can be composted. Woody prunings make a quick-burning kindling when dried. The branches are too soft and crooked for any functional use such as posts and stakes but they can be used for making flutes and baskets. The bark and leaves are rich in tannin and are used medicinally.

Other species of sumac with similar functions and products are: smooth sumac, *R. glabra*, grows to 20 feet; dwarf sumac, *R. copallina*, which generally grows to 12 feet and tolerates city air well; fragrant sumac, *R. aromatica*, which also provides oils, resins, and red dye. Poison sumac, *R. vernix*, grows in swamps and wet places. It should be avoided due to its poisonous properties. All sumacs are easily propagated by seed and transplanted root sprouts.

Ferns

If ever there were a plant to inspire artists with its form and beauty, balance and proportion, it is the fern. The sight of this plant, arching gracefully from the forest floor, each fragile frond spreading out in organic harmony to absorb the diffused light, has long awakened people to an understanding of the universal principles of order and harmony.

Mankind has utilized ferns since time immemorial. Native Americans were known to have used at least 20 species for food, variously eating fiddlehead, fronds, pith, and rhizome. Of the nearly 10,000 species of ferns, approximately 100 are native to the northeastern US. Most of these are widespread throughout the country and world. Ferns can be identified with a good field guide. Good information on uses for some ferns is found in various books on useful and edible plants.

Ostrich fern fiddleheads.

Please use extreme caution and be sure to properly identify any fern before eating it or using it medicinally. The growing environment and harvest time also may effect the safety of any wild foods. Cultures that use ferns for food may have had special preparation methods that made them a safe and important part of a seasonal diet. With the exception of the ostrich fern, as discussed below, we find their beauty and rarity restricts our harvesting them for other uses or sale. The information on specific species below is gathered and given in the interest of inspiring further research should you have these plants or wish to restore them to your landscape.

Ferns may be locally rare or endangered. Harvest and use of wild plants should not be an option unless you own the property or have the owner's permission and the plants are abundant and self renewing.

Another criteria is that the harvest be sustainable. We have established several propagation areas on our woodland property for ostrich fern. Each of these patches is in a small stream floodplain. They receive a fresh layer of sand and silt during large rain events, every few years. The ferns spread quickly here. Each year we can divide the spreading rootstock for establishing new plantings, and harvest a spring fiddlehead crop. We have been able to increase the total number of ostrich ferns in the propagation areas and increase our sales of them each year.

Many ferns are available from nursery suppliers. We recommend finding sources close to home. Royal fern, ostrich fern, cinnamon fern, and interrupted fern are sold as ornamentals. The last three all make excellent landscape plants because of their three to four-foot high vase-shaped clumps. Christmas fern is sold as a potted plant.

If you have a propagation area, transplanting in the fall or early spring while ferns are dormant is best. Ferns have a unique growing cycle. Spores first grow into a gametophyte, a flat green plant without leaves or roots. This is the sexual stage, having male and female organs. After fertilization, the egg grows into the sporophyte, the more familiar form. Once established, some ferns will live over a century. Ostrich, hayscented, and bracken ferns will spread quickly from rhizomes and can overrun a site.

Bracken or **Brake**, *Pteris aquiline*, is perhaps the most widely distributed fern, found throughout the Northern Hemisphere. In the Sierra Nevada Mountains it can reach a height of six feet but is generally about three feet high. It grows quite densely in low wet soil and can spread 10 feet or more each year.

Raw bracken contains an enzyme which destroys vitamin B1, thiamine, and should not be eaten in large amounts. Bracken fern may be carcinogenic and some sources, including the British Horticultural Society, recommend not eating them at all. However, various cultures have found ways to prepare bracken that they use in their diets. Caution and research is advised, as with all wild foods.

The tender unfolding fronds have been used worldwide as a pot herb and soup thickener. Pacific Coast Indians cooked and ate the thick rootstocks. Roots were used in Europe as flour to make a bitter bread during famine. While young bracken is useful spring pig forage, mature fronds have poisoned livestock. Bracken has also been used as a packing material and as thatch for roofing. Dyes ranging from green-yellow to gray are obtained from the shoots. The rhizomes are used as a substitute for hops.

Ostrich fern, *Pteretis pensylvanica*, is a beautiful fern found growing in large vase-like clumps on riverbanks and wetlands from Newfoundland to Virginia and northwest to British Columbia, and in Europe and Asia north to the Arctic Circle.

The thick succulent fiddleheads are excellent eaten cooked when under six inches. These are the classic fiddlehead fern and are in demand by chefs each spring. They should be thoroughly cooked before eating. Ostrich fern is easily propagated by division of rootstocks and will spread rapidly.

Royal fern, *Osmunda regalis*, is another tall fern (six feet) growing in vase-like clumps in sunlit, moist areas in Europe, Asia, Africa, and from South America to Canada. Unfurled fronds are eaten cooked. Fibers from the fronds are used to make cloth in Japan. The rootstock is used medicinally for cough medicine, tonic, and ointments for injuries. Royal fern will grow in shallow water if its crown is above the surface.

Cinnamon fern, *Osmunda cinnamomea*, and **interrupted fern**, *O. claytoniana*, have similar uses. Both have a small edible pith called fern butter in the center of the clump below ground level. Both have a fibrous root mass which can be made into extremely durable containers for growing orchids and other plants. Cinnamon fern produces a wool on the spore fronds which is used as an absorbent medicinally. Rhizomes of cinnamon fern have similar uses medicinally as royal fern, though not as powerful. It is also used to treat diarrhea. Cinnamon fern grows in most areas in forests and swamps in North America.

Sensitive fern, *Onoclea sensibilis*, is abundant in lowlands throughout the US. Young unopened plants have been used as a pot herb. Wild turkeys eat the spore fronds throughout the winter.

Male fern, *Dryopteris filix-mas*, grows in forests in Europe, Asia, and eastern North America. It is used as a taenicide, a worm medicine. Male fern should only be used with caution and knowledge of its properties.

Maidenhair fern, *Adiantum pedatum*, is a small delicate fern (16–20 inches) inhabiting moist, shaded places throughout the eastern US and Canada to the Northwest and in Asia. It has been used medicinally to make cough syrup and hair tonic. It is also dried and used as tea.

Common polypody, *Polypodium vulgare*, has been used as a worm medicine (with care), a fever reducer, and an appetite stimulant. It grows in moist shaded places and on stumps and logs throughout northeast North America.

Rattlesnake fern, *Botrychium virginianum*, found in the woodlands of North America and in the Himalayas and New Zealand, is eaten boiled when still unfurled.

A discussion of useful ferns would not be complete without mention of their relatives, ground pine, *Lycopodium* sp., and horsetail, *Equisetum* sp.

Ground pine is a running plant found in temperate regions worldwide. It grows in acid soils, particularly in abandoned pastures where it is a good ground cover and moisture conserver. Ground pine is mostly known for its use in wreaths but perhaps a more important use comes from its spores. These spores have a special electrostatic attraction. An object coated with them becomes almost waterproof, making them useful as an emollient, or skin softener and protector. Ground pine spores are highly explosive. They were used as flash powder in early photography. The development of the Xerox copy machine was based on the electrostatic principle of ground pine spores.

Horsetails are found in many bioregions worldwide. They are one of the most ancient plant families on the Earth. They reproduce by spores and are high in silica. Common horsetail, *Equisetum arvenses*, is an important plant in biodynamic agriculture, largely because of its high silica content. Several species especially rough horsetail (also known as scouring rush), *Equisetum hyemale*, have rough edges of silica deposits on their hollow stems. They work very well as scouring pads, and fingernail files. Probably many other uses for these sandpaper-like stems can be found. Some, if not all species of horsetail are poisonous to livestock.

The Hog Peanut, *Amphicarpaea bracteata*

Like its cousin the groundnut, the wild peanut is an unutilized legume with much potential for cultivation. A perennial native to eastern North America from Florida to New Brunswick, and west to Manitoba, the Dakotas to Texas, the wild peanut grows much like a pole bean, twining over shrubs and across the ground in moist, rich forests and along roadsides and fences.

The wild peanut has two types of flowers. The lovely pea-like white or lilac flowers along the vine produce an inedible seed pod with three or four seeds. From the base of the plant grow many thread-like runners with petalless self-fertile flowers. These flowers produce an abundance of subterranean pods, each containing a peanut-like seed. These seeds can be eaten raw or cooked and are said to be very good.

The wild peanut was an important food for some groups of American Indians, who would find mice caches of the peanuts and take them, leaving corn in its place. At one time wild peanut was cultivated in the southeastern US.

The great attraction of the wild peanut for permaculture is its habitat and the fact that it is a legume. It grows naturally as a ground layer plant in the shaded forest, where it contributes to the soil's store of nutrients by fixing nitrogen as well as producing a crop, at least for wildlife in a generally unused niche.

Besides providing snack food for direct human use, wild peanut provides forage for many animals. Pigs will forage for the underground seed pods, hence the name "Hog Peanut." The vines are browsed by livestock and probably deer. Both the aerial and subterranean seeds are eaten by quail, grouse, ring-necked pheasant, wild turkey, prairie chicken, chipmunk, mice, deer, and bear. It is especially important as a winter food where abundant. Wild peanut should fit very well into a rotational poultry forage system. Another variety of wild peanut, *A. pitcheri*, which has a stouter vine, is useful as a sand binder for erosion control. *A. pitcheri* has a similar range, habitat, and value.

I have found wild peanut vines in a mature woods, growing over small understory shrubs in a natural swale. The ground in this area is generally moist (not wet) and becomes a small drainage stream in a heavy rain. The bacteria nodules on the roots were numerous. The vine itself was thin and delicate in appearance and the pale green trifoliate leaves were very pretty.

Several methods of intensive cultivation are possible. Planting seeds in prepared beds of humus and leaf mold in woodlands and shaded areas should give good yields. Once established the peanuts can be harvested without harming the plant, which will live for several years. Wild peanut could also be brought into the annual garden, maybe as a companion to corn. Corn would shade the base of the plants and act as a trellis. Wild peanut would supply nitrogen to the corn. Cultivation in sunnier locations could be tried and may produce good results, though weeding may be more of a problem. This is a plant for adventurers, those willing to explore its possibilities.

Perhaps the best method of production would be to establish it heavily in a suitable place and let the mice harvest it for you.

CHAPTER FIVE

Tending and Growing a Forest Garden

Maintenance of the food forest landscape is not dramatically different from caring for any other garden system. The basic needs of the plants are the same: healthy soil, adequate water and sunshine, disease and pest awareness, pruning and harvesting.

In the food forest garden and in permaculture design, the long-term needs of the ecosystem and people are accounted for from the beginning, in the design process. Building and maintaining fertile soil, providing for water from rain and other natural features, practicing observation and preventative control for diseases and pests, and using efficient ways of pruning and harvesting are considered and factored into the design.

Doing this from the beginning and before every step we take is utilizing regenerative wisdom. The effort in being proactive pays off when it comes time to maintain the system.

Regenerative wisdom is defined by the Center for Regenerative Wisdom as "the insightful practice of thriving in peaceable harmony with the biosphere. By thriving thus, that individual simultaneously enjoys and fosters an upsurge of abundance for him- or herself, for the human world, for all life, and for the planet at large."

By observing nature and being keenly aware of our ecosystem and the interactions therein, we are able to save time and energy in the long run. Once again, this method of being present with the land calls for more investment upfront. We thoroughly assess the situation, explore different options, and then make the best decision that we can. This process is applied to every step, from initial site placement to cultivar selection, to soil building strategies, and so on. It is only possible to make progress from our current location, so use the information in this book and your own follow-up research to make the best decision. Do not be overwhelmed by not knowing everything. Look at missteps as valuable feedback and use them to move forward more boldly.

There is an alluring story of permaculture and food forests being totally natural, self-sustaining systems—and perhaps they can be depending on what you are growing. A food forest made up of native fruits and perennials or with the explicit intention of letting the plants grow without manipulation will need a relatively low maintenance system. However, with this method the plants will be exposed to everything nature has to offer, including diseases, pests, animals, and the general process of decay. And yields might be lower for an unmanaged system.

Designing food forests can utilize the 80/20 rule: 80 percent of the gains come from 20 percent of the actions. Those actions are based on regenerative wisdom that is cultivated and applied. Proper design helps to make the energy input effective. Working with nature is the premise of permaculture and food forest design. When we work with nature successfully, the system is already partly set up. We ensure the basics are covered and keep the amount of continual energy the landscape will need to a minimum. There are many and varied ways to do this.

Initial Site Preparation

The initial soil preparation will depend on the existing conditions and what is to be grown on the site. For example, a grass lawn can be converted to growing space through sheet mulching the ground in preparation for growing trees, shrubs, and other aboveground plants. Over time, this new soil layer will become fluffy enough to directly sow root crop seeds.

Building and Maintaining Soil Health

Soil health is probably the most critical factor when establishing your food forest system. With healthy soil, the plants will be provided with all the nutrients and organic material they need, proper water filtration, stability, and a diverse microbial community. Their roots can interact with the soil ecosystem in a way that brings in needed nutrients, water, and symbiotic relationships.

Soil is defined in the Soil Science Society of America's glossary as:

> The unconsolidated mineral or organic material on the immediate surface of the Earth that serves as a natural medium for the growth of land plants. (ii) The unconsolidated mineral or organic matter on the surface of the Earth that has been subjected to and shows effects of genetic and environmental factors of: climate (including water and temperature effects), and macro- and microorganisms, conditioned by relief, acting on parent material over a period of time. A product-soil differs from the material from which it is derived in many physical, chemical, biological, and morphological properties and characteristics.

Soil can be improved by spreading compost, composted manure, and planting cover crops. Sod is very competitive and can outstrip fruit trees for available nutrients so grass is not the best understory plant.

Fortunately there should be many basic ingredients onsite to build and maintain the soil's health. Raw materials to build soil and the compost system are often abundant onsite. This process of cycling returns the nutrients that were brought out of the soil back into it so that it can again feed the plants.

Here are some common materials to get your composting system going:
- Grass clippings
- Tree and shrub stems and twigs
- Leaf drop
- Plants after they have died back in the winter
- Detritus and decay that naturally builds

Occasionally you may want or need to add other amendments with essential minerals. Some of our favorite amendments include:
- Composted manures
- Fish emulsion for nitrogen

- Compost teas
- Herbal fertilizing brews
- Rock dust (pulverized limestone-calcium—used to raise pH; rock phosphate—phosphorus; greensand—potassium; azomite—multiple nutrients.)
- Kelp and seaweeds
- Urine for nitrogen

When preparing the site for a forest garden, you want to add the necessary non-water-soluble minerals based on soil test results. Some minerals are water soluble and need to be added continually based on future soil tests. The rock dusts last a long time and are less likely to leach out. Phosphorus and calcium may need to be supplemented every few years if there is abundant rain and leaching. In a forest garden, we set up dynamic relationships to prevent leaching. For example, accumulator plants keep minerals cycling in the garden and in a bioavailable form. The mycorrhizal fungi, carbonic acids, and high organic matter release the minerals to be available for the plants. The accumulator plants absorb nutrients that are released and prevent leaching. As we discussed in Chapter 4, annuals and herbaceous perennials play this role in a natural forest. In a food forest, we design to mimic that.

Using the terra preta concept (biochar: see Chapter 1) lots of organic matter provides reservoirs for these minerals once they are in the biocycle. The good soil structure also helps to hold these minerals.

As you manage the food forest, some plants will need compost teas and different minerals. The goal is to set up the system to be self-regulating over time with its own established nutrient cycles. The strategy is to add the right kind of minerals at the beginning so the cycle gets set up. A soil test and leaf analysis is recommended every three years to be sure your trees are not deficient in any nutrient. An overall picture of the nutrients the trees are taking up from the soil can be obtained through a foliar analysis.

In preparing your food forest location, whether a neglected garden space or a completely new area, the first few years will require ongoing preparation, focusing on the health of the soil and any existing trees or shrubs that will stay. Until the soil is in good health, the harvest will not be at its full potential.

The ideal pH for tree fruits is 6.5. Soil organic matter should be above three percent. Generally, a compost application of 55 pounds per tree every year in the spring is sufficient for fertility needs. If the tree is found lacking in a certain nutrient, such as boron, then amendments can be applied.

Manure is a great source of nitrogen. Incorporating it into the soil helps prevent nitrogen loss. The National Organic Program requires for organic certification that raw manure be incorporated into the soil 90 days (if there is no contact between the fruit and the soil) to 120 days (if there is contact) before consumption of the fruit. Though you may not have the goal of organic certification, the general guideline is sound.

It is important to keep tillage shallow when incorporating any organic amendments, to prevent damage to the roots and soil erosion. Soluble organic fertilizers (such as fish emulsion and kelp) are suitable for drip irrigation to supply quick supplemental fertility. Compost teas may also help increase fertility and contribute to disease control.

Compost

Compost is the finished product of decayed plant and other organic material that is used as a growth medium and fertilizer for plants. Most things in nature will eventually turn into compost. It is our good friend in building and maintaining soil health. Compost quickly builds the soil to healthy levels that will sustain abundant plant life. It can be made onsite from leaf droppings, debris, and other garden cleanup materials in addition to food scraps. So we are able to produce soil fertility in the garden, using materials from the garden, like a small miracle.

Mulching

Mulch is an organic covering made from carbon-heavy materials. In addition to being a weed management strategy, mulch provides habitat for beneficial insects, moderates soil temperatures, and provides for erosion control. Over time, organic mulches will improve soil quality. As they decompose nutrients

How to Make a Liquid Fertilizer Using Comfrey

Comfrey is a stellar food forest plant with many uses. If you have a plant that requires more nutrients or you just want to give it some extra love, comfrey brew is a good and free option. Its smell is horrifying, but often in nature there are many horrifying scents that mean fertility.

Ingredients

Comfrey leaves and roots (enough to loosely pack a five-gallon bucket)
Water

Materials

Large bins
Pruning shears, scissors, or knife
Gloves
Cotton fabric or metal screen

Directions:

1. Have a large bin or several five-gallon buckets ready. With the scissors or shears, chop the plant material up to small pieces. The smaller the pieces, the more quickly the bacteria will decompose them and the easier for the nutrients to be released.

2. Fill the bins with freshly chopped comfrey plant material (leaves, stems, and roots are all acceptable). The buckets or bins should be loosely filled to the top with plant material. Pour fresh water to cover the plants and stir with a large stick.

3. Cover the bins to prevent bugs from getting in. Air needs to be able to get in so if using a lid, leave it slightly ajar. Allow to steep for at least one and up to four weeks. Make sure to stir at least once a week to allow air into the mix. The brew is considered finished when it has a very strong smell of rot or manure.

4. When it is time to strain, place another clean bucket under the screen or cotton fabric and run the finished comfrey brew through it. The resulting liquid is your undiluted fertilizer.

5. It can be used straight but as it is very powerful, it is recommended to dilute it 1:10 parts water. Other plants can be used as well to make an herbal fertilizer brew, including dandelion leaves, plantain, and nettles.

are released and the residual organic matter improves soil structure and water-holding capacity.

The macronutrients nitrogen, phosphorus, and potassium are more available to trees in mulched systems than in unmulched systems. However, research done by the Natural Resources Conservation Service in 2012 states that certain high-carbon mulches, such as sawdust, can immobilize the nitrogen from being used by the plants.

Mulch should always be kept 8 to 12 inches away from the base of tree trunks to prevent mice from gnawing and to reduce the likelihood of diseases such as crown rot.

Sources of Mulch

Many types of mulch can be sourced directly from your garden. Here is a list of sources of mulch:

- Straw is particularly good for covering strawberries, potatoes, and tomatoes.
- Leaf mulch is an excellent soil builder and weed suppressor.
- Bark mulch gives a clean finish and is heavy enough to last a year.
- Plant mulch, such as chopped comfrey leaves, provides nutrients immediately as it decays. It is not the cleanest looking mulch but is simple and free. Use the "chop and drop" method of thinning plants to make use of plant mulch.
- Pine needles are great for mulching under blueberry or other bushes that need acidic soils to thrive.

Mulch Donut

The mulch donut is a common strategy for mulching trees. A donut-shaped circle of mulch is placed around the tree. In the early stages of tree establishment this mulch ring eliminates competition from grass, conserves moisture, and feeds the soil. Companion herbs and flowers can be planted in the mulch.

Credit: Sarah A. Jubeck

A mulch donut, or circle of mulch around a tree, helps get a newly planted tree off to a good start by reducing competition and building soil.

Credit: Michelle Czolba

Sheet mulching begins with covering the ground with layers of compost, paper, and cardboard.

Credit: Michelle Czolba

Layers of paper and cardboard are covered with mulch.

- For improving soil, hay, lawn clippings, leaves, and macadamia nut husks and shells are considered the best.

Sheet Mulching

A well-loved strategy for quickly building soil, conserving water, and suppressing weeds is called sheet mulching. The ground is covered with layers of organic materials and mulch. Add a bunch of rich organic material, such as compost, grass clippings, leaves, and aged manure. Top this with clean mulch. Then simply plant into it, usually by clearing space in the mulch and creating a hole in the layer of cardboard or newspaper. For the Hazelwood Food Forest, the sheet mulch layers consisted of compost, cardboard, and bark and leaf mulch. Essentially, sheet mulching mimics the process of leaf fall and decay in the forest.

The first step is to add a layer of compost, approximately three inches deep. This layer is worked into the existing ground lightly, using a garden rake. Other layers can then be added, such as fresh food scraps, manure, fish fertilizers, and other soil amendments. Alternatively, you can add these layers first then the compost on the next layer.

Next is the organic cover, such as cardboard, which will act to protect the soil from drying and runoff of nutrients. The layer of carboniferous material slows down evaporation and runoff of water. This way, a healthy soil system can be created to lessen the need for human energy inputs including watering, weeding, and constant input of new soil.

When putting the cardboard over the soil-building blend, be sure to overlap the pieces so that there are no spaces for weeds to come through. You can use one, two, or more layers of cardboard. One is most practical if you plan to plant soon thereafter, as it is easier to cut through one layer of cardboard to reach the soil level. More than one layer will prove more difficult to plant into.

After the cardboard is added, it is time for the mulch layer. Wood chips have been found to create more opportunities for fungal symbiotic relationships, which is important in the establishment of fruit orchards and forests. Leaf mulch works well under shrubs or around annual garden plants.

Materials for Sheet Mulching:

- Cardboard
- Newspaper
- Burlap
- Leaf mulch
- Wood chips
- Compost
- Manure
- Soil amendments
- Fresh food scraps

When sheet mulching to establish a food forest guild, the mulch can be laid in a cloverleaf or keyhole pathway pattern to allow for easy access and management of the understory.

Hugelkulture

Another method for sheet mulching to prepare raised beds is *hugelkulture*, a German word for a type of raised bed. As presented by Austrian farmer Sepp Holzer in his book *Sepp Holzer's Permaculture* (Chelsea Green Publishing, 2011), a hugelkulture bed is a mound of woody material and compost. These beds are often laid out on contour. Materials are layered and covered with soil and planted with a mix of perennial and/or annual crops. The woody material slowly decomposes in the mound, feeding the plantings and developing a high moisture retention capacity. This process mimics the natural process of a fallen tree in the forest, decaying over time and feeding a succession of plants over a long period of time. If you experiment with hugelkulture, as we have, we recommend keeping the woody material under a few inches in diameter and incorporating a balanced blend of carbon and nitrogen sources to build a healthy, productive soil. Larger logs can take a long time to breakdown and may be more useful for retaining the edges of the mound. This method is a good alternative to burning woody material when clearing brush and trees for establishing a food forest and garden landscape. Carbon is incorporated into the soil and as the woody material breaks down it is home to a good diversity of beneficial soil organisms. These include decomposers, mycelial fungi, and beneficial insects such as centipedes, millipedes, and ground beetles.

Ground Covers

Perennial understory cover crops help to suppress weeds, add organic matter, improve soil fertility (fixing nitrogen and bringing phosphorus from subsoil), attract beneficial insects, and conserve water. This is an example of stacking functions. A full ground cover is best to prevent soil erosion. Some possible issues with cover cropping the understory are competition with the trees and attracting rodents. On the other hand, clean cultivation has many disadvantages, including erosion, gradual depletion of organic matter, increased soil compaction, and decreased water infiltration.

Plants such as buckwheat, lupine, and sweet clover are noted for their ability to extract phosphorus from soils. Alfalfa is a green manure that can help scavenge nutrients as well. White clover establishes quickly and can compete well with weeds. Orchard grass, fescue, and other cool season grasses are valuable because they go dormant in the summer, thus minimizing competition for water.

Cool season legumes, such as fava or bell beans, vetches, and clovers add nitrogen into the system. For example, subterranean clover can fix from one to two hundred pounds of nitrogen per acre per year in a living mulch system. Other legumes can fix as much or more. However, organic apple growers on California's Central Coast only plant rye or other grass cover crops because leguminous crops contribute too much nitrogen, which can induce excessive shoot growth and decrease fruit production.

Planting perennial species will decrease the amount of tillage necessary to establish the cover crops and minimize the labor needed to maintain the understory. Instead of having one plant in the understory, a diverse set could also be grown to promote diverse insect habitat. Chickens can act as weeding animals and distribute manure throughout the orchard. Their manure is high in phosphates so this practice would be very useful if this is a deficient nutrient in the orchard. Animal manure should not be applied less than 90 days before harvest, so poultry can be allowed into the food forest after harvest through the following spring.

Living Mulches: Nitrogen Fixers

A living mulch is a specific type of ground cover that can be a valuable tool for food forest maintenance. Living mulch is a cover crop which is planted between or sown under main guild plants. White clover and alfalfa are great perennial living mulches.

Unlike a mulch that needs to be reapplied every year, living mulch will reproduce itself. Living mulches can provide all the benefits of other types of mulch plus continue to grow with the main crop year after year. Since they do not need to be replanted or reapplied every year, they are relatively low maintenance.

Credit: Lincoln Smith

A mix of wildflowers and legumes will build soil health and promote pollinators in the food forest.

A critical nutrient in food forest or any plant systems is nitrogen. According to the Charles Stuart University in Australia:

> Nitrogen is one of the main chemical elements required for plant growth and reproduction. Nitrogen is a component of chlorophyll and therefore essential for photosynthesis. It is also the basic element of plant and animal proteins, including the genetic material DNA and RNA, and is important in periods of rapid plant growth.
>
> Plants use nitrogen by absorbing either nitrate or ammonium ions through the roots. Most of the nitrogen is used by the plant to pro-

Nitrogen-fixing Plants and Microbes

In his article "Nitrogen Fixing Plants and Microbes," Paul Alfrey of the Balkan Ecology Project in Permaculture explains the two main groups of microbes plants use when nitrogen fixing and describes biological nitrogen fixation and the relationship with microorganisms (permaculture.co.uk/articles/nitrogen-fixing-plants-microbes).

Biological nitrogen fixation is an important component of organic gardening/farming, forest gardening and other agro-eco practices. Through a partnership with micro-organisms in their roots, some plants can turn atmospheric nitrogen into nitrogen fertilizers useful to themselves but also becoming available to their neighbors over time through root die back, leaf fall, and chop and drop pruning. These are known as the nitrogen fixing plants.

This is a mutually beneficial relationship with the plant providing carbohydrates obtained from photosynthesis to the microorganism and in exchange for these carbon sources, the microbes provide fixed nitrogen to the host plant.

While it does not replace the need to bring in other nutrients depleted by harvests such as phosphorus and calcium, nitrogen fixation provides a valuable biological source of an essential fertilizer.

There are two main groups of microbes that plants associate with in order to use the atmospheric nitrogen to fuel growth. They are *Frankia* and *Rhizobium*.

Frankia

Many plants partner with micro-organisms called *Frankia*, a group of Actinobacteria. These plants are known as the actinorhizal nitrogen fixers.

duce protein (in the form of enzymes) and nucleic acids. Nitrogen is readily transported through the plant from older tissue to younger tissues. Therefore, a plant deficient in nitrogen will show yellowing in the older leaves first due to the underdevelopment or destruction of chloroplasts and an absence of the green pigmented chlorophyll.

Given the importance of nitrogen in our systems and the inability of many plants to supply it or gather it from the atmosphere, it is standard practice to incorporate nitrogen-fixing plants into your design. These are plants which are able to supply the needed nitrogen for other plants.

Actinorhizal plants are found in many ecosystems including alpine, xeric, chapparal, forest, glacial till, riparian, coastal dune, and arctic tundra environments and can be found in the following plant families:

- Betulaceae, the birch family
- Myricaceae, the bayberry family
- Casuarinaceae, the Australian "pines"
- Elaeagnaceae, the oleasters
- Rosaceae, the rose family
- Rhamnaceae, the buckthorn family

These plants tend to thrive in nitrogen-poor environments and are often the pioneer species in plant communities playing an important role in plant succession.

Rhizobium

By far the most important nitrogen-fixing symbiotic associations are the relationships between legumes (plants in the family Fabaceae) and *Rhizobium* and *Bradyrhizobium* bacteria. These plants are commonly used in agricultural systems such as alfalfa, beans, clover, cowpeas, lupines, peanut, soybean, and vetches.

The *Rhizobium* or *Bradyrhizobium* bacteria colonize the host plant's root system and cause the roots to form nodules to house the bacteria. The bacteria then begin to fix the nitrogen required by the plant. Access to the fixed nitrogen allows the plant to produce leaves fortified with nitrogen that can be recycled throughout the plant. This allows the plant to increase photosynthetic capacity, which in turn yields nitrogen-rich seed.

Our Top Five Nitrogen-fixing Shrubs and Perennials

Supporting the overall ecosystem, fruit trees, and shrubs with nitrogen-fixing plants is key. They can be integrated into perennial agriculture systems to restore and maintain nutrient cycling and fertility self-reliance. Our favorite nitrogen fixers also have a host of other benefits.

1. Siberian pea shrub (*Caragana arborescens*) is ornamental, edible, and can be used in windbreaks. It generally does best in full sun. It is tolerant of adverse conditions, such as poor dry soils, extreme cold, salt, and wind.
2. Goumi (*Elaeagnus multiflora*) is edible and medicinal, growing well in full or part sun. It is suitable for poor soil and can tolerate atmospheric pollution.
3. Mimosa (*Albizia julibrissin*) is also known as silk tree. It is highly valued in Chinese medicine, as well as being quite beautiful. It prefers full sun.
4. Wild indigo (*Baptisia australis*) is a herbaceous plant which is also used to make a blue dye. It is aesthetically pleasing, having rounded green leaves and beautiful purple flowers.
5. Red clover (*Trifolium pratense*) is a perennial herb. It is medicinal, edible, and a bee-attracting plant. Red clover can thrive in poor soils and prefers sunny locations.

Diverse Plant Life Spans

Every plant has a life span that is completed in one or two years, or many more. Each plant is unique and the life span is also determined by the health of the plant and the ecosystem. In food forest design, we focus mostly on using perennials for the ecosystem benefits they provide and the lower maintenance required. Annuals are valuable in that the fruiting stage happens the first year. While mostly using perennials, annuals can be incorporated in the design allowing for immediate productivity. As the forest matures, the number of annuals decreases as the perennial plants ripen.

Three Steps to Creating a Dynamic Mineral-rich Ecosystem

Nutrient-rich food comes from nutrient-rich soil. So keeping the soil fortified with the right balance of minerals is essential for the health of the food forest and for our own health. The goal with mineralization is to keep the minerals cycling in-house as much as possible. This can be done to a large extent utilizing the principles of permaculture and ecology. The idea is to create a healthy ecosystem from the start.

1. Mineralize the soil with the appropriate amendments.

To get the system prepared and ready to feed the plants, the soil needs to be mineralized. See the list provided for how to select the best amendments for your site.

2. Plan to have dynamic accumulators on site.

In your design, be sure to put in dynamic accumulators (see Chapter 4). While there have not been any scientific studies to date verifying the process by which the accumulation process works, anecdotal evidence does support the dynamic accumulator theory. The best way to ensure adequate soil mineralization is to continually test your soils.

In the natural ecosystems which we seek to mimic, healthy rich soil is the bank. From this bank, some plants draw out resources and the dynamic accumulators reinvest the capital. There are many mysteries in nature yet. We can use the best information available along with our own experience to grow our plants.

3. Continually test the soil for mineral content.

We want to be sure that the accumulating plants are drawing the minerals out of the soil, making bioavailable forms, and delivering it back into the system for the plants that are not accumulators. The best way to check on this is to keep an eye on the soil test results.

For a comprehensive list of minerals found in plant tissues, check out Dr. James Duke's Phytochemical and Ethnobotanical Database at the USDA Agricultural Research Service site (ars-grin.gov/duke/plants) or this nutrient content spreadsheet (cdn.shopify.com/s/files/1/0248/9641/files/Dynamic _Accumulators_and_Nutrient_Contents.xlsx?723). Some of the plants included are common and high mallows, lambsquarter, stinging nettle, chives, mullein, borage, mugwort, red clover, sage, purslane, and many more. A snapshot of the spreadsheet appears on the following page.

Nutrients in Plant Tissue

		Macro (primary) nutrients			Macro (secondary) nutrients				Micro (trace) nutrients					
		N	P	K	S	Ca	Mg	Si	Fe	Mo	B	Cu	Mn	Na
Malva neglecta	Common Mallow	4,200												
Malva sylvestris	High Mallow	3,300	5,000			10,715			440					
Chenopodium album	Lambsquarter		36,833	87,100		33,800			250					250
Amaranthus	Pigweed		10,082	73,503		53,333	6,616		1,527			19		2,406
Urtica dioica	Stinging Nettle		6,800	37,220	6,665	33,000	8,600	6,500	418		36	15	172	491,400
Allium schoenoprasum	Chives		6,437	31,250		10,375	6,875		200					750
Verbascum thapsus	Mullein		5,700			13,300		74	2,360					760
Taraxacum officinale	Dandelion		4,583	27,569	3,300	13,000	2,500		5,000		125	12	130	5,278
Artemisia vulgaris	Mugwort		3,150	22,000	2,800	6,455			118			20	170	
Borago officinalis	Borage			67,210		5,005								
Trifolium pratense	Red Clover						8,100				23	18	464	
Helianthus tuberosus	Jerusalem Artichoke										30			
Chrysanthemum parthenium	Feverfew			39,385		5,810	2,400	46					81	48
Scutellaria lateriflora	Scullcap			21,800		4,550	1,130	48	250				47	160
Origanum vulgare	Oregano			18,647		18,794	3,016		598			9	47	205
Stellaria media	Chickweed			18,400	3,828	12,100	5,290	157	2,530				153	1,470
Equisetum arvense	Horsetail			18,000		24,000	4,370		1,230				69	560
Achillea millefolium	Yarrow			17,800		8,670	1,920	45					50	82
Cichorium intybus	Chicory			37,128		18,900	2,652		246					1,428
Salvia officinalis	Sage			24,700		17,957		31	305		41	8	31	1,080
Portulaca oleracea	Purslane				6,300									7,400
Oenothera biennis	Evening Primrose					23,400	3,900							
Thymus vulgaris	Common Thyme					16,700	4,360	202	1,508		48	9	79	1,490
Calendula officinalis	Calendula					30,400								
Rheum rhabarbarum	Rhubarb					14,400			250					
Rumex crispus	Curly Dock					10,000								
Symphytum officinale	Comfrey		242	1,870		1,980	77	1	1.3				0.6	12

Data Source: http://web.archive.org/web/20130126052424/http://www.ars-grin.gov/duke/; http://www.ars-grin.gov/duke/

Perennials and Biennials

Now we can discuss what plants will work well for the food forest design, serving specific functions. Perennials are the crux of food forest design. They have many benefits, some of which include soil stabilization, dynamic accumulation of nutrients which are then cycled back into the soil in the dormant season, as well as the functional uses for which they are chosen. Comfrey is an often used fast-growing perennial which is considered a dynamic accumulator.

Biennial taproot plants such as Queen Anne's lace, yellow dock, burdock, and plants like dandelion have a taproot through which they accumulate minerals and which, when they die, puts organic matter back into the soil as it decays. It also helps to aerate the soil and feed the soil ecology, thus keeping minerals in cycle. Much research needs to be done in the field of dynamic accumulators. What we know is that some plants are higher in certain minerals than others and so in growth and eventual decay they keep the minerals in a form usable by other plants.

Fungi

Fungi will occur naturally in a healthy soil. Many beneficial fungi work unseen in the soil's upper layers, accessing minerals and exchanging them with plants for hormones and nutrients. Mulches tend to promote fungi in the soil. You can also inoculate the food forest with purchased mycorrhizal inoculants. And you can "seed" useful fungi into the system. Edible mushroom spawn can be purchased and added following the supplier's directions. Wild mushrooms can be collected and tossed about the food forest to increase diversity. Edible boletes, puffballs, meadow mushrooms, and medicinal mushrooms all can find a home in your garden. We do recommend avoiding poisonous species. And of course never eat any fungi that you have not properly identified.

Space for Annuals

Where do annuals fit into the food forest system? Do they? In food forest design, we can incorporate annuals in several ways. They can act as understory plants to fill in gaps between perennials. A separate bed can be created only for annuals. It is also helpful to utilize annuals when the perennials and trees are still young and small, as they will keep land from being occupied by weedy plants, provide food, and can be incorporated into the compost pile at the end of the year.

Soil Fertility Ideas

White Clover As Multipurpose Ground Cover

White clover is a long-lived perennial that can be used as living mulch and ground cover to fix nitrogen. It also attracts and provides pollen for bees. It can be planted in the early spring and allowed to grow until late spring. It can then be mowed down, raked 12 inches from the base of any trees and left as mulch until before the tree begins to drop fruit in mid- to late fall. In late fall, compost can be added to facilitate quick decomposition of the mulch. Mulch left over winter could attract rodents. The next spring the clover will grow back and this cycle can be repeated.

Compost and Chickens

Another strategy for soil fertility is to add a five-gallon bucketful of compost to each tree in the early spring. Chickens can also graze the area until 90 days prior to harvesting any fruit. The manure will add phosphorus and other nutrients to the soil and allow the chickens to forage on the cover crop. Additionally chickens *love* insects and larvae and can clean up an area from any harmful pests. The chickens should be rotated as they will cause soil damage if left for too long in the same area.

Maintaining Plant Health: The Power of Observation

The permaculture principle of observation is defined by Bill Mollison as: "protracted and thoughtful observation rather than protracted and thoughtless labor." And by David Holmgren as: "observe and interact."

The essence of this principle is about *paying attention* and *giving something your awareness*. It is extremely powerful. We can choose where to place our attention, and often it helps that point of attraction to grow. Does this mean that if we pay attention to a disease that a plant is developing, we grow the disease? Yes and no. With the underlying intention of having a healthy tree, gathering information through observation, staring directly into the shadow aspect (disease), uncovering all parts of this, and dealing with it through action can be the way to the other side. On the other hand, it is far more powerful to focus our bigger attention on the abundant health of the system and seek ways to keep this level high.

Each of the trees and plants that you select for your food forest will have individual needs. It is wise to do a bit of research for each plant but no need to let this hold you back from beginning. Plant research is part of the design process and you want to do enough to choose the best varieties and the best location.

Information is abundant and when issues arise you can troubleshoot and problem solve. By creating a healthy foundational system, many issues will be averted and when any arise, they may not be as devastating as if the ecosystem was out of balance. Healthy soil, proper site selection, appropriate cultivar choices, and symbiotic relationships between plant, animal, insect, microorganism, and human go a very long way.

One pattern that may become apparent at some point is that certain plants will be better suited to your site than others. This may hold true even if all the visible factors indicate they should fit. If certain plants are not thriving and others dying altogether, some possible reasons include:

- some plants are more delicate than others and simply require more direct care
- unidentified factors in the soil do not agree with the plant
- just as there are companion plants, there are also plant combinations that do not do well
- there is an energetic exchange between people and plants and this relationship may not be a good fit
- mysterious factors yet to be named!

Regular visual inspection of leaves, tree, and fruit are your first-tier tools in maintaining a healthy ecosystem. This is the principle of observation that you used throughout your initial design process and is very important for keeping the system healthy. When something is awry, use your information bank to hone in on the problem and the ways to address it. Routine leaf analysis is an option as well if you want to dive deeper into nutritional analysis.

Managing the Food Forest Ecosystem

Here is a rundown of how to keep a watchful eye on the health of your ecosystem. It is a graduated approach beginning with the most gentle methods and going to the most invasive. It is loosely based on the Integrated Pest Management (IPM) approach.

Each plant will be prone to different pests and diseases, with much crossover in plants in the same genus. Once you get to know the plant in its healthy state, you will be able to notice any issues that may arise.

1. **Monitor and observe:** As we have discussed, the first step in pest and disease control is to observe what is going on. Get to know the plants in their healthy state so that you can be aware when imbalances happen.
2. **Identify and study life cycles:** If you notice a pest or disease, take some time to properly identify it and get to know its life cycle. Many times the

Case Study: Organic Apple Tree Pest and Disease Control

The goal of managing your forest garden is to produce healthful harvests. A full crop of perfect fruit is not always easy to produce. If you are like us and believe consuming pesticides is not part of a healthful diet, you will prefer a few worms in your apples to pesticides in your diet. Similarly, use of chemical fertilizers can disrupt the health of the soil and throw your systems off balance. So organic methods are preferred, and perhaps some pest damage is tolerable. There are, however, strategies for getting a great harvest with the least the amount of damage. As your experience grows and your management skills evolve you will learn to minimize pest damage and control disease.

It is important to know that most insects in an orchard are not pests. Some provide essential services like pollination and many others actually eat pest insects. The important thing to notice is damage to orchard plants caused by insects or disease: look for discolored leaves, unusual growth, holes in leaves, stems, or fruit, etc. Also look out for squirrels and other non-insect pests that may be damaging crops or plants.

Each pest or disease may have a different treatment strategy, from hand removal to predator release to spraying of water or soap.

Soil Health

Healthy soil is the beginning of healthful harvests. Soil should be deep, six inches at a minimum, well drained, with a steady balanced fertility, including the correct minerals in balanced proportions. Trees growing in good soil can better resist diseases and pests.

Crop and Varietal Selection

Choosing the right variety for your area is important. Study your nursery catalogues carefully for most effective management will be to intervene or leverage an opportunity in the pest's life cycle.

3. **Cultural controls:** Though this is step three, some of these actions need to be considered before planting anything. Good design equals fewer problems. Choose a site with good drainage, plant resistant cultivars, provide adequate nutrients (such as compost), and prune out dead, weak, and extraneous limbs. Genetic controls for the disease include growing resistant varieties.

4. **Physical controls:** Raking and destroying the previous years' fallen leaves can help eliminate scab inoculums. Liming leaves, flail-mowing and

varieties that grow best in your area. Ask your friends and neighbors what grows best for them. Doing research before you buy plants can greatly increase your success.

Microclimate

Finding the perfect spot to plant your food forest is a key, if you have a choice. A south-facing slope warms early in the spring and stays warmer longer in the fall, and may be hotter in the summer. When the soil warms too early, trees may flower and leaf too soon and be caught in a late frost. If the soil stays warm into the fall, trees may take longer to go dormant. For this reason many consider a north slope to be ideal for fruit planting. However, much depends on your chosen varieties and your local growing season.

The main thing is to keep microclimate in mind as you develop your site. If it is less than ideal you can still work around limitations by choosing varieties and management practices that suit the site.

Ecosystem Management

And, of course, creating a healthy ecosystem in and around the food forest will help ensure success. Promoting balance and health in the larger landscape with bird habitat, beneficial insect habitat, and other supporting species can help create a proper environment for success. Some things will be beyond your control. If you neighbor has prized cedar trees that harbor cedar apple rust, there is not much you can do to control the source of the disease. But you can choose varieties resistant to the disease and work to keep your plantings healthy.

spreading compost can also be effective means of deterring the spread of apple scab.

5. **Organic/Biological controls:** Within the organic program, commonly used fungicides are: sulfur, lime-sulfur, and Bordeaux mixture (copper sulfate and lime). All of these fungicides must be applied before the spores germinate or else the tree will have to be sprayed all season. When sulfur spray is utilized, spray coverage should be renewed two to three weeks following the formation of tight clusters.

6. **Chemical controls:** Applying organic fungicides—mixtures of copper and sulfur—at regular intervals throughout the season can prevent apple

scab infections. These can provide a protective coating over the fruit and foliage, preventing spores from landing and infecting the tree.

Managing Cedar Apple Rust (*Gymnosporangium juniperi-virginiana*)

This fungus is a serious threat to apple orchards. Wind can carry spores of cedar apple rust from cedar trees to apple trees up to a mile away. The infection can lead to poor growth and even the death of young apple trees. The fungus can eliminate the trees' return bloom.

Managing Sooty Blotch and Fly Speck

These are two different pathogens that affect the aesthetics of apples and are treated similarly. They overwinter on the bark and twigs of woody plants with waxy cuticles and can infect the apple blooms. While these diseases may account for shortened storage life of apples, they do not cause decay; yet they do affect the apples' market value due to the perceived unacceptable appearance of fruit.

Life Cycle

These fungi are commonly found on the twigs of many woody plants, including apple shoots. Infections may occur on fruit as early as two to three weeks after petal fall, yet are more prevalent in mid- to late summer. Infection most likely takes place during periods of frequent rainfall, poor drying conditions and high humidity.

Monitoring

These diseases usually appear on apples late in the season. The first signs of infection can be seen by early to mid-July. Fungicides or organic sprays should be applied to fresh fruit showing any infections.

Cultural Control

Orchard sanitation is important to managing this disease; this includes dormant and summer pruning to help dry out leaves and branches of the apple trees. Pruning improves air movement and allows for better spray coverage and improved fruit quality. Thinning of clustered fruit is also helpful. Brambles and wild blackberries in the orchard and surrounding hedgerows should be removed as they act as hosts to these fungi. Fruit should be cooled after harvest to slow down the occurrence of the disease.

Organic and Biological Controls

Equesitum spray will enhance the light energy that gets to the tree, encouraging a stronger waxy cuticle. Stylet oil is also effective in protecting trees against sooty blotch and fly speck.

Life Cycle

Cedar apple rust overwinters as galls on red cedar branches. Spring rains wet the galls, initiating the expansion of spore horns and the production of basidiospores. These spores are carried to the apple trees infecting leaves and fruit during extended wet periods Ten to fourteen days after infection, lesions will begin to appear. Spores produced on the lower surface of infected apple leaves will reinfect the foliage of nearby cedar trees in late summer.

Following the next full growing season, these infections will develop into galls and produce spores in the spring. These galls produce spores for only one season. Apple tree lesions all result from spores produced on the cedar; there is no secondary infection within the apple tree.

Monitoring

Apple trees leaves are susceptible to cedar apple rust when three to seven days old and from pink until three weeks after bloom. Orchard monitoring during this time is essential.

Cultural Control

Delicious varieties are nearly immune to cedar rust infection. The life cycle of cedar apple rust can be interrupted by removing cedars located within a two-mile radius of the orchard; this makes control with sprays more effective. The removal of all cedars within four to five miles of the orchard will eliminate the problem of this fungus in orchards all together.

Organic Control

Stylet oil can be used on early lesions.

Plan for Abundance

The two-fold approach to planning for abundance is: 1) implementing practical strategies to minimize loss and 2) planting extra in different areas of the garden.

While the idea of birds eating all of your blueberries before they have ripened may make you cringe, imagine that you have all the blueberries you could possible want or use and you feel generous about feeding the birds

Diversity: As a general rule, as sustainable systems mature they become increasingly diverse in both space and time. What is important is the complexity of the functional relationships that exist between elements not the number of elements.

— Bill Mollison,
*Permaculture:
A Designers' Manual*

with your extra yield. You can use netting to keep the damage down and also plan for repetition, diversity, and abundance. This way if one plant gets wiped out from a fungus, you have other plants that are harvestable. If one plant gets eaten by a deer, there are other plants to fall back on. So building this into the design right from the beginning is inherent in food forest systems.

Planting a Tree

Once you have created your design, you will know where the trees will be planted. Make sure you have amended the soil as needed to be the site of the fruit tree, through adding compost or sheet mulching.

Credit: Michelle Czolba and Juliette Olshock

Newly planted trees should be protected from rabbits and deer with adequate fencing.

Generally, spring is the best time to plant trees, followed by fall. Fall tree planting is a bit riskier as the tree needs enough time to stabilize the root system before the freezing cold comes on. However, many trees are hardy enough to withstand this.

You will want to plant the tree soon after you purchase or it is shipped through the mail. This is especially true if you purchase bare rootstock which do not have protection for the roots. They are much easier to handle, though, as they weigh much less. Ball and burlap trees are also an option but are very heavy as they include soil around the roots.

Once you have identified your location, dig a hole as wide as the root system, without the roots being bent or bunched. The depth of the hole should accommodate the tree right below the bud union.

After the hole is dug, place the tree in it. If balled and burlapped, remove the burlap first. Have one person hold the tree upright while the other shovels dirt back into the hole, lightly tamping it as you go. Move the tree very gently up and down as the soil is being added, to prevent air pockets from forming.

Fill with soil up to the ground level. Press the soil down firmly so that the tree is held in place. Water it deeply, with up to five gallons of water. Cover the site with mulch using a donut formation.

Pruning Techniques

Pruning and Thinning

For most fruit trees, pruning should be done in the dormant season, from February to April. Pruning should be done for the life of the tree. In the beginning it's done to train the tree in a certain manner. The purpose of ongoing maintenance pruning is to remove dead, broken, crossing, or competing limbs. This helps to increase fruit size and the amount of nitrogen reaching the growth point. Always be sure to remove low-hanging limbs as well. To produce high-quality fruit, the light environment should not be lower than thirty percent of the available sunlight throughout the canopy.

Producing trees may send up strong shoots from the main scaffolds and these should be removed, as they will block light from reaching the lower limbs. The weak shoots can be left, as they can fruit but will not create shade. Cuts can be made to remove the tall, upward growing shoots to maintain a low height.

When a tree has not been pruned, the fruiting buds tend to form up and out due to decreasing sunlight in the interior. To maintain a practical, healthy, and efficient harvesting system, the tree should be pruned in a shape the follows the particular species' natural habit. For example, an apple tree tends to grow into a more rounded shape, while a pear tree has a more pyramidal growth habit. Following the natural form of a tree helps prevent the need for excess pruning.

The major problem in a tree that has not been pruned regularly is the excess of limbs, which create shade. To properly prune a mature tree, many of the limbs should be removed entirely. Several large limbs can be removed, but make sure it is not the major limb of the tree. The cuts should be made as smooth as possible and without scarring the limbs that are left. The ones that are left should be shortened, as they will become stiffer and better able

Knowing the size and natural form of the trees you plant can help you visualize how your food forest will look when the trees mature. *Top row (left to right)*: columnar, conical, irregular, open; *middle row*: oval, pyramidal, round; *bottom row*: spreading, vase, and weeping.

to hold fruit that way. After a major cut, suckers will form from the cut and they should be removed when six to eight inches long. This can be done immediately; it does not have to wait until the dormant season. When a tree is pruned this much, do not apply fertilizer for at least a year as it will cause too much vigor and stunt fruit growth.

There is also a practice of summer pruning which improves fruit color, quality, and storage life. It is initiated once the terminal bud development is evident. It is done by removing some of the current year's growth to open the canopy for light and to reduce crowding. This practice is only to be done if deemed necessary by visual observation.

The more you prune, the more you have to prune. Open-vase pruning, a standard practice in commercial orchards, keeps the center of the tree wide open with three main branches. This system requires intensive pruning. A more natural tree shape can be kept open with less effort. Judicious pruning as the tree develops is done to prevent branches from crossing and to allow air to circulate and some sunlight to penetrate the canopy.

Masanobu Fukuoka, in his writings on natural farming, says that you should not have to prune a tree if it is allowed to grow from a seedling. In our experience, this may be a worthy experiment, but may not be best for all tree crops. When managing a food forest, a moderate level of pruning will allow for fruit production and let more light penetrate to the ground for other crops. What we advocate is keeping with the tree's natural form but preventing it from turning into a dense tangle of branches.

How We Prune

Make sure to always use sharp, clean pruning tools. Remember that pruning is causing a wound to the plant tissues so you want to make it an aseptic technique to the best of your ability. The shears do not need to be sterilized but be aware that during pruning it is easy to transfer pathogenic bacteria and fungi to the plant's inner tissue.

The cut should always be smooth and clean, leaving about an inch or less of stub. The main idea is to not get too close to the main branch so that the cut piece can form a callus and heal easily. Wounds can be covered with grafting wax to prevent pathogens from getting in. Pruning should be done when plants are dormant whenever possible to help prevent pathogen infection.

Thinning

The two main purposes for fruit thinning are: 1) to increase fruit size and uniformity and 2) to remove pest larvae and diseased fruit. It also prevents biennial bearing, where trees crop heavily one year and then produce little or nothing the next. For these reasons, thinning is necessary to yield a marketable crop. There are three ways to thin apple trees, one of which uses a chemical method and will not be described. Another is to remove extra blossoms when they form. The third, most effective way, is to hand remove immature fruit.

This is more labor intensive but feasible for a small orchard. It allows you to determine the exact amount of fruit to leave on the tree to ensure adequate space. It also allows for the removal of any small, deformed, or insect-injured fruit, ensuring a healthier crop. Fruit should be spaced about six inches apart on a branch unless abnormally large. Thinning by hand should be done 7 to 14 days after bloom or when developing fruit reach a half-inch in diameter, prior to the June drop and approximately 35 days after full bloom/petal fall. The largest and best-looking fruit is left on each cluster.

Harvest

Harvest is an ongoing activity in the food forest. For plants that go to seed, you want to harvest the usable parts before they do. For fruits and vegetables, there will be a succession of harvesting times throughout the season. Harvesting of nutrient-accumulating plants strictly for the purpose of fertilization (for example, comfrey) can and should be done continually to encourage more growth. You can use the chop and drop method if the plants are healthy and disease free. This entails cutting the plant above the growth line and leaving it around the area it grew or distributing it as mulch under other plants. It can then decompose in place or you can put leaf or wood chip mulch over top.

Be sure to harvest all fruit from the trees and clean up fallen fruit to prevent spread of any disease or insects. If you have integrated animals into your system, chickens are excellent at cleaning up fallen fruit as well as fertilizing and eating harmful insects and larvae. They can be put in certain areas after you are done with the seasonal harvest to clean up and fertilize. If you are doing the cleanup by hand, be sure to compost the dropped fruits in a high-heat pile to be sure to destroy pathogens.

Fruit Tree Care

Fruit trees inherently are high maintenance. For best fruit production and tree health, they require annual pruning, soil conditioning, regular visual checks for insects and diseases, mulching, weeding, and harvest and cleanup. Also, fruit drop can attract animals such as rats or lizards.

Disease-resistant Varieties

One suggestion is to do research into your local disease-resistant varieties of fruit trees. This will tremendously decrease your potential future problems. At the Hazelwood Food Forest, we planted a Cresthaven dwarf peach tree and it performed really well. Peach trees are notorious for fungal issues and we avoided most of those through proper variety selection. We chose varieties known to be disease resistant and suited for our climate zone.

Maintenance Schedule

Throughout this chapter, we have highlighted and discussed all the basic requirements for maintaining your beautiful food forest system. Putting it all together into a schedule can help with a big picture overview of what needs to be done and when. Below you will find a general summary for how to organize your activities. Of course, your seasons and special needs will modify this list.

With these general guidelines, we hope to get you started towards a productive and fruitful ecosystem:

- Spring: monitoring, watering as necessary, weeding, fertilizing, mulching, pruning, harvesting.
- Summer: monitoring, watering, weeding, mulching, thinning, harvesting.
- Fall: monitoring, watering as necessary, weeding, mulching, harvesting.
- Winter: pruning.

Water Source Development

One of the most important activities in food forest care is regular watering. Young plants need frequent watering when there isn't adequate rainfall, especially during the summer. Each watering should be generally equal to an inch of rain or 5–10 gallons per tree.

Additionally, the design of the food forest will conserve water in many ways. Sheet mulching techniques incorporate layers of organic material and protect the soil from desiccation. If the site has a minor slope, swales should be contoured into the land to hold rainwater and release it more slowly as needed. Ground covers act as living mulches and protect the soil from sun and wind.

First Year

Spring Plantings: Water every other day for the first three weeks. Water twice a week for the second three weeks and then once a week through the end of October. Perennials and ground covers may need more frequent watering in their first season.

Fall Plantings: In dry weather, water twice a week through the end of November.

Second Year and Beyond

During warm weather, orchards should be watered once a week when they don't receive one inch of rainfall. Older, established food forests may need watering only in severe drought conditions.

Soil Preparation

Healthy soil is the ultimate key to happy orchard plants. The most important time to improve soil quality will be during planting, but it will also be necessary to do so in following years. It is recommended to test the soil every two years to find out what nutrients may be needed.

As illustrated throughout this chapter, using compost, sheet mulching techniques, and regular mulching will greatly help to build the soil in the early stages and throughout the life cycle of your food forest.

Weeding and Mowing

Weeds can be a major competitor for water, light, and nutrients. Food forests, especially in their first year, should be weeded fairly frequently to give more delicate plants the best chance to succeed. Always attempt to pull weeds out with their roots. As the food forest matures and its understory and ground covers fill in, fewer new weeds will appear.

A few times in the summer and once in the fall, the ground covers that are planted may be cut and worked back into the soil.

Harvesting

Harvesting is another essential and, of course, rewarding orchard maintenance activity. Every edible plant has its own harvest time and a food forest will produce food from spring through fall. Each fruit has it own unique handling methods. Soft fruits, such as mulberries, strawberries, raspberries, and blackberries are easily bruised and will not keep long after harvest. They will need to be picked almost daily while ripening and should be eaten fresh, frozen, or otherwise processed as soon as possible. Other berries, including elderberry, currants, gooseberries, aronia, blueberries, huckleberries, and

Applesauce

One of my fondest childhood memories is making applesauce each summer with my father. For several weeks in July we would collect Yellow Transparent apples from our backyard tree until we had enough for a full five-gallon pot. On Saturday my father would core and cut the soft, slightly sour apples into large chunks, skin and all. We filled the pot full and added enough water to get them started cooking, about a quart. Then, while the pot simmered over a low heat, my brothers and I took turns stirring the apples with a long wooden spoon.

In a short time the chunks of apples transformed into sauce. We preferred to leave a few chunks to give the sauce texture, but a few more minutes of cooking would make a smoother sauce. When nearly done we would sweeten the applesauce with sugar—now I use honey—to taste. Again, we all preferred it slightly tart. After we feasted on the sauce my mother would freeze the excess for later Sunday dinners. She always tried to save a quart for Thanksgiving dinner.

Cider

October is cider time. Cider, in the United States, is fresh-pressed apple juice. In England the term cider is used for fermented apple juice, what we call hard cider. The term *perry*, by the way, refers to a fermented pear juice. Cider and perry connoisseurs have their preferred varieties and combinations of fruits for making the best cider.

Most of the apples at Three Sisters Farm are grown for our sweet (not fermented) cider. We collect our apples, Golden Russet, Northern Spy, Greening, Liberty, and assorted wild apples gleaned from abandoned orchards nearby, when they are ripe and begin to fall off the trees. The best apples are set aside and stored for fresh eating, sauce, and baking through the winter. We often add some of our Seckle pears to the mix for a special flavor.

Cider day is a good adventure. Apples are sorted one more time to pull out any fruit too badly bruised and then loaded in the truck. We try to get to the cider press early but usually need to wait in line an hour or so. While waiting we chat with other cider press customers about the apples they grow and watch the process. Apples are dumped into a hopper. As they ride the conveyor up to the mill they are tumbled over brushes and rinsed with clean water. The mill grinds the apples into a sauce consistency and pours it down into cloth-lined trays. The press operators fill the trays, stacked several high, until all the apples in the batch are milled. Then the final tray is covered and the press lid lowered. The sweet brown juice is pressed out of the pulp and drains into a storage tank, passing though an ultraviolet light along the way to kill any potential bacteria. Naturally occurring yeast, that will turn the cider hard and eventually to vinegar, is not affected by the light. When all the apples are pressed the juice is pumped into jugs, barrels, or other containers to transport home for drinking, sharing, and freezing. Some might even become hard cider or apple wine.

juneberry will keep for longer in the refrigerator, but again, it is best to use them or process them when fully ripe to preserve maximum nutritional content. Stone fruits, including peaches, plums, and cherries will keep a little longer if harvested promptly but should also be used or processed when ripe. Pears and apples vary with the variety. Yellow Transparent apples and Summer Crisp pears, for example, are picked when just about ripe, stored or left out to ripen, and processed as soon as possible. Other varieties will keep for many months with proper refrigeration. Golden Russet, Red Delicious, Liberty, and Northern Spy have kept all winter into early springtime for us at Three Sisters Farm.

Credit: Darrell E. Frey

In cold climates the tender fig tree can be buried underground for the winter and replanted in early spring. This fig has been pruned, buried, and replanted every year for over 40 years.

Nuts are usually collected promptly when they fall off the tree, and before the wildlife beats you to them. Hazelnuts, chestnuts, pecans, and hickory nuts generally come cleanly out of their husk. Walnuts and butternuts require the husk to be removed and the shells allowed to dry before shelling. Acorns are easy to collect but require the nut meats to be soaked in several changes of water to remove tannins before consuming. Fallen fruit should be picked up to avoid attracting pests to the orchard and recycling diseases.

Maintaining your food forest will be much easier with a plan. Using the information in this chapter as well as your personal observations will move you in the direction of success. Flexibility and responsiveness is always important as the landscape changes over time.

CHAPTER SIX

Propagating Your Food Forest Garden

Propagation is the act of making new plants. The term includes sexual reproduction, as in planting seeds, and asexual reproduction—rooting cuttings from stems, dividing clumps of existing plants, and grafting stems from one plant onto another. This chapter provides guidance for propagation of plants to aid you in creating your food forest from local resources. It also discusses obtaining and purchasing plants. Advice for would-be nursery enterprises is given.

Learning to propagate your own plants has a number of benefits: economy, satisfaction, community building, and varietal selection among them. Foremost is cost savings. Plants are expensive. Propagating your own can save hundreds of dollars. There are, of course, costs to plant propagation, which we will discuss below. As always, scale is important. If you are just adding a few herbs as understory to existing trees it may be cost effective to buy plants. But if you want to turn your property into a diversified permaculture landscape, buying propagation tools and supplies is a sensible investment and propagating your own plants can be cost effective and fulfilling.

Growing your own plants is indeed satisfying. In a hectic world where many occupations do not always allow us to see the fruits of our labor, successful plant propagation provides tangible results. Tasting the first fruit of a tree you grafted is a pleasure that can not be easily explained. Gathering seeds in the wild, preparing them to germinate, nurturing and planting the young seedlings to maturity takes a little skill and experience, and can be very fulfilling. In truth, a green thumb is not required, just the right techniques and tools. While it is true that some people seem to have a bit of plant magic about them, everyone can enjoy the satisfaction of propagating plants successfully.

Trading and sharing plant materials is an ancient tradition among gardeners. Many gardeners save seeds of favorite varieties and collect herbs and flowers. New gardeners can often get plants by helping more experienced gardeners tend their garden in the spring. Sharing and trading plants with friends and neighbors allows you to obtain locally adapted varieties and find unusual cultivars. In the long term, the most productive food forests will be those developed using locally and regionally adapted varieties and selected native plants.

The intrepid plant explorer can find and propagate locally adapted varieties. When I am out foraging or hiking, I am always on the lookout for interesting selections of wild plants. Nannyberry, juneberry, elderberry, and wild blueberry all have potential for the refinement and selection of improved cultivars. Elderberries, for example, have a wide range of ripening times, size of fruit, and flavor. Finding a locally adapted wild elderberry with good flavor and productivity is an ongoing goal of mine.

As the forest garden matures and expands, propagating your own plants can save a lot of money. And of course it is fun and empowering to harvest plants you started from seeds or traded with friends. When a plant in your garden has a backstory, it adds to the rewards of tending the garden. Twenty years later you will still remember who gave you a particular cultivar.

Cost savings can be considerable when you propagate your own plants. Potted herbs can range from $4 for a small pot to $15–$20 or more for larger pots. Fruit tree prices continually rise. Bare rooted trees cost a minimum of $30 at the time of this writing, and potted plants may cost much more. When planting a food forest, even the small pots can add up to a considerable sum.

The costs of propagating your own plants are mostly your investment in tools, equipment, and supplies. When starting seeds you will need flats and pots and potting soil mixes. You may also need grow lights and a place to set them up.

A sterile potting soil may be needed to start plants from seedlings to avoid damping off disease. When making cuttings, you can use potting soil or a light garden soil. For dividing perennials garden soil works fine.

You will need a variety of sizes of nursery pots. You can save money by reusing pots you or your fiends purchased plants in. Recycled pots should be thoroughly washed in soapy water, and perhaps disinfected with hydrogen peroxide to ensure you do not introduce plant pathogens. Dedicated pruning shears and grafting tools might be required. Grafting tools are discussed below.

Propagating plants also requires space and time to tend them. A semi-shady area of the garden can be dedicated as a propagation area. Laying down a thick layer of mulch under the planting area will help prevent your plants from getting lost in the weeds. The space should be level and fenced to keep out rabbits and deer. You will need to water your nursery plantings regularly so that the plants thrive.

Buying Plants

Purchasing plants for your food forest is the easiest way to get started. Purchasing plants is an annual ritual for many gardeners. Many towns and organizations host spring plant markets, where local growers sell plants. Sometimes you can find or even organize plant trading events. We suggest supporting local nurseries that grow and propagate their own plants. If you have an organic plant supplier, that is even better. Many garden centers and big box stores sell plants that have been shipped a long distance and may be treated with a variety of chemical compounds that you may not want on your plants. Other than local suppliers, there are many nurseries that ship nation wide.

Considerations When Buying Plants

Know the source. When you know where your plants come from you can be better assured of their quality and history. Ask the grower about how they propagate plants and what their potting medium is made of. Organically grown plants will be free of pesticides and are likelier to be in a health-promoting potting mix. A good mix will include a bulk organic material, such as peat moss or decayed leaf mold, minerals such as limestone, greensand, and rock phosphate, coarse sand for drainage, and compost. At Three Sisters Farm our potting soil mix is as follows:

- 10 gallons peat moss
- 5 gallons vermiculite
- 5 gallons compost
- 2½ gallons coarse sand
- ½ quart pulverized limestone
- ½ quart rock phosphate
- ½ quart greensand

All materials are mixed thoroughly in a wheel barrow.

Buying locally allows you to develop a relationship with the nursery growers and support a strong network for continued development of regional food systems. Regionally grown plants can be more likely to be hardy in your location. Many larger plant sales locations simply import mass-produced plants from distant locations. A good plant nursery that grows their own plants will probably be choosing varieties of seeds, rootstock, and cultivars that will be likely to succeed in your food forest. Shopping around at different nurseries and plant sales will give you a sense of what is available in your area.

When selecting plants you want to look for those with good leaf color, sturdy stems, and a generally healthy appearance. Avoid plants that are root-bound, stunted, or overgrown for the pot. Also check for insect pests. It is quite easy to bring home a new problem when buying plants. Aphids, white-flies, scale insects, and other pests may be present on the leaves or lurking in the soil. Check a number of plants in the nursery to see if any pests are present.

It is important that you do not buy more than you can plant and tend each season. It is not unusual to get carried away and buy more plants than you can tend. When plants languish in pots too long they can get rootbound, use up available nutrients, and suffer from water stress when you forget to water them. So plan carefully each season what you will buy and where whey will be planted.

Growing Your Own: Tools and Methods

Tools

Plant propagation tools include spades and trowels for dividing and transplanting, pruning shears, grafting knives and grafting wedges, and seedling propagation systems. We will examine each of these below as we discuss the various propagation methods. Plant propagation tools should be reserved for that use and stored clean and dry when not in use. Proper storage ensures they are ready to use when you need them. Cleaning tools after use and between uses helps prevent spread of plant diseases.

Plant Division

Many plants with multiple stems can be propagated by digging up and dividing the plant. Perennial herbs can benefit from being moved, or thinned and fertilized. Every few years it is helpful to give them a new start in fresh soil. Early spring is a good time to divide herbs such as comfrey, chives, garlic chives, mints, French sorrel, sage, lavender, and oregano. Shrubs and small trees with multiple stems are best divided when still dormant in late winter or early spring. These include figs, willows, serviceberry, lilac, and bay laurel.

When dividing herbs it is often best to work in the morning or evening, so as not to stress the roots and plants with too much sunlight. Work at a good pace. At times you may divide by leaving most of the plant in the ground and just cutting off sections from the outer edge of a clump. This is especially done with spreading plants like bamboo, comfrey, sorrel, daylilies, and ground cover plants like sweet woodruff, mints, and ajuga. When dividing plants in the ground, you should refill the empty spaces you create with compost-enriched soil.

Generally, herb plants can be removed from the ground and divided. Using a garden spade, cut into the soil all around the plant. Cut a little wider than the plant's top growth to preserve as much of the roots as possible. Gently lift the plant out of the ground. Using a sharp garden knife or your garden spade cut the plant into sections. Be sure each section has a strong root connected to a strong stem. If you are not placing the plants in the ground right away, place them in a good potting mix in pots large enough that their roots are not crowded. When planting in the ground, replant at the same depth as they were growing originally. Whether in pots or in the ground the divided plants should be watered well with a bit of liquid seaweed added to the water. The seaweed has hormones to promote root growth and a lot of minerals and nutrients for general plant growth. When put in the ground plants should be top dressed with a rich compost, mulched, and watered every few days for a week or two until the root systems recover from the transplant shock. Shade cloth may be used if your weather is too hot and dry, but generally, if you are careful to preserve the roots when replanting, shade should not be necessary.

Plant Rescue

Self-seeding plants and shallow-rooted spreading plants can be potted up or thinned and replanted with a hand trowel. Each spring we obtain dozens of seedlings of bronze fennel, pansy, violets, tansy, anise hyssop, catnip, and other plants this way. As we weed and mulch the food forest garden in mid- to late spring, these plants are thinned and rescued for sale, trade, or replanting. We occasionally rescue plants from roadsides this way as well. Many wildflowers and useful naturalized herbs sprout up in roadside ditches each year. If you can beat the road crew, you can dig them up and replant them in safer places.

This is not to advocate collecting plants from the wild. As a firm rule, native wildflowers should not be taken from the wild. Many plants are endangered or threatened. Collecting plants in the wild can add to the stress on native ecosystems. It is far better to buy wild plants from established nurseries or start them from seeds. When we speak of plant rescue, we are talking about saving plants from destruction by development or land use.

Examples are if a woodland or meadow is being cleared for development, or a new highway or pipeline is being built—then it is a good thing when one can go in ahead of the heavy equipment and rescue plants for replanting.

Cuttings

Most perennial herbs, many shrubs, and some trees can be reproduced by cuttings. The process is simple. A branch or section of stem is cut from the plant and placed in a potting soil mix or propagation bed. Herb cuttings should be three to four inches long. Strip off the lower leaves and push the stem an inch or two into the soil. Water with a seaweed mix to promote root growth and keep the soil moist. In a few weeks they will begin to grow roots. Herb cuttings can be made anytime, from actively growing or dormant stems. Shrubs and trees vary in their ability to root from cuttings. Shrubs may be more successful. Hardwood trees are not likely to root from cuttings. Exceptions include aspen and willow trees.

Hot Beds

A greenhouse is helpful if you want to propagate a lot of plants, but it is not absolutely necessary. Plants can be started in outdoor propagation beds as well. In the centuries prior to central heating, a fossil fuel use, compost-heated propagation beds, or hot beds, were used to root cuttings through the winter months.

A hot bed is a variation on a cold frame that has a layer of composting material covered with around six inches of soil. The intensity and duration of the heat produced by decomposting organic material depends on the ratio of carbon to nitrogen. Composted manure, with a high proportion of nitrogen, heats up quickly as the microorganisms feast on the bounty. Within a few weeks the temperature drops and the compost process slows down. Depending on the plants being propagated, some manure or green plant materials can be added to speed up the composting. If you use animal manure in the mix you will want to compost and be sure it is over 130 degrees for several days before you layer it in the hot bed. This will insure pathogens are killed.

A hot bed is set about a foot or so into the earth and a wooden frame with a translucent cover is set on the ground. The bottom is filled with moist organic materials at least six to eight inches deep. Soil is layered six to eight inches on top of the composting material. After a week or two of initial heating, the compost settles down to a steady warmth and can stay that way through the winter months.

Garden writers of the late 18th and early 19th centuries describe a form of hot bed called a "bark stove" which is heated by composting tree bark. Shredded tree bark, with a lower ratio of nitrogen to carbon, heats more slowly and can stay warm for a longer period of time. A bark stove is prepared in the fall. The slowly composting bark of a bark stove will provide bottom heat to keep cuttings of roses, grapes, figs, perennial herbs, and other plants warm and happy, stimulating root growth. In the spring they will be ready to pot up or plant out into the garden.

Layering

Some plants propagate from tip layering. Currants, black raspberries, and vines especially reproduce well this way. Simply peg the tip of a branch or bramble into the soil in the fall, cover with a little mulch and watch it come back in the spring. Roots will be formed and the plant can be cut from the mother plant and moved to a new location.

Seed

Growing perennial plants from seeds can be a little more complicated than growing annuals. But with a little knowledge it will soon seem easy. Perennial herbs are the easiest to grow. Most are seeded just like you would start your vegetables. Seeds of many wildflowers, shrubs, and trees may require cold treatment, known as stratification, to germinate. Some fruits, including the stone fruits—cherries, peaches, plums, and nectarines—may be true to seed if self fertilized. But apples, pears, and many other fruit will not bear true to seed. Nuts are also not likely to be true to seed. It is best to buy or graft selected varieties of these.

The majority of perennial herb seeds will germinate and grow just like your vegetable seedlings. Start your herbs in the same soil mix as your vegetable seedlings. A slightly sandy soil mix, for good drainage, is best for Mediterranean herbs, like rosemary, sage, thyme, oregano, and marjoram. Keep the seedlings moist as they germinate and begin to grow. Make sure they get adequate light to not get leggy and a bit of draft to help them grow sturdy. Feed them with a rich compost tea or liquid seaweed and fish emulsion to keep them healthy. Pot the seedlings up to larger pots as they grow. Some herb seeds, like rosemary, do not remain viable for long, so be sure you buy fresh seeds.

Many native wildflower seeds, and seeds of fruiting shrubs and trees, need to be stratified to germinate. Stratification is the practice of chilling

Credit: Darrell E. Frey

Stratified paw
paw seeds.

seeds for a period of time in a moist soil medium. Many seeds have a built-in dormancy period so they do not germinate before spring. In the wild they would lie on the ground surface, or be buried by ants or animals. Autumn leaf fall covers these seeds, keeping them from drying out. The normal cycles of freeze and thaw from autumn until spring breaks their dormancy and they germinate when the soil temperatures rise in spring or summer.

When we stratify seeds we mimic this process. Seeds are stored in damp soil in a refrigerator or in a sealed container buried under light mulch in the garden for the winter.

For wildflowers we plant seeds in seedling flats of moist soil, cover them with a layer of plastic, and put them in a refrigerator or cool place for six to eight weeks. Then we set them in the sunny propagation tables in the greenhouse or under grow lights. They then germinate vigorously.

Stone fruit seeds, paw paws, and nuts are stratified as soon as we gather them. The seeds are layered with soil mix or leaf mold in sealed plastic bags or containers for cold storage.

In the early spring we begin to watch the seeds for signs of sprouting. When the seeds begin to split open and the first roots poke out, it is time to put them into pots.

Grafting

Grafting is the joining of living plant tissue from one plant with living tissue to another plant of the same species. The art of grafting goes back thousands of years in Europe and Asia. Primarily, it is used to propagate a desired variety. Seedlings may not produce the same fruit as the parent tree. Grafting ensures you get the variety of fruit you want. As discussed above, some fruits may be true to seed. However, grafting is a far more certain way to get the

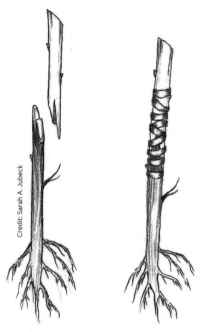

Whip and tongue grafting is used to securely join scionwood to rootstock.

Cleft grafting is used to add new scionwood to an existing tree. It involves cutting a branch or small tree trunk, splitting it with a cleft graft wedge, and inserting scionwood into the split branch with cambium layers in contact.

desired fruit. If your space is limited it is best to be sure you are getting what you want.

The terms you'll come across most often in grafting are rootstock and scionwood (pronounced like "science").

Rootstock is what it sounds like, a small tree with roots. Different rootstocks provide the tree with different characteristics. Specific rootstocks may produce trees that are dwarf, semi-dwarf, or standard-size trees. Within these divisions various rootstocks are selected for soil type, soil drainage, and hardiness. Rootstocks are grown by coppicing a standard rootstock tree so that is produces many stems. While the stems are young, soil is piled around the stems so they grow roots. The rooted stems are then cut from the base when they are dormant and stored for later use. Some rootstocks are patented or otherwise proprietary, requiring a license to propagate for sale.

Scionwood refers to twigs cut from a tree or shrub for the purpose of grafting onto rootstock or another tree. Scionwood is gathered when the tree is dormant. Wrap the cut end of the scionwood in damp paper and store in a sealed plastic bag in the refrigerator until ready for use.

The main goal when grafting is to be sure that the cambium layers, the green inner bark on the scionwood, is in contact with the cambium layer of the rootstock. This allows the two parts to grow together into one.

Grafting is generally done in the spring when plants are breaking dormancy, just before leaves emerge. You can add new varieties to an existing tree of the same species. Grape vines can also be grafted. This is called field grafting or top working. For adding scion to larger branches a cleft graft works well. For younger branches use a whip and tongue graft.

Bench grafting is more common. Bench grafting is done on the workbench with dormant rootstock and scionwood. Rootstock is purchased dormant and kept cool until ready for grafting. Using a grafting knife, the rootstock is cut at a sharp angle (see illustration) and sliced a bit in the center of the cut. Scionwood of similar diameter as the rootstock is cut to match the rootstock and the scion is united to the rootstock. The splice is wrapped with grafting tape or a strip of rubber band. Then the graft union is covered with grafting wax. The wax, often a mixture of beeswax and pine pitch, helps seal in moisture until the cambium layers can grow together. Some types of wax need to be melted and applied with a paint brush. Another type of grafting wax can be warmed in your hands and applied by hand. When doing a lot of grafts it is quicker to brush on melted wax. The tape or rubber band help to hold the union together in strong winds until the woody parts fuse. By summer's end the wax and rubber band will fall off.

Cleft grafting is a method of top working existing trees with new varieties. A larger branch or the main stem of a young tree is cut across the branch. A cleft grafting tool has a wide wedge that is hammered into the branch to make a slight split in the branch; a smaller wedge is used to hold the split open to receive the scionwood. Scionwood is cut into a pointed wedge shape and pushed into the split branches so that the cambium layers make good contact. Then the small wedge is removed from the split branch and the branch closes, holding the scion firmly. The graft union is coated in grafting wax to seal all exposed wood.

Bud grafting is done in the summer when trees are actively growing. Most fruit trees produce the buds for next year's new branches by mid-summer. These can be cut off the branch of the desired tree and grafted to rootstock or added to existing trees. When cutting a bud for grafting, be sure to cut into the wood a little. A shield-shaped cut will give a lot of cambium layer surface on the bud. Keep the bud moist until it is grafted. On the receiving tree or rootstock, cut a T in the outer bark and peel it back enough to insert the bud. As with other grafting methods it is necessary to be sure the green wood or cambium layers have good contact. Wrap the bud graft with a rubber band and seal with grafting wax or tape. Be sure to mark your bud grafts with ribbon to remember which bud you added. The following winter prune away any growth above your bud graft. In subsequent years keep pruning out unwanted branches.

Heirloom Fruit

As we rediscover local food systems it is a good idea to seek out regional selections and local favorite fruit varieties. In our area homesteaders and Amish farms have been trading an old variety of peach called Rare Ripe, perhaps since the area was first settled. Rare Ripe peaches are a bit smaller than modern varieties but they are a sweet and flavorful yellow peach. The small

Credit: Darrell E. Frey

The Rare Ripe peach is a hardy, disease resistant heirloom variety kept alive by farmers and homesteaders in northwestern Pennsylvania since the early 19th century.

trees bear abundant fruit while withstanding long cold winters in northwest Pennsylvania. Other old fruits found here include Stanley plum and Concord grapes. Common apple varieties known to do well here include Yellow Transparent and Northern Spy. Many others do well too, but these were the standby varieties for applesauce and apple pies.

A Nursery Business!

Once you have a thriving food forest with a broad diversity of plants and have a base of experience tending and growing plants, you might consider beginning a nursery business. Business management is a complex endeavor that requires a lot of planning and organization. If you are inclined to self-employment, managing a small business can be rewarding on many levels. And if you have a growing collection of useful plants, and skills in plant propagation, a nursery business might be for you.

Managing a plant nursery is a year-round enterprise. Dedicated spaces are needed for storing supplies and materials. Potted seedlings, cuttings, and young grafted plants need to be kept moist by regular watering. A common strategy for managing plants on a large scale is to set potted plants into deep mulch, wood chips, or shredded bark to keep the roots cool, reduce water loss, and to keep plants from becoming lost in weed patches.

Plants must be protected from marauding critters that will want to eat them. Even the seeding pots require protection. We have had dozens of newly planted paw paw seeds stolen overnight by chipmunks. As plants grow you will need to remain vigilant for pests and diseases. Keeping plants properly watered with adequate soil nutrition will help keep plants healthy. Feed your potted plants weekly by adding fish emulsion and seaweed extract or compost tea when you water them. When caterpillars, aphids, mites, and other insects attack your plants be sure to remove the pests on first sighting. Most insects can be killed with a spray of soapy water. We prefer a liquid castile soap for preparing insecticidal soap. Diseased plants should be removed. Try to identify the disease so you can study the disease's life cycle and prevent its reoccurrence.

Rules and Regulations

The first thing you will need to know is whether there are licenses required in your state or province and any regulations you need to follow. If you wish to be certified organic in the United States you will need to research and follow the National Organic Program regulations. In Canada, you will follow the Canadian Organic Standards. Additionally, patent laws may apply to certain cultivars and rootstocks.

Most states in the US regulate plant sales. Here in Pennsylvania the state Department of Agriculture charges a small annual licensing fee to cover some of the costs of inspecting nursery enterprises. Basically they are interested in assuring that businesses selling plants are not spreading pests and disease. If there is a problem the inspectors generally try to be helpful, but they do have an important job to do. If you have a problem they may be likely to provide advice to remedy it or avoid it in the future. A good nursery business will have a pest and disease control strategy and not sell plants that have problems.

Organic certification regulations are intended to provide the consumer with assurances that the product being sold is produced according to a minimal standard. The grower contracts with a certification organization to send an inspector each year. The inspector reviews the grower's annual records of seeds and plants purchased, products produced and sold, and interviews the grower about materials used in crop production. Disease and pest control strategies, soil management systems, and other issues relevant to organic production are reviewed. If you buy plants that are not certified organic, you must grow them with organic methods for a year before you can harvest or propagate them to sell as organic. As stated earlier, good organic practices go far beyond simple regulations. Conscious land and crop management require a diligence on the part of the gardener to maintain a rich healthy soil, preserve water quality, and promote biodiversity. The organic gardener judiciously chooses soil amendments and pest control strategies to ensure as natural, healthful, and clean a product as possible. In a world full of toxins and pollutants, our gardens and landscapes offer an opportunity to regenerate the earth and rejuvenate ourselves. The organic nursery, growing plants in rich, healthy soil mixes, is the starting point for this process. Healthy soil leads to healthy plants, and as they say at the Rodale Institute, healthy people.

Plant patenting regulations are an unfortunate fact of our existence. However, if you spend a lot of time and money developing new plant varieties, you may want to profit from your efforts. While the merits and politics of plant patenting is debatable, the fact remains that a commercial producer is required to pay a fee or purchase a license to propagate and sell a number of plants. So, if you do propagate patented plants, be sure to obtain the proper permission. The same applies to rootstocks. If you propagate rootstock for your nursery stock, again, be sure to have the proper permission as necessary.

Many start-up nurseries will buy dormant bare rooted plants in bulk, pot them, and resell them as potted plants. Be sure to know your source and only buy certified disease-free plants. Bare rooted seedlings should be kept in moist sawdust and potted with a good soil mix as soon as possible after receiving the plants and kept moist as the new roots begin to grow.

Your nursery enterprise can start slowly, with annual propagation of seedlings and cuttings and plant divisions. As you gain experience you can add grafted plants to your offerings. The bulk of a nursery's business is done in the springtime. Some nurseries offer plants again in the fall. If you do choose to keep plants in pots through the year, some summer sales are possible. But a well-planned business should expect to be busy in the spring rush of planting season.

Shipping plants has its own complications and regulations. We do not have experience with this and suggest before you aspire to that scale of production you should thoroughly research the issues involved.

CHAPTER SEVEN

A Tour of Food Forests in Various Climates

I currently have a city apartment. My landlady, an older Italian immigrant, has had the beginnings of a forest garden in her backyard for 40 years. A ten-foot-tall fig tree towers over her garden of broccoli, peppers, tomatoes, garlic, and basil. The parking spot between the house and garden is covered with an arbor of green grapes. Both the grapes and figs bear fruit continuously from August through the killing frost.

Everywhere I look I see perennial polycultures. Many are ornamental in nature, or unharvested except for foraging wildlife. But most have the potential to be adjusted for productivity.

In the final pages of this book we will look at a number of food forests in a variety of climates. These are meant to inspire you wherever you may live.

Drylands

Drylands comprise over 40 percent of the land surface of the Earth. The United Nations Food and Agricultural Organization (FAO) classifies drylands as arid, semi-arid, and dry sub-humid. This does not include hyper-arid deserts, where the potential for agriculture is negligible. Drylands are found in many climates across the globe, from equatorial to subarctic areas, and in many land forms, from below sea level to high mountainous regions. The primary characteristic of drylands is either low annual rainfall or very high rainfall evaporation rates.

Credit: Darrell E. Frey

Nopale and wild bean vine.

Worldwide 37 percent of the Earth's people live in drylands. Both population pressures to overuse water resources and changing climates have increased and will likely continue to increase the range of drylands worldwide. Climate change is expected to increase the intensity of rainfall in some areas and drought in others.

Continental drylands, such as the southwest and central plains of North America and central Eurasia, and tropical drylands, like sections of central Africa, Australia, and South America are characterized by a variety of ecosystems, from deserts to grasslands, savannas, and woodlands.

Mediterranean climates have long, dry, hot summers and cool, wet winters. The primary Mediterranean climate areas are the Mediterranean basin (southern Europe, the Middle East, North Africa), most of California, western and southern Australia, central Asia, Chile, and southwestern Africa. These areas are classed as drylands due to extended periods of minimal rainfall, often as much as four to six months. Due to a long growing season and minimal freezing weather, these areas have high productivity when their seasonal water resources are well managed.

Historically, mismanagement of these lands, with deforestation and overgrazing, has led to soil loss and the expansion of desert areas. There are, however, many examples of traditional sustainable land use throughout the world's deserts and drylands. Vast terrace agriculture systems in Yemen and

Oman on the Arabian peninsula, desert oases throughout North Africa, and tree crop agriculture throughout the Mediterranean region attest to ancient stewardship practices that supported thriving communities for centuries.

When designing forest gardens in dry climates a number of factors come into play. Rainfall, daily temperature extremes, and seasonal weather patterns all influence successful efforts.

Water management is essential in drylands. Strategies to capture and store water are critical in dry lands. As described in Chapter 2, the use of swales, terraces, and rain gardens to collect rainfall should be incorporated into designs. Roof runoff should be directed into storage in cisterns or the ground. Soil should be enriched with organic matter and biochar to enhance its water-holding capacity. And mulches should be used when possible to conserve soil moisture.

As with more humid lands, dryland ecosystems are built around natural polycultures. Would-be dryland forest gardeners are highly encouraged to study the work of Gary Paul Nabhan, and particularly his book *Growing Food in a Hotter Dryer Land—Lessons from Desert Farmers on Adapting to Climate Uncertainty* (Chelsea Green, 2013). This book provides a wealth of information on growing food in dry climates worldwide, with a particular focus on the American Southwest and northern Mexico.

Nabhan describes the role of the nurse tree in desert ecology. The nurse tree is a pioneer tree, often a legume, such as mesquite, carob, honey locust, palo verde, or desert ironwood. These trees grow in the full sunlight, and as a legume their bacterial companions help them fix nitrogen from the atmosphere and make it available for other plants in the ecosystem. The shade provided by the nurse tree allows for a wide range of desert plants to become established, and the nitrogen helps them thrive.

The nurse trees (what we call the overstory tree) in the dryland food forest described by Nabhan serve a number of functions in the system. Primarily they create a microclimate, providing cooling shade in hot seasons and protective cover in colder weather. Many add nitrogen-rich organic matter when they shed their leaves and fruit. They help the whole system gather and store seasonal rainfall, and attract a diversity of pollinating insects and songbirds.

Nabhan gives many good examples of dryland polyculture designs in this book, most of them under a canopy of a leguminous tree. Understory plants include fruiting cacti, such as prickly pear, which also produces the edible pads known as nopales, maguey, agave, and a range of berries and herbaceous plants. Wolfberries, a native type of goji berry, is a common native understory plant in the southwest.

Central Mexico Food Forest: El Huizachal

In June of 2016 I traveled with a small group to a native village in central Mexico. Our journey to El Huizachal was planned to allow us to continue to study the Xi'ui farming methods and to help add diversity and selected varieties to the local food system.

El Huizachal is a Xi'ui village in the rugged Sierra Madre Oriental mountain range of Central Mexico. The Xi'ui, also known as the northern Pame Indians, are an indigenous people who settled in these mountains in the mid-16th century while warring with the invading Spaniards. Since then the Xi'ui have been farming the stony fields and mountain slope, raising crops of corn, beans, and squash with hand tools in the deep soil amid the boulders.

In keeping with long-established tradition, new sections of mountainside fields are burned in the early summer to turn the slashed scrubland trees and underbrush to ash. When the rainy season begins, frogs begin to breed in any available pool of water and the farmers plant their seeds in pockets of soil between the rocks. Three corn seeds are planted together, with clumps of corn spaced three to four feet apart. Beans and squash are interplanted among the corn, with the beans climbing the corn stalks. Fruiting trees are tended among the patches of annual crops. Each household tends a garden near their home, and the home landscapes generally include a mix of perennial fruits, vegetables, and herbs.

This region has abundant natural tree crops. Dozens of legume tree species are present. Some of the notable edible varieties include:
- A small tree called Chicharon pea locally, elsewhere known as pigeon pea, that produces pods of small round edible peas.
- Mesquite, which has edible pods and seeds.
- Guamichi, also known as Guamuchil, *Pithecellobium dulce*. A small tree

with edible pulp in the seed pods. The pulp is sweet and is similar to coconut in texture.

- Cirguela, a native "plum," *Spondias purpurea*. Also known as jocote.
- Mangos, *Mangifera indica*.
- White zapote.
- Perennial pepper. These small peppers grow semi-wild among the gardens and trees. They are usually dried and used to flavor sauces and salsas.
- Nopale cactus. Grown for its edible pads and fruit, prickly pear, and known in Mexico as "tuna."

Other cultivated fruits include:

- Avocado
- Lemon
- Mandarin
- Banana
- Plantain
- Fig
- Guava
- Chayote—a gourd with edible fruit, roots, and leaves
- Chaya—a perennial shrub with edible leaves when cooked
- Patol—a leguminous trees with edible flowers
- Moringa—tree with edible leaves and seeds

Of particular note was the farm belonging to Amansio Ramirez, a native Xi'ui. Now in his late sixties, Amansio had been managing his farm for many decades. His main milpa was a one-acre low-lying field with few stones. They had been removed many years before to make stone walls around the farm. This field was used to grow corn, beans, squash, and a few other crops. Rising up from the milpa was a series of small terraces. On various levels were the small house, outbuildings, and outdoor kitchen and many other smaller gardens, trees, and shrubs. Each terrace was designed to maximize the collection of water as it ran downslope through the farm in the rainy season. Plantings included herbs like rosemary, mints, and perennial pepper, numerous flowers, and many perennial trees and shrubs. These included lemon, lime, orange, plantain, mango, jocote, avocado, chayote, figs, nopale, and numerous leguminous trees and shrubs with various uses.

Rich bottomland has been cleared of stones for annual crops of corn, beans, and squash. The rocky hillside has been terraced for perennial crops.

The house and other buildings are set on leveled terraces amidst a fruitful landscape.

Terraces are planted as a food forest featuring many crops.

Papaya is a common food forest crop in central Mexico.

Food Forest Around Luis and Carla Hurtado's House

This property is a medical clinic located in El Huizachal. It is an excellent example of the food forest landscapes common among the Xi'ui. The entire property surrounding the clinic and second-floor home of Dr. Luis Hurtado and his wife Carla and their two children is an edible landscape.

The roadside plantings at the property entrance include a leguminous tree known as patol. This tree's large red flowers are an ingredient in local cuisine in the springtime. A passionfruit vine climbs through its branches, laden with fruit. Beneath this tree is a prickly pear, bearing both fruit and nopale pads. A huizachal shrub bears seed pods for the local birds and adds nitrogen to the system. Across the road a seasonal pool is home to several species of toads and frogs in the early summer rainy season. A kitchen garden of annuals and perennials includes lemon, moringa, rosemary, lemon verbena, lavender, and other kitchen herbs. A grapevine twines along the fence. The backyard includes ciguela "plums," mango, lemon, maguey, and several large shade trees. The side yard includes a guamichi tree, producing a tasty pulp and adding more nitrogen to the system.

The guamuchil tree is a leguminous tree that produces a sweet edible pulp inside the seed pod.

The chaya produces abundant and nutritious edible leaves. They must be cooked before eating.

These lovely vines grace the front yard of Luis and Carla Hurtado's food forest landscape.

The passionfruit vine produces many delicious fruits as it twines through the trees.

Temperate Continental Climate: Perennial Polycultures at Three Sisters Farm

Three Sisters Farm has a number of perennial polycultures. Each is designed to fit into the larger farm plan in various ways.

Spiral Garden

The Spiral Garden at Three Sisters Farm has evolved over 25 years from a mix of annuals and perennial herbs and flowers to a fruitful forest garden.

True to good permaculture design, in which each element in the plan provides multiple functions in the landscape, we wanted the Spiral Garden to be part of our windbreak system to shelter our bioshelter (greenhouse), provide habitat for beneficial creatures, produce marketable crops, and be a beautiful centerpiece of the farm.

The layout of the garden was planned to allow for continuous productivity through the succession of plants. Similarly to the milpa of the Maya, this 400-square-foot garden began as primarily an annual garden for the first four or five years as the trees and shrubs were established. As the shrubs on

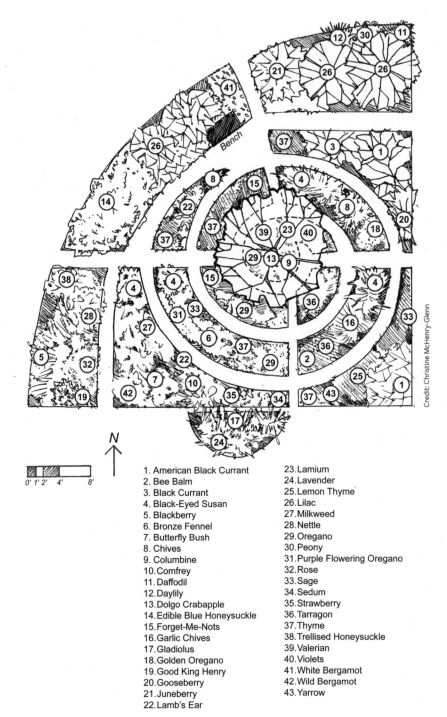

Food Forest plantings
at Three Sisters Farm
Spiral Garden.

0' 1' 2'   4'   8'

N

Credit: Christine McHenry-Glenn

1. American Black Currant
2. Bee Balm
3. Black Currant
4. Black-Eyed Susan
5. Blackberry
6. Bronze Fennel
7. Butterfly Bush
8. Chives
9. Columbine
10. Comfrey
11. Daffodil
12. Daylily
13. Dolgo Crabapple
14. Edible Blue Honeysuckle
15. Forget-Me-Nots
16. Garlic Chives
17. Gladiolus
18. Golden Oregano
19. Good King Henry
20. Gooseberry
21. Juneberry
22. Lamb's Ear

23. Lamium
24. Lavender
25. Lemon Thyme
26. Lilac
27. Milkweed
28. Nettle
29. Oregano
30. Peony
31. Purple Flowering Oregano
32. Rose
33. Sage
34. Sedum
35. Strawberry
36. Tarragon
37. Thyme
38. Trellised Honeysuckle
39. Valerian
40. Violets
41. White Bergamot
42. Wild Bergamot
43. Yarrow

Credit: Darrell E. Frey

For the first several years of the Spiral Garden, annual crops were grown while the perennials were established.

Credit: Darrell E. Frey

A food forest takes shape.

Credit: Darrell E. Frey

The Spiral Garden
food forest matures.

the west and north edge of the garden grew tall and filled out, they served
as a suntrap and windbreak, developing a sheltered microclimate. These
shrubs included lilac, juneberry, edible honeysuckle, and rugosa rose hips.
The understory to these shrubs included daylily, peony, bergamot, beebalm,
various mints, Good King Henry, and a few wildflowers.

The Dolgo apple tree planted in the center was lightly pruned to allow for
a natural canopy that was not too dense. This small tree produces abundant
white blossoms each spring and small deliciously tart fruit each August. Beneath the tree flowers and pollinator plants include violets, valerian, lamium,
ajuga, lamb's ear, and bronze fennel. Arcing around the apple tree from east
to south to west are small berry crops: gooseberry, red currant, black currant, American black currant, and bush cherry. Interplanted herbs include
oregano, thyme, lavender, chives, garlic chives, purple coneflower, gladiolas,
tulips, crocus, iris, and various other flowers.

Tree Line

When we started developing Three Sisters Farm in 1983, the north and east
borders of the property were lined with 20- to 30-year-old trees, including

wild black cherry, red maple, and red oak. There was no understory to speak of. Crop fields from a neighboring dairy farm bordered our five-acre property on the north and east. Allowing the tree line to mature and develop an understory was a priority, both to serve as a break from the prevailing winds for the farm as a whole and to mitigate the potential for pesticide drift from the neighbor's field onto our own land. Allowing for a diversity of native plants to fill in the tree line also greatly promoted the songbird populations on the farm.

Within ten years the tree line developed a dense understory of mostly dogwood shrubs (grey dogwood, *Cornus racemosa*), with a number of juneberry trees, spaced about 50 feet apart along the 1,500-foot length of the tree line. Other trees that grew naturally include slippery elm, ash, staghorn sumac, and seedlings of red maple and wild black cherry. We added to the mix at various times, planting nannyberry, butternut, heartnut, sour cherry, white pine, balsa fir, and various types of raspberries.

This tree line is now over 40 feet wide in some places. We have established campsites and put up hammocks and swings for children in several clearings. Various woodland wildflowers are growing among the trees and shrubs. This tree line has great potential for our continuing addition of useful plants below the larger trees and along the outer edge.

A second tree line, about one hundred feet long, was established a hundred feet west of the bioshelter to slow winds from the west. This tree line also shelters our compost yard. Over time we have included a number of species in and among this tree line. The main trees and shrubs, from north to south, are two plum trees, Waneta and green gage, and two large highbush cranberry shrubs, a stone pine tree, and a patch of high bush blueberries. The northern half of the hedge includes damask rose bushes. Beneath the plums we planted thornless blackberry, black raspberry, Heritage red raspberry, and ground nuts. Jerusalem artichokes fill in at various locations along the tree line. Nearby a maturing basswood tree provides bees with copious nectar each spring as it shades the compost yard from morning sun. Beneath the basswood we have established the nutrient-accumulating plants stinging nettle and comfrey. These are chopped and added to compost piles each year before the nettles set seeds.

At Three Sisters Farm, we have a row of a dozen mature mulberry trees separating our yard from the east garden. The trees are watered by a swale leading from the northeast portion of the bioshelter roof. The mulberries yield a high quality fruit from mid-June through early July most years. Each spring and fall we harvest shade-loving salad crops from beneath the trees. Wild violet leaves are a main ingredient in our spring and early summer salad mix. Chervil, chickweed, and dandelion also self-seed here and are harvested for the salad. Current plans are to establish more gooseberries in the partial shade of the mulberries and interplant them with more perennial salad plants, including sorrel, Good King Henry, ramps, salad burnet, chives, and others.

For the Bees: A Bee Yard Design

Honeybees are an important asset to a fruitful landscape. Bees can thrive best if the proper habitat is established. A perennial polyculture designed for bees might include a hedge from the west to the northeast (or whichever direction your prevailing winds originate from) and an open mowable or mulched yard for the hives open to the east and south for morning sun. Morning sun allows the hive to become active early in the day. Bees also require a nearby source of water. And of course bees want regular sources of nectar and pollen. Nectar provides carbohydrates, the basis for honey, and pollen provides the bees with protein and fats, plus a wealth of vitamins and minerals. A diversity of pollen and nectar sources are essential for bee health, and therefore bees should have plenty of options from which to choose their forage.

Honeybees can be parasitized by both tracheal mites and the larger varroa mite. Suggested treatments include essential oils of mint and formic acid. Formic acid is found in stinging nettles. Plant-derived essential oils that have been suggested for mite control include spearmint, peppermint, wintergreen, rosemary, and tea tree. Growing these plants near your hive could allow for bees to self-medicate. And when the beekeeper manages the hives, she can gather the fresh herbs close at hand and place crushed herb bunches around the hive entrance to expose the bees to fresh essential oils. These herbs are also good sources of nectar and pollen for the bees, and so they also benefit from the essential oils when they forage these herbs.

Trees and Plants for Bees

- Black locust
- Honey locust
- Catalpa
- Tulip poplar

- Pea shrubs
- Raspberries
- Goldenrod
- Aster

- Clovers
- Sweet clovers

Native Pollinators

All these plants that are good for honeybees are also good for native pollinators. Mason bees, metallic bees, bumble bees and hundreds of other species of bees and wasps all need pollen and nectar in their lifecycle. Each is active at specific times of the year. So a healthy ecosystem has a range of plants that flower at different times, from winter-flowering witch hazel and skunk cabbage, through autumn's asters and goldenrods.

Some Food Forests in Pennsylvania

Paw Paw Haven

Early in my explorations for regional permaculture plants I learned of Tom Mansell and his Paw Paw Haven, near Alliquipa, Pennsylvania. I contacted Tom and was invited to tour his property in time to taste my first ripe paw paw. Tom was in his mid-80s and in failing health. So he had cut back on his plant propagation activities. For many years Tom was an active plant collector and paw paw breeder. His paw paw cultivar Kirstin is available still.

Tom was an active member of the North American Fruit Explorers for many years. He told me he had maintained 22 varieties of paw paws. His property, a little less than an acre perched high above the Ohio River just downstream from Pittsburgh, had been planted with the paw paws, 80 varieties of apples grafted onto 25 semi-dwarf trees, Illinois Everbearing mulberries, and multiple cultivars of hazelnuts, filberts, heartnuts, butternuts, Chinese chestnuts, black walnuts, raspberries, plus assorted other fruits.

I was gratified and astounded to meet Tom and amazed at this example of what I would call permaculture that had been planted and maintained from the 1950s through the 1980s. I was sad that I met him at a time when he was no longer able to maintain his collections and I was not prepared to carry on his work. (He passed away within a year or two of our meeting.)

I left Paw Paw Haven with a grafted seedling of Tom's Kirsten paw paw and the inspiration of seeing his food forest landscape first hand. The paw paw I bought from Tom has thrived and turned into a small thicket along a wooded stream.

Paw paw haven.

Nancy Martin's food forest and biodiversity landscape begins in the front yard.

LIPP Homestead

Nancy Martin's LIPP Homestead is a one and a half-acre parcel in a suburban neighborhood just north of Pittsburgh, Pennsylvania. LIPP (Living in Peace and Prosperity) is a small-scale example of permaculture in action. The property has been Nancy's home for over 12 years. The house is the original homestead in the neighborhood; surrounding farmland has long since been developed, first into victory gardens and finally into streets and houses. The house and property are secluded, hidden behind mature pine trees and down a small lane from the street. When Nancy renovated the house she used locally sourced hemlock lumber and siding, maintaining the historic feel of the house.

The property is divided into three use areas. Zone One includes a fenced front yard for the two dogs to enjoy, and a side yard patio and garden. Zone Two is a wooded landscape of pine trees, fruit, compost bin, shiitake logs, and native habitat. Zone Two includes a rain garden stormwater basin to collect and slowly release the house's roof runoff into the ground. Paths through Zone Two lead to

Herbs, flowers, and useful trees grace the front entrance to the house.

Credit: Nancy Martin

Zone Three, an open area with a fire pit and outdoor seating. Beyond Zone Three lies a wood-fired sauna surrounded by locust, oak, sumac, beech trees, paw paw, and ferns bordering a 500-acre native woodland in a deep, undeveloped stream valley.

Nancy's fruitful landscape includes several varieties of grapes, paw paws, hardy kiwi, blueberries, elderberry, several mulberries, cherry, black walnuts, raspberries, and many useful herbs. Native shrubs, including service berries, wild black cherry and chokeberry provide song bird forage.

The entire property is landscaped with both native and edible plants. The house is landscaped with native wildflowers, ferns, Virginia creeper vines, wild grape, sweet woodruff, milkweed, chicory, burdock, nettles, and other useful plants. The front yard is an open area lined with a mixed bed of flowers, elderberry and raspberry on the west, and white pine trees, mulberry, and elderberry on the south. A long arbor of wine and table grapes leads through the front yard to a garden gate in the east.

Nancy takes her garden design cues from nature. The land suggested that the garden design merge the feminine and masculine. To this end the main forest garden's raised beds take the form of a serpent snaking across the yard to represent the masculine meeting a triple spiral representing both the feminine (maiden, mother, crone) and a symbol in honor of water. In practical terms, the triple spiral raised bed design slows and holds water for absorption. The serpent bed emerges from beneath a hardy kiwi vine in the northwest edge of the garden and weaves around a series of blueberry bushes, then brushes past a Chinese silk tree and continues to wind across the yard into full sunlight in the southeast corner of the garden where the triple spiral dominates the landscape. The silk tree and a mulberry tree are the dominant trees in the garden. The leguminous mimosa tree provides a light shade allowing good growth beneath. The flowers of the silk tree are a lovely silky white with pink tufts. These blossoms can be dried and are traditionally used in Chinese medicine as a calmative.

The entire serpentine bed is interplanted with herbs, blueberries, and flowers. Plantings directly beneath the tree include blueberry, Egyptian onions, comfrey, nettle, garlic, echinacea, evening primrose, bee balm, and various herbs and flowers. The triple spiral annual beds are variously planted with peas, strawberries, kale, tomatoes, garlic, and other kitchen garden crops each year. Nearby, an 1,150 gallon aboveground cistern covered with trumpet vine stores roof water for garden use. The trumpet vine attracts native pollinators and hummingbirds while shading the water to prevent algae growth and warming.

The Zone Two wooded area includes a number of plantings around the rain garden basin. Black walnuts, cherry, mulberry, chokeberry, sumac, and an apple tree surround a grove of young white pine trees. Several paw paw trees interplanted with pine are beginning to form a thicket. The pines will be thinned to accommodate the spreading paw paws. Shiitake mushroom logs are stacked beneath the pines and a porcelain bathtub allows for soaking the shiitake logs as desired to induce fruiting.

LIPP Homestead is filled with examples of thoughtful and functional design. A thicket of paw paws produces fruit along the forested stream that defines the northern edge of the property. A small mulberry along the south wall of a workshop building on the site is interplanted with annual flowers. Tall evergreens shelter the house from winter winds, while rhododendrons, a red bud tree, and bushes give privacy to the front porch. Visiting Nancy's home and garden feels more like visiting a country retreat than a suburban home. With minimal management Nancy's landscape provides easy access to a seasonal succession of fruit, foraged edibles, and herbs. Living in peace and prosperity with beauty and abundance looks easy at LIPP Homestead.

Mary Beth Steislinger's Landscape

Mary Beth Steislinger has created a mini-farm in a quiet Pittsburgh neighborhood. Her home landscape is a reflection of her personal values, learned and developed over a lifetime of work in permaculture, environmental action, and community development. She views her small urban homestead as a part of a neighborhood food system and encourages networking and trade of fruit and produce among her neighbors. She has been working to plant a block orchard, giving fruit trees to neighbors for births, deaths, and special occasions. She says that within a block radius of her house, there are now well over a dozen fruit trees, mainly pears, cherries, and plums as there were already three productive apples that produced an overabundance.

Her own double lot is a productive landscape graced with an artist's eye for beauty and detail. The yard includes assorted fired-clay sculptural elements and rough-cut finish on fence and garden shed. Three small

Credit: Darrell E. Frey

Art and horticulture merge: cherry tree with currants, comfrey, and herbs.

crabapple trees across the front of the property produce a type of small, sweet apple each autumn good for jams or eating raw. Numerous wild flowers frame the narrow front yards. The backyard is laid out to maximize productivity while allowing for a semi-private space where large gatherings, intimate dinners or meditations are hosted regularly. Thornless blackberries are trellised along the outside of the back-alley fence. A productive mulberry shades the well-managed compost piles tucked in along the back fence.

In the northwest corner a small garden shed includes a 10-foot by 10-foot greenhouse that produces winter greens and shelters several laying hens. A small chicken run lining the north side of the yard is shaded by hazelnuts and elderberry. A sweet cherry tree overhangs a grape arbor. The grapes, brought from Italy by the prior owners of the property, provide fruit and shade for relaxing beside currant bushes and a red raspberry patch. An adjoining yard includes an annual garden for Mary Beth and her neighbors. Elsewhere in the yard are blueberries and various flowers and culinary herbs, both annual and perennial.

All the components on the property flow together in a whole system. Rainwater is captured and overflows to

Credit: Darrell E. Frey

A grape climbs the arbor beneath the cherry tree, with gooseberry and raspberry.

water parts of the garden. A photovoltaic array on her roof transforms sunlight into electricity, supplying the modest needs of the house and feeding excess into the power grid.

The scale of this cottage garden landscape is small and intimate. Space is maximized to provide a portion of the household needs for fresh food while allowing room to relax and enjoy the ambiance. A balance is achieved between beauty and productivity, creating a quiet retreat in the middle of the city.

Subtropical America: South Florida Food Forests

Koreen Brennan, Director of Grow Permaculture, is a permaculture designer and teacher based near Fort Myers, Florida. We will discuss one of Koreen's food forest projects, Hibiscus House.

Hibiscus House, a residence with one third of an acre of land, is being developed as a permaculture homestead featuring a number of perennial polyculture plantings and a small tropical food forest, with annual gardens in among the trees. Koreen placed emphasis on functional arrangement.

A primary goal of the Hibiscus House is to demonstrate the possibilities of permaculture design in a subtropical suburban lot. Koreen wanted the food forest to support the whole-systems approach to homestead design.

Cranberry hibiscus.

The list of plantings gives you a sense of the scope of the work. An incredible array of foods and useful plants have been placed in functional arrangements, both to experiment with polycultures and to provide food and materials for the home.

Koreen focused early and continually on soil building and resource conservation. The nutrient cycle includes household compost, gathered mulches, and cut and drop pruning. Rainwater collection, water conservation, and drip irrigation, combined

Credit: Darrell E. Frey

Site map of the
Hibiscus House food
forest landscape.

Credit: Koreen Brennan

Front yard of Hibiscus House includes elderberry, banana, and sweet potato ground cover.

Credit: Koreen Brennan

Cranberry hibiscus, with edible leaves, graces the landscape with its purple leaves beneath towering banana leaves.

with mulches and productive ground covers, such as sweet potatoes, help maximize water usage.

Koreen has provided the following lists of gardens and plants to describe Hibiscus House.

Microclimates/Gardens

Jungle/semi-tropic food forest—southeast corner, backyard.

Understory food forest—under oaks, southwest corner, backyard.

Bamboo food forest—northeast corner, front yard.

Stone fruit food forest—northwest section of front yard, south of pollinators

Aquaculture—pond in front yard.

Banana circles—shower area, area near pond in front.

Native pollinator section—northwest corner, front yard, near mailbox side, front yard.

Elderberry stand—flooded area near street, northeast, front yard.

Kitchen garden—near carport, spreading out from backyard sidewalk (east), behind cottage.

Groundcover—sweet potatoes.

Chaya hedge—east.

Hardscape Food Elements

Sunburst garden—mix of mostly perennial with some annuals; colorful, landscaped.

Trellises/arbors—leading to back kitchen garden; north side of kitchen garden; between cars and front yard garden; on east stone wall inside backyard picket fence; on south wall of house.

Statues/sculpture, benches, paths—aesthetic and attractive.

Nursery/Propagation Area

Food processing area—drying, fermenting, etc.

Chickens—southwest corner, run extends out from coop along side of garage.

Food

Backyard, Summer, Fall

Beans/bean greens, sweet potato, boniato, katuk, chaya, basils, turmeric, ginger, mild hot peppers, lemongrass, mint, yam, chayote, roselle, cranberry hibiscus, Mexican tarragon, basils, amaranth, molokhiya, moringa, lufa, papaya.

Backyard, Winter, Spring

Cilantro, lettuce, brassicas, watercress, tomato, peppers, basils, blueberry, banana, cucumber, peas.

Front Yard, Summer, Fall

Sweet potato, boniato, turmeric, ginger, moringa, grapes, mulberry, cherries, chaya, lufa, Seminole pumpkin.

Front yard, Winter, Spring

Brassicas, sweet potato, boniato, herbs, fruit trees.

Front Yard, Fruit

Mulberry, surinam cherry, barbados cherry, jujube, peach, avocado, loquat.

Beans

Perennial

Winged beans for leaves, pods, seeds; pigeon peas.

Summer

Long beans for beans; lablab for seeds; velvet for fodder, mulch; iron clay for leaves; cowpeas for seeds, leaves.

Winter

Bush beans, fava beans, Christmas lima beans.

Greens

Perennial Greens

5 chaya plants, 3–4 katuk bushes, 10 moringa, 3 cranberry hibiscus, 3 edible hibiscus, collard (short term), purslane, Okinawa spinach, longevity spinach, Ceylon spinach.

Summer Annuals

Molokhiya, roselle, amaranth, beans, sweet potatoes.

Winter Annuals

Kale, cabbage, collards, lettuce, parsley (can be perennial), watercress, arugula, mustard.

Other Vegetables

Perennial

Hot peppers.

Summer Annuals

Lufa, long beans, lablab beans, bitter melon, chayote, watermelon, daikon radish.

Mid-Atlantic Food Forest

When landscape architect and permaculturist Lincoln Smith was employed in an architectural firm he felt something was missing. The projects he worked on did not seem to integrate people with the ecosystems around them. Housing development projects, even those that were LEED certified, had a big ecological foot print. He felt that there was more he could be doing with his skills and passions for the Earth and for people.

Lincoln began to study food forest design. He read all he could on the topic, including David Jacke's multivolume *Edible Forest Gardens*. He attended talks about food forests by Jacke and traveled to England to meet with Martin Crawford and tour his food forest. Crawford shared his success and challenges and inspired Lincoln to go home and grow a food forest.

The high cost of land in the mid-Atlantic region near Washington, DC, was a deterrent to his goals—part self-funded research, part entrepreneurial startup—so Lincoln found a local church with property to rent long term. Located near Bowie, Maryland, this ten-acre site included five acres of woods and five acres of former hay and tobacco fields. Along with the land he found a small community to support the project.

Land secured, in 2012 Lincoln, his wife, and associates began developing the food forest. Their progress is documented on their website: forested. us. A food forest CSA offers subscribers various seasonal greens, assorted vegetables, shiitake mushrooms, sea kale, and herbs such as anise hyssop, chives, and fennel. Lincoln has been developing recipes for acorn flour products. In 2015 he collected 1,000 pounds of acorn.

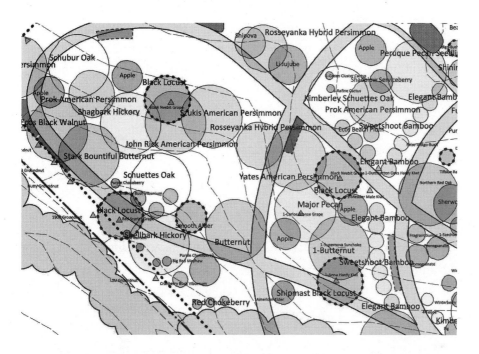

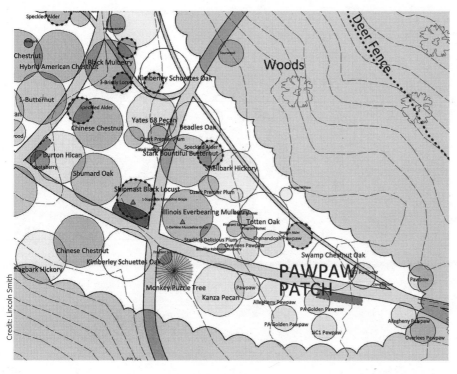

Credit: Lincoln Smith

Details of Mid-Atlantic Food Forest design plan.

Each spring they plant 40 to 50 new trees. His associate Ben Fritton works at the food forest part time. Volunteers help them plant and mulch the plantings. Species planted include basswood, paw paws, persimmons, pear, Asian pears, various apples, cherries, and numerous berries and small fruits. Nitrogen-fixing legumes, herbs, and vegetables are interplanted with the trees. A resident flock of duck and geese forage among the plantings.

In addition to managing the food forest and the CSA Lincoln and Ben offer classes and tours of the property. Lincoln uses his training as a landscape architect and permaculture designer to consult and design on sustainable land use and food forest design throughout the region.

Suzi's Natural Food Forest and Permaculture Gardening—Texas Style

Suzanne Fields is a natural gardener. The urge to plant, tend, and process the harvest is integral to her being. Perhaps being a single mother of two in her twenties provided a necessity to create a home food system, but Suzi's continuing drive to create abundance is drawn from a deeper well.

Suzi first developed her knack for gaining sustenance from the soil when

Fall apple with comfrey and wildflower understory.

Credit: Lincoln Smith

she lived on a few acres in western Pennsylvania. Learning homesteading skills from friends and neighbors and her own research, and from her studies of environmental science and permaculture at Slippery Rock University, Suzi advanced, in a few years, from a small garden plot to a well-developed home food system. Her basement larder was well stocked with home-canned foods, a small flock of hens provided eggs, a goat provided milk, and she sold crops to restaurants and a food cooperative in Pittsburgh.

When her son and daughter grew up and moved away, a job opportunity offered a chance to relocate. Suzi decided it was time to leave western Pennsylvania for the warmer climate of San Marcos, Texas. Not long after arriving in Texas, Suzi became a driving force in her local community garden and a sustainable San Marcos group. Eventually she found her own house and plot of land and immediately began to put down roots—suburban permaculture Texas style.

Today Suzi's urban homestead is an oasis of abundance. Her one-third of an acre home landscape contains chickens, fruit trees, herbs, and vegetable gardens laid out in a well-designed integrated system. Seven years of work

Credit: Suzanne Fields

Side yard view of Suzi's food forest.

Many fruits fit into this suburban lot.

Credit: Suzanne Fields

has transformed this property from yard to food forest. Her navel orange, Brown Turkey fig, and Meyer lemon tree produce huge, flavor-filled fruit. Other trees include three types of peaches, low-chill apples such as Fuji and Yellow Transparent, and plums. Passionfruit and two types of grapes twine along the fencing.

The list of tree crops grows each year: pomegranate, jujube, mulberry, mandarin orange, and pineapple guava are all producing good harvests. Bay laurel provides fragrant culinary leaves. A Kaffir lime, grown for its fragrant leaves, is grafted with several varieties of citrus. Interspersed with her deciduous trees are numerous perennial herbs, flowers, and vegetable gardens. Oregano and scented geraniums have spread under the peaches and plums. When the citrus trees were young, vegetables and herbs were interplanted in the mulch around them. As they grew larger the evergreen citrus cast too much shade for good understory production, so Suzi moved the companion beds to the drip lines. Many of her herbs and roses are used on products she makes for Suzi's Naturals—soaps, shampoos, lotions, salves, teas, and other herbal products.

Suzi cans, dries, and freezes her crops. Root crops and greens not eaten fresh are fermented into kimchi or otherwise pickled. Excess produce—like the 600 pounds of Meyer lemons she harvested in 2015—is sold through farmers markets along with Suzi's body care products.

Suzi's suburban livestock includes laying hens and the occasional chickens for meat. (Local ordinances allow for eight hens.) Every year she gets fertile eggs from a friend to be hatched by one of her hens. These provide a new laying flock and the best hens are kept for the new year's layers. Chickens eat excess produce and their manure is added to the kitchen compost to keep fertility high. It all begins with the soil, Suzi explains. Kelp and greensand provide mineral nutrients needed for healthy plants to provide healthful harvests. Compost and mulch are added annually to conserve moisture and feed the soil's microbiome. Annual crops are rotated and her vigilant eye is quick to notice any pests. These are dealt with using organic control methods.

The San Marcos growing season is nearly year round. A typical annual crop cycle is a lot different than her Pennsylvania garden. The heat of July and August make gardening difficult. Fall through early summer are the main gardening seasons. She does get cold spells and frosts in mid winter, but after March 15 there is little chance

Each winter Suzi sells and shares her bountiful harvests at local markets.

Satsuma orange.

Credit: Suzanne Fields

Navel oranges and
Meyer lemons.

of frost until almost December. When the summer heat slows down, vegetable and fruit irrigation is required to keep the food forest happy.

Suzi Fields continues to add to her food forest and gardens each year, and continually experiments with new crops, new recipes, and new ways to preserve the harvest. She also propagates figs, roses, and other plants to sell at the local farmers market. And she continues the work of promoting local food security that she began when she first arrived in San Marcos about 15 years ago. Local permaculture students and new gardeners seek out Suzi to tour her gardens, buy her products, and volunteer to help tend and harvest the bounty of a West Texas Food Forest.

Pacific Northwest: Beacon Food Forest

The Pacific Northwest is blessed with a mild climate and plentiful rain that allows for a wide variety of fruits and useful plants. The Beacon Food Forest, located in Beacon Hill, Seattle, Washington, is perhaps the best known food forest project in North America. Early in the process of planning and establishment, this ambitious project received national press attention as an innovative community project. A key aspect of the project has been its goal of continuing community engagement and that the fruits of the Beacon Food Forest be available freely to members of the local community.

The Beacon Food Forest Permaculture Project germinated in a permaculture design course that Jacqueline Cramer and Glenn Herlihy took in 2009. They then built on research and designs they had begun in the permaculture course. They found a non-profit organization, Grow Northwest, to partner with them to help shepherd the food forest to fruition. They organized public meetings to present their proposal to the ethnically diverse community and established a steering committee to help guide the work. Long-term access to the seven acres of open land was secured from Seattle Public Utilities and the Seattle Parks and Recreation Department. Early funding allowed the formation of a design team that included experienced permaculture designer Jenny Pell and landscape architect Margarette Harrison, who worked with the Friends of the Beacon Hill Food Forest to refine the design and implementation plan.

The plan that emerged includes an edible arboretum, a nursery, a food forest orchard, a food forest nut grove, a children's area, community gardens, and a community gathering space. Since 2010 hundreds of volunteers

Site map of Beacon Hill Food Forest.

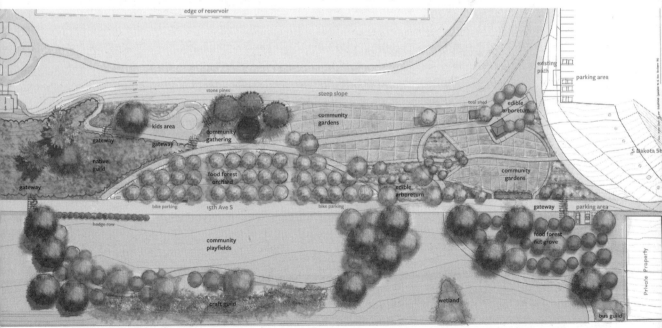

Credit: Glenn Herlihy and Jacqueline Cramer   16th Ave S

Scale: 1" = 20'

harrison design
landscape architecture
911 western ave suite 406
seattle wa 08104
206.840.2540

Credit: Darrell E. Frey

Early development of Beacon Hill Food Forest included construction of terraced planters on the sloping site.

Beacon Food Forest Plant List

Indian plum	Thimbleberry	Salmonberry
Red huckleberry	Beaked filbert	Lingonberry
Salal	Tall Oregon grape	Low Oregon grape
Sea buckthorn	Gooseberries	Currants
Kousa dogwood	Cornelian cherry	Elderberry
Blueberries	Raspberries	Blackberries
Goumis	Autumn olive	Aronia
Blue honeysuckle	Evergreen huckleberry	Red flowering currant
Lonicera	California wax myrtle	Weeping mulberry
Chilean guava	Dwarf blue Korean pine	Strawberry tree, compact
Yew	Sweet shoot bamboo	Ceanothus
Siberian pea shrub	Lupine	Willow
Red twig dogwood	Red osier dogwood	Mock orange
Sword fern	Sitka alder	Yellowhorn Xanthoceras

and community members have participated in work days and education programs as the food forest continues to evolve and grow. The project also has strong connections to a number of local organizations and schools. The Beacon Food Forest offers a full calendar of classes, work days, and community events as it engages the community and continues to plant, tend, and harvest.

Hazelwood Food Forest Revisited: Where Is It Now?

In Chapter 1 Michelle described the design and creation of the Hazelwood Food Forest. It grew for five years with all-volunteer help. Some of our most loyal volunteers were Seth Nyer, Matt Peters, and Jim McCue. We were amazed at the productivity of the food forest in such a short time.

Sadly, the tides of the neighborhood became more desirable to development and we moved, with funding assistance and some volunteers, to another site.

On the bright side, we created a good partnership with a local church to transplant many of the thriving plants and trees, and we are in the process of developing an extensive training program to hand off the food forest to the congregation and community.

We were able to relocate many of our plants. However, it was very hard to see the food forest that we put so much time and love and resources into get torn down and covered with concrete—no doubt about

A mulch donut builds soil and reduced weed competition around a young walnut tree at the Beacon Hill Food Forest.

Salmonberries.

that. In some ways, though, it was our answer to the ongoing issue of maintenance. One of our stipulations for leasing the land from a public entity was that we could not legally sell anything grown on the site. This became an issue down the line. When there is nobody getting compensated for the work, it becomes draining and difficult to keep it up.

If I had to do it again, my most intense focus would be on the long-term maintenance and sustainability element, or, basically, a business plan. I would make sure there was a way to generate funds from the site, so that it could continue.

Food Forests in the Sustainable, Regenerative Society

As we have seen with the work of the Hazelwood Food Forest and the Seattle food forest, these perennial polycultures have a role to play in the regeneration of our local landscapes and food systems. There are many possible ways these systems can be integrated into our communities. Some examples include edible parks, foraging along hiking and biking trails, community tree planting, and co-operative neighborhood food forests.

Gardens of Millvale

A current client, a small-town suburb of Pittsburgh, in a steep valley in view of the Allegheny River, has retained our services to develop community food forests on vacant lots and in several town parks. Their goal is simple and yet also farsighted. The town's eco-district plan includes the development of an integrated local food system and sustainable energy production. They are combining community garden space with urban farming enterprises in their town. The gardens are leased to managers for sales to local restaurants and markets. Food forests, community gardens, community composting, storm-water management, urban aquaculture, restaurants, and farmers markets will be linked through the suburban eco-district plan to create a more resilient and revitalized community

Closing Thoughts

Plant a tree. Tend it. Nurture it. It will reward you with a harvest, with shade, with biodiversity. It will take carbon from the atmosphere and improve local air quality. Tended well when young, it may well endure after you are gone. These things are certain, at least proven in the past. Today the future seems less certain. Changing climates, mass migrations, economic uncertainty, and other concerns are part of the daily news. More than ever there is a need to put down roots, to create islands of sanity, and to nurture the land. The food forests we profile and suggestions we make in these pages are only a sampling of the food forests, forest gardens, and edible landscapes being created worldwide. We encourage you to be inspired, to be daring, to create, plant, tend, and harvest. Experiment. Experiment with new crops, new patterns of planting, new ways of cooking.

Nature has been creating polycultures for millions of years. People have been selecting crops, interplanting, and tending productive polycultures for millennia. It is only in recent times that we have come to embrace monoculture. It is time to rediscover and revive and renew this ancient art into countless new forms.

Plant a tree. Plant another. Tend them well. They will reward you.

Compost Remediation for Lead Contamination

For the reader working in an urban landscape or in a heavily polluted area, the following information will prove useful in your goals to first clean up the soil so that food can be grown safely. We have provided a fair amount of technical detail so that interested readers can consider how to apply this simple yet effective technology in their own community. We hope to provide enough information to show that the lead pollution that is common throughout industrialized areas can be remediated using relatively inexpensive and simple methods.

In order for urban agriculture to be viable, lead contamination needs to be addressed in a cost-effective, ecologically sound manner. While using compost for remediation is still in the research phase, case studies and research done to date clearly demonstrate its effectiveness.

Likewise, in situ treatments have numerous benefits over costly removal methods of the past. In situ compost bioremediation treats the lead onsite by applying a three-inch layer of compost over the contaminated ground. Soil amendments, including organic materials, can inactivate the lead (Pb), reducing bioavailability to humans and uptake by plants. The benefits include reduced treatment costs, reuse of organic materials used to make the compost, and a decreased rate of soluble lead. There are also less regulatory requirements and logistical concerns with in situ treatment.

Many vacant lots and backyards in urban environments can present a public health problem because of the likely presence of the heavy metal. The Environmental Protection Agency's (EPA) Lead-Safe Yards program recommends levels below 400 parts per million (ppm) in soil that is going to be used for growing food or as play space for children (Table 1). The content of soil lead includes factors such as: historical traffic patterns, city size, age of city, prevailing industries, and the soil type ("Effect of biosolids processing on lead bioavailability in an urban soil," S. Brown, R.L. Chaney, et al., *Journal of Environmental Quality* 32(1):100–8, January 2003). Elevated lead levels are also the result of lead-based paints used for housing prior to 1978, automobile emissions, and local industry.

Table 1: Soil-lead levels adapted from the EPA's Lead-Safe Yards program

Soil-Lead Level (Parts per Million)	Rating
>5,000	Very high
2,000–5,000	High
400–2,000	Moderately high
<400	Urban background

After addressing the importance of the issue to public health, we will present the possibility of using compost to inactivate the soil lead, reducing bioavailability to people, plant root uptake, and leaching into groundwater. We will then explain an implementation procedure for compost bioremediation.

Background

Lead poisoning is the most common and serious environmental disease affecting young children. For children under six, an elevated blood lead level is 10 μg/dL (micrograms per deciliter), though there is increasing evidence for detrimental health effects at lower levels. There is a higher prevalence of lead poisoning for inner-city children and the relationship of blood lead levels to soil lead for children in urban areas ranges from 1.1 to 7.6 μg/dL blood per 1,000 milligrams lead per kilogram soil.

Along with health issues such as anemia and kidney, gastrointestinal, and neurological problems, lead poisoning has also been linked with increased rates of behavioral problems and juvenile delinquency. Though the specific biological mechanism is still a mystery, it is known that lead acts at a large number of central nervous system sites, some of which are involved in impulse control.

Diet plays a large role in the likelihood of lead poisoning. Though the mechanisms that affect lead solubility and absorption by receptors in the body are not fully understood, the following are known dietary patterns:

- Low iron in the diet causes greater lead absorption.
- Low calcium increases lead absorption and distribution.
- Diets low in calories, protein, zinc, and vitamin C or high in fat increase lead absorption.
- High phosphorus, phytates (antioxidant compounds found in whole grains, legumes, nuts, and seeds), and fiber in the diet reduce lead absorption.

With a particular focus on urban gardening and lead contamination, it has been shown that the greatest risk of lead poisoning comes from ingestion of the soil itself rather than crop uptake. One study compared garden vegetables and soil as potential sources of lead to children and showed that the risk is greater through direct soil ingestion.

It is important to treat the lead in the soil when embarking on gardening projects. Children may be involved in these projects and airborne dust or direct ingestion is always a possibility. Likewise, soil on crop surfaces can be directly ingested. Extra care and precaution should be taken when washing homegrown produce, particularly with root crops where fine soil particles can adhere to peels and contribute substantial lead.

Chemistry

The goal of using compost to bioremediate is not to remove lead from the soil but to decrease its bioavailability. *Bioavailability* refers to absorption into systemic circulation. It is related to *bioaccessibilty*, which refers to a measure of physiological solubility of the metal at the portal of entry into the body.

This means that insoluble metals with low bioaccessibility have low bioavailabilty. If the lead cannot get through the digestive tract (bioaccessibility), then it cannot get into systemic circulation (bioavailability) and will thus be eliminated from the body without negative consequences.

Bioavailability is determined by measuring the fraction of lead (Pb) that is absorbed following ingestion by a test animal. Bioaccessibility is another way to find out if lead will be absorbed in the body, by using an in vitro, chemical testing method which simulates the conditions of the gastric tract.

The levels of both soil lead contamination and soil microorganisms are important in determining bioavailability. The mineral form of lead ingested either in a soil matrix or as pure mineral can alter the rate of lead absorption. Therefore, by changing lead's mineral structure, its bioavailability can be manipulated. For instance, rats fed urban garden soil with 1,000 ppm lead in one study showed that bone lead was only about 20 percent as high as when equivalent lead acetate (a salt form) was fed. Likewise, lead in a contaminated soil matrix was 75 percent less bioavailable than a lead acetate-amended diet. It is still unclear how lead behavior in the soil system relates to its behavior in the gastric tract.

Soil can adsorb lead. *Adsorption* is an electrochemical process where positively or negatively charged organic molecules bind with their charge-opposite counterparts in organic matter and clay.

The primary forms of soil lead are: sulfate, sulfide, carbonate, and oxide. In order to be metabolized by plants or animals, lead must be in a soluble form. In the soil, soluble lead is generally 60 percent of the total lead present. Lead oxides and carbonates are soluble forms, whereas lead sulfide (galena), lead phosphate (pyromorphite), and lead combined with soil organic matter are less soluble. Lead immobilization is primarily known to be through formation of pyromorphite. Lead usually remains near the surface of the soil and so contamination becomes less of an issue deeper into the soil.

Manganese, phosphorus, and iron have demonstrated the ability to decrease lead's bioavailability, as has organic matter. It has been shown that compost made from biosolid waste with high mineral content has the same effect.

With composting, a two-fold compost chemical process has been identified in which phosphorus, manganese, and iron bind with lead while the compost increases levels of humus. Humic substances provide more (and more active) sites for adsorption of lead. In urban soil with high lead levels, the addition of high-iron compost reduced the lead's bioavailability by 37 per-

cent and 43 percent in both in vivo (fed to rats) and in vitro (chemical ex-
traction process) studies, respectively. The iron content (active iron oxide)
was 113,900 ppm. In this study, compost was added to the soil at 10 percent
dry weight ratio to reach a total weight mix of 1.25 kilograms (1.125 kilograms
dry soil mixed with 125 grams dry compost).

Compost Remediation Procedure

Soil testing is an important first step in the remediation process. Lead levels,
pH, organic composition, and nutrient levels are important parameters to
measure.

A layer of compost about three inches deep is required. This measures
out to 400 cubic yards per acre. Compost can be found locally at a nursery
or a compost business in your area. We also recommend beginning to make
compost on site if at all possible.

For an ⅛-acre site (that of a typical city lot), 50 cubic yards are necessary.
Once the compost has been applied, it needs to be worked into the soil,
either with hand tools or a rototiller.

After the compost is worked into the top three inches of soil, a cover
crop can be seeded. Cover crops can be chosen based on your goals. A green
cover crop will be a nitrogen producer and will help to enrich the overall
quality of soil for growing other plants. Green cover crops are legumes and
include cowpeas, soybeans, clover, and crotalaria. Non-legumes can also be
grown, primarily to provide biomass, smother weeds, and improve soil tilth.
Examples include sorghum, millet, buckwheat, and oats.

Alternatively, at this point plants for phytoremediation can be sown.
Phytoremediation is the technique of using plants to remove pollutants from
the soil. Plant the seeds according to the package, making sure to cover
with an adequate amount of soil to prevent bird predation and desiccation.
Thoroughly water the site to encourage adequate germination. Add finely
chopped straw on the ground at about one to two inches depth to further
protect the seeds.

Post-treatment sampling should be conducted two months and six
months after treatment. After a year's time, follow-up samples can be taken
though most of the pyromorphite formation will take place immediately. The

EPA has set less than 400 parts per million as the acceptable level of lead in the soil and the goal of remediation should be under this quantity.

Steps to Implementation

1. Perform initial site evaluation including measuring the lot size, visual observation of rubble or concrete and any other notable features that may affect delivery and distribution of compost.
2. Familiarize field team with safety precautions and follow the suggestions listed in the EPA's Safe-Yards Program (listed below).
3. Remove rubble and other trash and debris.
4. Perform initial soil testing including lead levels, organic matter, nutrient levels, and pH.
5. Wet the soil if dry to prevent inhalation of lead air particles.
6. Apply manure-based compost at a rate of 400 cubic yards per acre.

EPA Safe-Yards Program Health and Safety Recommendations (Environmental Protection Agency, 2007):

Primary route of entry of lead into the body is ingestion:

a. Lead can enter the body through normal hand-to-mouth activities.
b. Small amounts of lead left on hands or clothing can impact blood lead levels.
c. Lead-contaminated soil can be transferred to the interior of dwelling (by pets, shoes, clothing).

Preventive measures:

a. Avoid dust-generating activities.
b. Dampen soil to minimize dust generation.
c. Keep children and pets away from area where work is being done.
d. Wear leather or comparable work gloves to minimize hand contamination.
e. Do not smoke or eat while in work area.
f. Wash face and hands before smoking or eating.
g. Remove shoes/boots before entering a dwelling to limit contaminated soil transfer.
h. Wash work clothing separately from other clothing.

7. Lightly work the compost into the top three inches of soil with a roto-tiller or hand cultivator.

8. Sow the cover crop or plant for phytoremediation; tamp down seed to insure it is held in the soil; cover lightly with compost.

9. Cover the site with one to two inches of finely chopped straw and water thoroughly.

10. Conduct follow-up testing for lead immediately after, two months, and six months after implementation.

Index

About the Authors

DARRELL FREY holds Diplomas in Permaculture Design and Permaculture Education from The Permaculture Institute of North America (PINA) and was among the "first wave" of permaculture practitioners. He established Three Sisters Farm and Nursery in northwest Pennsylvania as a permaculture research project in 1983. The five-acre plot has been a research project in right livelihood and permaculture design. Darrell's previous book, *Bioshelter Market Garden: A Permaculture Farm,* is a detailed study of year-round market gardening and the role of small-scale market gardens in sustainable food systems. He facilitates workshops and delivers keynote presentations on permaculture design, perennial polyculture management, and ecological land use planning, and has been a sustainable community development consultant and permaculture teacher for 30 years. For more information on Darrell Frey see www.threesisterspermaculture.com.

MICHELLE CZOLBA is co-owner of Pittsburgh Permaculture and co-founded the Hazelwood Food Forest. She has extensive experience in the design and maintenance of perennial polyculture. Her formal training includes biology, chemistry, and herbalism, and she has earned a B.Sc. in Environmental Science and a M.Sc. in Sustainable Systems. After obtaining her Herbal Certification Michelle founded Wildly Natural Skin Care, and developed her own full line of handmade, wildcrafted and organic skin care products.

A Note About the Publisher

NEW SOCIETY PUBLISHERS (www.newsociety.com), is an activist, solutions-oriented publisher focused on publishing books for a world of change. Our books offer tips, tools, and insights from leading experts in sustainable building, homesteading, climate change, environment, conscientious commerce, renewable energy, and more—positive solutions for troubled times.

Sustainable Practices for Strong, Resilient Communities

We print all of our books and catalogues on 100% **post-consumer recycled paper**, processed chlorine-free, and printed with vegetable-based, low-VOC inks. These practices are measured through an Environmental Benefits statement (see below). We are committed to printing all of our books and catalogues in North America, not overseas. We also work to reduce our carbon footprint, and purchase carbon offsets based on an annual audit to ensure carbon neutrality.

Employee Trust and a Certified B Corp

In addition to an innovative employee shareholder agreement, we have also achieved B Corporation certification. We care deeply about *what* we publish—our overall list continues to be widely admired and respected for its timeliness and quality—but also about *how* we do business.

For further information, or to browse our full list of books and purchase securely, visit our website at: **www.newsociety.com**

New Society Publishers
ENVIRONMENTAL BENEFITS STATEMENT

For every 5,000 books printed, New Society saves the following resources:[1]

33	Trees
3,009	Pounds of Solid Waste
3,311	Gallons of Water
4,319	Kilowatt Hours of Electricity
5,471	Pounds of Greenhouse Gases
24	Pounds of HAPs, VOCs, and AOX Combined
8	Cubic Yards of Landfill Space

[1] Environmental benefits are calculated based on research done by the Environmental Defense Fund and other members of the Paper Task Force who study the environmental impacts of the paper industry.

MIX
Paper from
responsible sources
FSC® C016245